Y0-BRS-537

PR
3001
.B37
1987

Bradshaw, Graham.

Shakespeare's
scepticism

$35.00

DATE		

DAVID GLENN HUNT
MEMORIAL LIBRARY
GALVESTON COLLEGE

© THE BAKER & TAYLOR CO.

SHAKESPEARE'S
SCEPTICISM

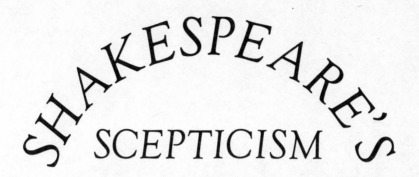

SHAKESPEARE'S SCEPTICISM

GRAHAM BRADSHAW

Lecturer in English
University of St Andrews

ST. MARTIN'S PRESS
New York

DAVID GLENN HUNT
MEMORIAL LIBRARY
GALVESTON COLLEGE

© Graham Bradshaw, 1987

All rights reserved. For information, write:
Scholarly & Reference Division,
St. Martin's Press, Inc., 175 Fifth Avenue, New York, NY 10010

First published in the United States of America in 1987

Printed in Great Britain

ISBN 0–312–00964–X

Library of Congress Cataloging-in-Publication Data

Bradshaw, Graham.
  Shakespeare's scepticism.

  Bibliography: p.
  Includes index.
  1. Shakespeare, William, 1564–1616—Philosophy.
2. Scepticism in literature. I. Title.
PR3001.B73   1987   822.3′3   87–9479
ISBN 0–312–00964–X

For Ann

Contents

Contents

Preface

Ted Hughes has described the Complete Works as a torture chamber in which Shakespeare carries on an endless quarrel about the nature of Nature. The plays themselves do indeed show how opposed visions of Nature yield opposed accounts of value, and the first chapter of the present study traces Shakespeare's explicit and developing preoccupation with that issue which Troylus so impetuously broaches when he asks, 'What's aught, but as 'tis valew'd?' This, I take it, provides one way of beginning to characterise Shakespeare's scepticism.

However, the relation of the second chapter to the first is intended to be corrective and complementary. Here my main concern is to emphasise those respects in which the processes of poetic-dramatic thinking are not like those of logical-discursive thought. For example, we need to understand why the fact that a Falstaff or Thersites speaks only in prose is itself a constituent of dramatic meaning—regardless of whether this presents a consciously purposive creative decision, or the more or less instinctive reflex of a poetic dramatist used to thinking *through* his medium. Here my argument is in some ways parallel to that in Joseph Kerman's pioneering *Opera as Drama:* just as Kerman insists that, although the libretto of a music drama provides its conceptual references, the drama is articulated through the music, *poetic* drama is articulated through its poetry. The kind of poetry or prose a character speaks, and its place within the poetic drama's system of reciprocal relationships, contribute to our thinking—to the way the play is thinking—about the character and his or her potentialities. Here Shakespeare's scepticism reveals itself not in the explicit 'play of ideas' found in dramatists like Shaw or Lessing, but in a subtly appraising play of intelligence. One result, as I try to show in discussing Hal and Hotspur, is that a single speech may prompt opposed valuations of a character or of an issue like 'love' or 'honour'; in such cases, the process of thinking may be all the more challengingly exploratory, in being non-linear.

Criticism itself is necessarily linear and discursive, so that one or the other of these chapters had to come first. Yet my argument depends, ultimately, on the proposition that the relationship between Shakespeare's concern with acts of valuing and his poetic-dramatic perspectivism is irreducibly complex. Neither of these two ways of characterising Shakespeare's scepticism properly precedes the other, since neither is to be seen as the other's cause or effect. Rather, they are complementary and interdependent, representing an essentially interrogative mode of radically sceptical 'thinking' which makes it appropriate to recall Blake's great maxim, 'As a man is, so he sees', or Nietzsche's constant insistence that we interpret the world as we interpret a text.

Because Shakespeare is in this respect his own deconstructionist, we short-circuit the process of poetic-dramatic thinking whenever we give a particular character or speech a privileged, supra-dramatic significance. Nowadays, few would defend E. M. W. Tillyard's habit of doing this, when, as a kind of wartime effort to be compared with Olivier's wartime film of *Henry V*, he leant on whatever speeches might make the plays seem to present a sustained hymn to Order and Degree; but it may be less obvious that those 'radical' critics like Jonathan Dollimore or John Drakakis, who are riding a contemporary Zeitgeist in their 'materialist' readings, are not so much correcting Tillyard's approach as standing it on its head, by privileging those anti-humanist, anti-essentialist perspectives which most threaten Tillyard's Elizabethan World Picture. In either case the exploratory, interrogative effect of Shakespeare's perspectivism is defeated, when the critic determinedly identifies one perspective with that of the author or (more warily) that of 'the play'.

That the final version of this book makes so little attempt

to set Shakespeare's thought in the context of Renaissance ideas may surprise or disappoint some readers. There are several reasons for this, and showing is better than telling; but one very pressing reason for feeling that I had to start rewriting the first draft of this book as soon as I had finished it was my increasingly vexed sense of the problematics of 'matching' supposedly analogous ideas.

To take just one instance: it *may* be helpful, when we are pondering Hamlet's 'There's nothing either good or bad, but thinking makes it so', to consider Montaigne's essay 'That the taste of goods or evils doth greatly depend on the opinion that we have of them', or Donne's observations that 'There's nothing simply good, nor ill alone . . . The only measure is, and judge, Opinion' (*The Progress of the Soul*) and that 'There is no externall act naturally evil' (*Biathanatos*). And yet before we can know what might enter into, and justify or qualify, any such comparison we must first decide what meaning Hamlet's utterance takes within the poetic drama. In context, Hamlet's assertion sounds more like a painful question than Troylus's question, 'What's aught, but as 'tis valew'd?', which sounds more like a glib assertion. Nor would the content of Hamlet's utterance be quite the same, if it were spoken by Thersites, Iago, Edmund, or the Belmont Portia who observes that 'Nothing is good I see without respect'. Some critics assume, like Harry Levin, that Hamlet says what he means; others assume, like Harold Jenkins (who objects to the supposed parallel from Montaigne), that Hamlet cannot mean as much as he says. Nor should we suppose that there is general agreement about what Donne or Montaigne 'really' mean and believe.

The immediate point of these remarks is to suggest why this book offers so little discussion of discussions of Shakespeare's and other Renaissance writers' 'thought': my concern is not with a body of ideas which supposedly corresponds with Shakespeare's 'thought' or even his 'beliefs', but with the processes of the plays' poetic-dramatic thinking. Similarly, although I develop a distinction between terminal or dogmatic scepticism and what I call radical scepticism, the distinction's relevance to the experiential process of watching or reading a Shakespearean poetic drama must be established first—whether or not we go on to consider its relevance to the difference between Charron and Montaigne, or between the so-called 'libertines' and Donne.

Anybody who has written a book on Shakespeare will know, all too well, that collecting one's sense of indebtedness is impossible. Certainly, I should begin by expressing my gratitude to John Spiers and to Sue Roe for showing so much faith in the book. Some material appeared in the *London Review of Books;* in an essay on Ted Hughes and Shakespeare which was included in Keith Sagar's *The Achievement of Ted Hughes* (Manchester University Press); and in a discussion of Verdi and Boito as 'translators' which provided the Epilogue in James Hepokoski's *Verdi's Falstaff* (Cambridge University Press). I am grateful to Karl Miller, John Banks and Michael Black for granting permission to reprint (or restore) this material.

The works to which I refer in the book itself are listed in the Select Bibliography, but this cannot reflect my deep indebtedness to some critics I should mention here. A. P. Rossiter's *Angel with Horns* still seems to me the most illuminating critical book on Shakespeare to be published in the period separating Bradley's *Shakespearean Tragedy* and Norman Rabkin's *Shakespeare and the Problem of Meaning.* Both Rabkin's book and Wilbur Sanders' *The Dramatist and the Received Idea* have been crucial in shaping my sense of what makes the Shakespearean 'play of ideas' so distinctive. What I say about reflexivity draws on Anne Barton's *Shakespeare and the Idea of the Play,* J. L. Calderwood's discussions of Shakespearean 'metadrama' and Stephen Booth's work. There is a more general indebtedness to S. L. Goldberg's *An Essay on King Lear,* and to Jonas Barish's discussions of style.

My extensive obligation to the editors of the *New Arden Shakespeare* and other modernised texts should be emphasised, since it may be obscured by my decision to quote from (and on occasion silently correct) Folio or Quarto texts. This, largely for the reasons that would be taken for granted in any scholarly or critical work on a lesser writer of this period; the arguments for playing safe and quoting from a respected modernised text are in my view good but not compelling. For the reader's convenience I have supplied line references from Peter Alexander's one volume edition of Shakespeare.

I am grateful to the University of St Andrews for a period of study leave and to my various hosts in Australia when I held a Visiting Fellowship at the Australian National University's History of Ideas Unit. Being able to try out some of this book's arguments both at the Unit and at the Universities of Sydney, Monash and La Trobe was invaluable. Special thanks are due to Wilbur Sanders, Harriett Hawkins, Jonas Barish and Marta Gibińska for their comments on some parts of the book, and to my students and colleagues in St Andrews. But the greatest indebtedness is to Michael Tanner, S. L. Goldberg and Jane Adamson, for sacrificing many hours and many days to going through a book which was even longer before they finished with it.

It might be said—every poet does no more than find metaphors for his own nature. That would be only partly true. Most poets never come anywhere near divining the master-plan of their whole make-up and projecting it complete. The majority cling to some favoured corner of it, or to remotely transmitted Reuter-like despatches, or mistranslate its signals into the language of a false nature. Shakespeare is almost unique in having unearthed the whole original thing, learned its language, and then found it such a cruel riddle that he could not rest from trying to solve it.

Ted Hughes

ONE

Nature and Value

Look round this Universe. Whan an immense Profusion of Beings, animated and organiz'd, sensible and active! You admire this prodigious Variety and Profundity. But inspect a little more narrowly these living Existences, the only Beings worth regarding. How hostile and destructive to each other! How insufficient all of them for their own Happiness! How contemptible or odious to the Spectator! The whole presents nothing but the Idea of a blind Nature, impregnated by a great vivifying Principle, and pouring forth from her Lap, without discernment or parental Care, her maim'd and abortive Children.

David Hume, *Dialogues Concerning Natural Religion*

Troylus's question

'What's aught, but as 'tis valew'd?', asks Troylus—with little sense of what makes his question terrifying. Hector's reply is prompt, and shows a confidence to which the play he inhabits gives little or no support:

But value dwels not in particular will,
It holds his estimate and dignitie
As well, wherein 'tis precious of it selfe
As in the prizer: 'Tis madde Idolatrie,
To make the service greater then the God,
And the will dotes that is inclineable
To what infectiously it selfe affects,
Without some image of th'affected merit.
(Troylus and Cressida, 2.2.53–60)

On this view values are in some sense 'out there', where they can be judiciously appraised and recognised, or, as some modern philosophers put it, 'read off'. In this Trojan debate

1

both Troylus and Hector are jockeying for position; Hector's speech is intended to establish the superiority of his judgement, and his immunity to 'infection'. By seeing value as a property of the valued, existing *in* the prized 'as well' as 'in the prizer', Hector asserts that the human mind—or his superior mind—is able to establish and measure any discrepancy between imputed value and inherent value.

Hector's clever play on *infect* and *affect* recalls Theseus's no less confident distinction between *apprehending* and *comprehending* in *A Midsummer Night's Dream*. Lovers, lunatics and poets are all subject to 'shaping phantasies, that apprehend/ More then coole reason ever comprehends' (5.1.5–6), and the 'tricks' of 'strong imagination' ensure that 'if it would but apprehend some joy,/ It comprehends some bringer of that joy' (19–20). Indeed, this suggests why Hector's use of the word 'image' does not help his argument: in Theseus's speech the sense of *comprehend* shifts, to allow that the object of supposedly rational comprehension may itself be one of 'fancies images', a product of 'shaping phantasies'. Moreover, Theseus's use of the word 'trick' anticipates the way in which the word 'cheat' would be used, nearly a century later, in two instructively complementary passages. In his preface to *Religio Laici* (1682), Dryden opposes reason and imagination:

> The Florid, Elevated and Figurative way is for the Passions; for Love and Hatred, Fear and Anger, are begotten in the Soul by shewing their Objects out of their true proportions; either greater than the Life, or Less; but Instruction is to be given by shewing them what they naturally are. A man is to be cheated into Passion, but to be reason'd into Truth.

Dryden assumes, like Hector, that reason can establish the true proportions of things and show what they *naturally* are. Eight years later *An Essay Concerning Human Understanding* appeared, and in his discussion 'Of the Abuse of Words' (Book III, Chapter 10) Locke writes:

> All the artificial and figurative applications of words Eloquence hath invented are for nothing else but to insinuate wrong *Ideas*, move the Passions, and thereby mislead the Judgement, and so indeed are perfect Cheat . . .

And while these passages are before us I shall add one more, to pose a question which seems all the more pressing as we ponder the basis for Troylus's disagreement with Hector. F. R. Leavis's essay 'Tragedy and the Medium' includes this arresting remark on 'the tragic experience':

> It is as if we were challenged at the profoundest level with the question, 'In what does the significance of life reside?', and found ourselves contemplating, for answer, a view of life, and of the things giving it value, that makes the valued appear unquestionably more important than the valuer, so that significance lies, clearly and inescapably, in the willing adhesion of the individual self to something other than itself. (1952:132)

Just what sense should be attached to Leavis's use of the word 'appear' in relation to what he regards as 'clear and inescapable'?

I shall return to that question later, but we may observe here that Leavis himself is in some danger of making 'the service greater then the God'. My immediate concern is with that difficult triad, *value, valuer* and *valued*. To see how Shakespeare—not the man with laundry bills, but the disposing, directing intelligence at work within the works—keeps returning to Troylus's question is a good way of attending to the plays' imaginative integrity and creative continuity: so I shall argue in this chapter. And once we try to trace this continuing creative preoccupation with the act of valuing, two closely-related points emerge.

The first is this: in very varied ways, Shakespeare repeatedly exposes what may be called a process of *disjunction*. Once someone or something has been endowed with value a disjunction occurs, so that the value *appears* to be inherent in the valued and detached from the valuer. Perhaps, if Dr Johnson had not been so convinced that values are 'out there', he would have been less quick to object to a supposedly mixed metaphor in *Othello*—which actually represents the process of disjunction in a precise and moving way:

> But there where I have garner'd up my heart,
> Where either I must live, or beare no life,
> The Fountaine from the which my currant runnes . . .
> (4.1.58–60)

3

The idealistic Othello first endows, or invests, Desdemona with unique significance, garnering up his heart by making her his storehouse of value; and then he sees her as the fountain or source, from which his life *derives* significance and value.

The second point is that different views of the nature of Nature yield different accounts of value. To see why this so important we might consider a passage from one of Wordsworth's letters, which A. P. Rossiter quotes in *Angel with Horns* (295):

> What I should myself most value in my attempts is the spirituality with which I have *endeavoured to invest* the material universe, and the moral relations under which I have *wished to exhibit* its most ordinary appearances.

The italics are of course mine not Wordsworth's, and the italicised phrases show a process of disjunction so blissfully complete as to be altogether immune to irony or doubt. After observing that it is hard 'to see how anyone who *thinks* about Nature can have any faith in the famous lines' from *Tintern Abbey* about how 'Nature never did betray/ The heart that loves her', Rossiter recalls Dorothy Wordsworth's end as a paralytic imbecile and comments: 'Nature *does;* Nature did' (305, 310). The main thrust of Rossiter's fierce assault on 'the national park of Wordsworthian Nature' is that Wordsworth's vision of Nature and 'humanity' is 'so highly selective and exclusive' because it suppresses or fails to see that *under-nature* which is so terrifyingly present in *King Lear* and 'invites artistic expression in terms of agony, distortion, clashing paradox, diabolism'. The passage from Hume at the start of this chapter presents the conflict between two mutually exclusive visions of the nature of Nature in a clashing paradox which recalls *Hamlet* and Montaigne's essay on Sebonde.

In Shakespeare this conflict is closely connected with, and gives incomparable urgency to, his presentation of the idealists, cynics and nihilists who figure so prominently in the plays produced in the first decade of the new century. On the one hand, there is the sustaining humanistic vision of *natura naturans*, of 'great creating-Nature'; but there is also the utterly amoral 'Goddess' to whom an Edmund can appeal, and whose 'multiplying Villanies' will (if any 'Divell-Porter' opens the gate) 'swarme upon' a Macbeth, Angelo or Othello. The two visions yield opposed accounts of value. In the affirmative, humanistic view of Nature, Nature itself provides a sanction for human values, which then appear to be discovered, or recognised: they are, as Hector professes to believe, somehow 'out there'. So, for example, in *De conscribendis* (which Shakespeare certainly knew from the English version in Thomas Wilson's *Art of Rhetorike*, and drew on in his sonnets) Erasmus wrote:

> Naye sir (you will saye) we muste folowe vertue, rather then Nature. A gentle dishe. As thoughe anye thinge can be called vertue that is contrary unto Nature. (116)

But the opposed view of Nature allows no such affirmation: on the contrary, man is 'unaccommodated', exposed to the terrors of what Rossiter called the Shakespearean *undernature*, and values appear to be created or invented.

Hamlet's honour

A few examples should suggest how and why these creative preoccupations are so closely related. I shall take my preliminary examples from plays which are later examined in more detail, since I can here only indicate briefly how the local effect of the examples depends on their dramatic context. We see this, for instance, when Hector wants to deflect Troylus's question with an account of value which many of Shakespeare's contemporaries would have been ready to take for granted. The audience knows, although the assembled Trojan council in 2.2 does not yet know, of that challenge which Hector himself sent to the Greeks in 1.3: Hector has *already* committed the Trojans to a course of action which his arguments against Troylus would prohibit. And this means that, even as the crucial discussion of the problematic nature of valuing is released into the play, the audience must regard Hector's more attractively conventional argument with some unease. If Hector *believes* that Helen is 'not worth what she doth cost the keeping' (2.2.52), and that the moral laws of nations both coincide with and by implication derive from universal moral laws of Nature (184–90), why has he sent that challenge? Conversely, if he does not really believe his professed 'opinion' of the 'truth' (189–90), what principles or motives actually direct his actions? If we were taking this scene in isolation and attending to its philosophical implications, we could suppose that it presents a debate between a thoroughgoing sceptic and a man who believes in those natural laws of which Aristotle writes in the *Ethics* (V.7) and which Hooker assimilates to Christian belief in his *Laws of Ecclesiastical Polity* (I.iii–x); and the terms of such a debate are indeed relevant to Shakespeare's play. But the play introduces a further complication, and a deeper uncertainty about principles and motives, by suggesting that neither Troylus nor Hector is unequivocally committed to the opposed philosophical positions which they appear to represent.

Here *Troylus and Cressida* recalls *Hamlet*, and might even be regarded as that play's afterbirth; but there are less provocative ways of pointing to *Hamlet's* pivotal place within the *oeuvre*. One point is so obvious as to be easy to forget: by the end of the sixteenth century Shakespeare's fame and not inconsiderable fortune were based on the series of 'histories' and romantic comedies, and he might, like so many writers who become established and successful, have stopped trying to break new ground. *Hamlet* shows a remarkable redirection of creative energy, and was followed by a remarkable period of restless, radical experimentation. Moreover in *Hamlet*, the collision between opposed views of Nature and value is not only terrifyingly extensive; it is also internalised, to an unprecedented degree, so that the protagonist's own fractured view of the nature of Nature is at the centre of the play's nervous system.

One locus is provided, ironically enough, by a sentence which Ian Macdonald, a government spokesman during the 1982 war between Britain and Argentina over the Falklands/Malvinas, saw fit to lift from the 'How all occasions' soliloquy:

> Rightly to be great,
> Is not to stirre without great argument,

But greatly to find quarrel in a straw
When honour's at the stake.
                                            (4.4.53–6)

Quoting this sentence was incautious, not merely because
President Galtieri might equally have put it to the same
use, but because in the immediately preceding exchange with
Fortinbras's Captain, Hamlet takes a very different view of
this expedition to the Polish Malvinas. Here the word 'straw'
registers sorrowing contempt, not admiration:

Captain: Truly to speake, and with no addition,
We goe to gaine a little patch of ground
That hath in it no profit but the name
To pay five duckets, five, I would not farme it;
Nor will it yeeld to *Norway* or the *Pole*
A rancker rate, should it be sold in fee.
Hamlet: Why then the Pollacke never will defend it.
Captain: Yes, it is already garisond.
Hamlet: Two thousand soules, & twenty thousand duckets
Will not debate the question of this straw:
This is th'Impostume of much wealth and peace,
That inward breakes, and showes no cause without
Why the man dies. I humbly thanke you sir.
                                            (4.4.16–28)

The First Folio text of *Hamlet* gives only the first ten lines
of 4.4, omitting the conversation and soliloquy. In dramatic
and moral terms, rather than those of state propaganda, what
is most interesting about the sentence Mr Macdonald quoted
is the considerable inner division and doubt it reveals—as
soon as we try to trace the soliloquy's trajectory of thought
and feeling.

In proposing two criteria by which to establish what is
'rightly' great, the sentence *seems* logical enough. Hamlet
first reflects that a truly great prince will exercise his god-
like faculty of reason by refusing to go to war without 'great
argument'; he then goes on to allow that merely rational
considerations must none the less be set aside when 'honour'
is engaged, so that the ability to recognise what concerns a
prince's or a nation's 'honour' will be the second mark of
true princely greatness. But here the difficulty appears, since
Hamlet's soliloquy throws out two sharply opposed conceptions of 'honour' without showing how the gulf between

7

them might be bridged. For Hamlet to feel *shamed*, as he says he is, by the 'example' of Fortinbras's resolution presupposes that the Norwegian expedition should be regarded as something other than an insane waste of life in a worthless cause. Yet if 'honour' is merely a 'fantasie and tricke of fame' (4.4.61)—whether in general terms, or just in Fortinbras's particular case—then leading two or 20,000 men off to their imminent deaths is an obscene act of madness, and the 'How all occasions' soliloquy loses its own ostensible 'occasion': far from justifying the soliloquy's melodramatic and bloodthirsty conclusion, the 'example' shows why it so important to think precisely before embarking on any course of violent action.

Characteristically, Hamlet begins the soliloquy by lurching into the large question of what gives life value:

> What is a man
> If his chiefe good and market of his time
> Be but to sleepe and feede, a beast, no more . . .
> (33–5)

No less characteristically, he affirms that what makes men more than beasts is their sovereign faculty of reason:

> Sure he that made us with such large discourse
> Looking before and after, gave us not
> That capabilitie and god-like reason
> To fust in us unusd . . .
> (36–9)

Given that Hamlet's first response to the Captain's words showed shock and moral revulsion, we might expect that he will go on to criticise that Norwegian prince in whom reason does 'fust unused'. Nor is there any suggestion that Fortinbras's second expedition is supported by a greater argument than his earlier attempt to invade Denmark.

But of course, the soliloquy does develop differently, as Hamlet begins to arraign *himself*. He declares that he does 'not know' whether 'Bestiall oblivion' or 'thinking too precisely' has made him refrain from that revenge to which 'examples gross as earth exhort me'—and now Fortinbras enters the soliloquy, as a gross example:

8

Witness this Army of such masse and charge,
Led by a delicate and tender Prince,
Whose spirit with divine ambition puft,
Makes mouths at the invisible event,
Exposing what is mortall, and unsure,
To all that fortune, death, and danger dare,
Even for an Egge-shell. Rightly to be great . . .
                                        (47–53)

Even this is equivocal: should the actor give weight to 'puft',
which would call for a correspondingly sarcastic inflexion on
'delicate', 'tender' and 'divine'? This would suggest a moral
outrage like that Hector professes over a comparably futile
war: like Helen, the barren patch is not worth what it costs
to keep, and Hamlet appeals, like Hector, to reason as the
faculty which determines worth or value. Yet such ironies
would also deprive the speech of its 'occasion': the sentence
which appealed to Mrs Thatcher's spokesman is as Troylus-
like in its second half as it is, or seemed, Hector-like in its
first.

The whole speech is pulling in contrary directions. Hamlet
is indeed disposed to draw a shaming contrast between
Fortinbras's resolution and what he sees as his own
contemptible procrastination; but to make Fortinbras's readiness to go to war over a 'straw' or 'Egge-shell' the *proof*
of honour and greatness leaves no room for any positive
conception of the function of reason. In his next sentence
Hamlet declares—by now very excited, and multiplying his
first figure of 2000 by ten—that 'twenty thousand men' must
die 'for a fantasie and tricke of fame'. This fails to provide
any positive conception of *honour*, and even recalls Falstaff's
'catechism' (*1 Henry IV*, 5.1.126–40). There is a logical
impasse, for if 'honour' is no more than a 'fantasie'—if there
is nothing either honourable or dishonourable, but thinking
makes it so—the waste of life in a worthless cause is entirely
absurd. As Hector tells Troylus, 'bad success in a bad cause'
brings no honour; and even if it were merely Fortinbras's
conception of 'honour' which is an affront to natural and
God-given reason, Hamlet's contrast collapses.

At no point could Hamlet be accused of thinking too
precisely. That he claims to have 'cause, and will, and
strength, and meanes' to kill Claudius only adds to the air

of unreality in these reflections: he is after all being led from
Denmark by an armed escort—albeit a considerate escort,
which retires when he needs to soliloquise. The gulf between
reason and honour becomes ever more problematic, and by
the end of the soliloquy god-like reason is cutting its own
throat: instead of showing how reason might establish what
has or has not 'worth', Hamlet is reduced to howling, 'My
thoughts be bloody, or be nothing worth!' And by the end
of the play he is still disposed to approve, somehow, of
Fortinbras. He gives him his 'dying voice', which might have
been better employed, since Fortinbras shows that he can be
relied upon to see and seize his 'vantage'; that national
disaster which was once averted by Claudius's diplomacy
now takes place after all, so that Danes can henceforth be
led off by the thousand to die 'for an Eggge-shell'.

However, this logically tormented, self-tormenting soliloquy is also remarkably coherent: what comes through the
convulsive contradictions, and actually directs each twist in
the argument, is the intensity of Hamlet's disgust with
himself and the world. His attempt to make himself admire
Fortinbras proceeds from his determination to revile himself,
while the clash between concepts of 'honour' bears witness
to a more comprehensive collision between incompatible
views of Nature and value. In later plays, Shakespeare
frequently separates these opposed views by presenting them
as symbolic confrontations between different characters,
groups of characters, or cultures. Here, because the conflict
is internalised, there is no need for an Iago, Edmund or
Thersites: it is Hamlet himself who feels, voices and finds
his very hold on life is shaken by, a sickening apprehension
of all that is 'rank, and grosse in Nature'. Indeed, the soliloquy in which that phrase occurs also shows a *logical* deadlock which needs to be understood in relation to the speech's
emotional dynamics and Hamlet's self-division:

How weary, stale, flat, and unprofitable
Seemes to me all the uses of this world
Fie on 't? Oh fie, fie, 'tis an unweeded Garden
That growes to Seed: Things rank, and grosse in Nature
Possesse it meerely.

(1.2.133–7)

By speaking of what is 'rank' and 'grosse in Nature' Hamlet implies that there *is* some natural hierarchy of values admitting higher possibilities, just as his immediately preceding reference to 'the Everlasting' implies the existence of a supranatural order. Yet he is also saying that 'this world'—everything that is, in Nature—is entirely possessed by its weeds. 'Meerely' has an emotive, rather than logical, force, revealing the extent to which Hamlet is disposed to look for a hierarchy of values even as he denies its visibility. Similarly, the word 'seemes' is at odds with the sweepingly dismissive effect of 'all' and 'meerely': it allows for—even as Hamlet appears to deny—the possibility that his despairing view of the external world is determined by his own inner state. Later, when he tells Rosencrantz and Guildenstern that:

> this goodly frame the Earth, *seemes to me* a sterill Promontory . . . why, it *appeares* no other thing *to mee*, then a foule and pestilent congregation of vapours. . . . What a piece of worke is a man! how Noble in Reason . . . and yet *to me*, what is this Quintessence of Dust? (2.2.298–307)

the phrases I have italicised allow, once again, for the subjective nature of Hamlet's vision, even as he insists on the overwhelming imaginative reality of these negative apprehensions.

The earlier Hamlet whom Ophelia describes (3.1.150–61) had been the very embodiment of a humanistic ideal, the glorious epitome of the Renaissance polymath prince. These speeches allow us to measure the gulf which separates the man Hamlet was from the man he has become. His earlier mental habits still persist, as the customary reflexes of a resourceful, trained mind: it is still *natural* to Hamlet to appeal to first principles, to recall 'he who made us', to commend 'god-like reason', and to look for notions of inherent 'worth' and true greatness. But now his thought cannot keep to its old trajectories: recoiling from voids and horrors, it slides into illogicality, despair and violence. The speeches show, in a dramatically immediate way, that change which Ophelia describes in temporal, retrospective terms:

> that Noble, and most Soveraigne Reason,
> Like sweet Bels jangled out of tune, and harsh,

11

That unmatch'd Forme and Feature of blowne youth,
Blasted with extasie.

(3.1.157–60)

The earlier, harmonious and humanistic view of Nature and
Value has been displaced, but not replaced, and the 'How all
occasions' soliloquy shows why Hamlet cannot convert his
own worst apprehensions into settled cynicism, or dogmatic
nihilism. Too idealistic to dismiss the notion of 'honour'—
as would an Iago, Falstaff or Thersites—Hamlet is none the
less unable to arrive at any more positive, stable conception,
from which to resist the threatening idea that honour is a
mere 'fantasie' or mental fabrication. Similarly, Hamlet
cannot suppress the thought that 'There is nothing either
good or bad, but thinking makes it so' (2.2.248–9), but will
not surrender notions of value and deny the baffled aspirations of his own idealistic nature. The internalised collision
of opposed views of Nature and Value throws out these
painfully discrepant views of 'honour', and testifies to a more
comprehensive split between the internal and the external:
Hamlet is unable to project his moral needs and imaginative
aspirations back onto the world with any conviction. The
'Noble mind' is indeed 'o'erthrowne' by its fracturing vision
of a morally unaccommodated universe; the 'blowne youth'
has outgrown his strengths.

If we see this as a paradoxical and painful advance—for
although some critics do condescend to Hamlet as a 'case', it
is hard to think that the earlier, polymath prince was so profound—we might further reflect on this play's pivotal place
within the *oeuvre*. Hamlet's moral and imaginative disturbance could never be resolved by killing Claudius, nor should
the peculiar circumstances (the father's death, the mother's
remarriage) which precipitated the mental crisis obscure its
representative significance, in relation to the momentous
changes on which Donne reflects in *The First Anniversary*:

    new Philosophy calls all in doubt . . .
'Tis all in peeces, all cohaerance gone;
All just supply, and all Relation . . .

(206, 213–14)

For Ophelia to see Hamlet as a blown rose—the 'Rose of
the faire State', now a 'blowne youth,/ Blasted with extasie'—

is all the more poignant if we remember how in the early sonnets the symbol of the rose was associated with the humanistic idea of a serenely ordered and harmonious creation: it is this optimistic sense of divine and natural sanctions which is 'all in peeces'. Here, as has long been recognised, Hamlet's moral and imaginative crisis corresponds with the disturbance caused by a new astronomy which decentred man, by Machiavelli's challenge to traditional notions of degree, and by Montaigne's radically sceptical questioning of natural law.

Moreover, *Hamlet* and the plays that follow show another kind of shift or redirection of creative interest—first towards, and then away from, protagonists who are highly 'intellectual'. The first Quarto of *Hamlet* tells us that it was performed at the Universities of Oxford and Cambridge; moreover, although there is no evidence that *Troylus and Cressida* was performed on any popular stage in Shakespeare's lifetime, many critics and scholars have suggested that it was staged in what was in all but name the third University—that is, in the Inns of Court, where young and disaffected intellectuals like Donne were well placed to feel the alienating effects of 'new Philosophy'. If Hamlet is obviously Shakespeare's greatest 'intellectual'—with no precedent in the earlier plays, unless we allow Brutus—a marked intellectuality is also apparent in Ulysses, Hector and Troylus; in Angelo and Isabella, the youthfully inexperienced novices of *Measure for Measure;* and even, to some degree, in the heroine of *All's Well That Ends Well*, and in the Lafew who so ironically reflects on the irrational hubris of 'modern' rationalist philosophers (2.3.1–6). The critical habit of splitting these plays off into different generic groups has tended to obscure the extent to which they make successive approaches to Troylus's question. But then there is another shift: however formidable we find them in other respects, it would not occur to us to describe Othello, Macbeth, Lear, Timon, Coriolanus or Mark Antony as 'intellectuals'. In these later plays intellectuality, of the kind displayed by Hamlet at his most corrosive, is more likely to characterise the antagonists or *villains:* Othello is the first of these unintellectual protagonists and is (as Iago sardonically observes) decidedly 'unbookish'.

Othello mediates another complementary development, since the 'pilgrimage' of this 'erring Barbarian' has brought him to a society as ripely civilised, or indeed over-ripe, as the 'worlds' of *Hamlet, Troylus, All's Well* and *Measure*. These are all highly developed, complex societies within which (to appropriate Freud's relevant insight) civilisation has produced its own strains and discontents. Here the sharp, jolting contrast is provided by *Lear* and *Macbeth:* both the *Lear*-world and the *Macbeth*-world are terrifyingly primitive, although the removal from civilisation's costly amenities is predominantly temporal in the one case and geographical in the other. There are the worlds elsewhere—'France' in the one play and 'England' in the other—but the glimpsed higher possibilities are like distant rumours, and the unintellectual protagonists must find their way in violently primitive, unevolved societies. But these complementary developments, which suggest a Nietzschean interest in the 'genealogy' of man's moral and imaginative aspirations, also show a remarkable continuity in presenting different perspectives on the colliding visions of Nature and Value: Othello, Lear and Macbeth are all brought to a terrifying vision of what Rossiter called Shakespeare's *under-nature*—like Hamlet, Troylus, and even Angelo, who must confront what he has it in him to become.

Double vision

Here we may return to those lines from *Othello* which I quoted earlier, to illustrate Shakespeare's unnerving insight into the process of disjunction. They do indeed show how the 'valued' appears 'unquestionably more important than the valuer' (at least to the valuer), after 'the willing adhesion of the individual self to something other than itself'. To reapply Leavis's words to a play which he viewed very differently is provocative, but then, if we are to see how *Othello* returns to Troylus's question, we need to see how Shakespeare makes the contrast between Iago and Othello so absolute and comprehensive. Moreover, since the reductive, materialistic Iago presents what could be called the 'alternative account' of Othello's idealistic aspirations, it is particu-

larly instructive to see how Leavis's own account of the Moor
unexpectedly overlaps with Iago's.

For Iago, the prodigiously successful Othello owes his
success to his capacity for deceiving himself and others: 'Not
I for love and dutie' (1.1.60) establishes one of this play's
main antitheses, in opposing Iago's nihilistic materialism to
Othello's idealism. Love, for Iago, is 'merely a Lust of the
blood, and a permission of the will'—a 'sect' or 'scion' of
lust, and a product of 'the blood, and baseness of our Nature'
(1.3.325–44). It is 'merely' lust in fancy dress: by dressing
up both the lover's base appetites and the loved one, it
provides another example of those 'shaping phantasies' which
(as Theseus insisted, in a play more genially concerned with
the operations of blind Cupid) allow us to 'comprehend' the
'bringer' of the 'joy' we would 'apprehend'. Iago's use of the
word 'merely' is both like and unlike Hamlet's in his first
soliloquy, since Iago *exults* in his habitually destructive
reductivity, and takes a paradoxical pride in his fancied ability
to see through self-deceiving fancies: for Iago, 'gain'd knowledge' (1.3.378) consists in an awareness of the consistently
ugly truths which others evade. Othello's more elevated
conception of love necessarily depends on a quite different
conception of the nature of Nature, but for Iago this is
further proof—like the Moor's 'horribly stufft' epithets and
'bumbast' (1.1.13–14)—of Othello's intolerable self-esteem:
the uppity Moor cannot allow himself to acknowledge any
'base' or ordinary appetite, and instead projects his absurdly
inflated sense of the importance of his desires onto the desired
object. Paradoxically, Leavis's essay sets out to demote Iago's
'diabolic intellect', but promotes a view of Othello as a self-
deceiving egotist which very largely corresponds with Iago's
own judgement.

In Act 1 Iago has special reason to 'hate' the Moor whose
successes have coincided with his own failure to achieve
promotion. Iago cheers himself up by preparing the scenario
for a comedy which will be (on the best Jonsonian principles)
utterly unlaughable but highly instructive. It will show how,
'If the balance of our lives had not one Scale of Reason, to
poise another of Sensualitie, the blood, and baseness of our
Nature would conduct us to most preposterous Conclusions'
(1.3.323–8). First Cassio, and then Othello himself, will be

'conducted' to conclusions which are as preposterous as they are bloody; each will be 'now a sensible man, by and by a Foole, and presently a Beast' (2.3.295), and these horrible transformations will *demonstrate* the 'baseness of our Natures'. Like some subtle psychologists in our own century, Iago assumes that the practical success of a course of treatment establishes the truth of the diagnosis; our pressing difficulty is that of establishing why this is *not* the case—unless we think, like Leavis, that it is, in at least Othello's case.

The 'tragedy' may thus be said to contain its own very black parody, and an alarmingly dry-eyed view of its untragic elements. We are confronted with comedy, of a particularly nasty kind, when Othello rails that 'we can call these delicate Creatures ours,/ And not their Appetites' and then proceeds, like Leontes, to console himself with the thought that losing possessions in this way is 'the plague to Great-ones' (3.3.272–7; compare *The Winter's Tale*, 1.2.190–200). Iago has no difficulty in reconciling Othello's earlier, soulfully idealistic 'provulgations' with this ugliness: self-deceiving portentousness is now giving way to the *truth*—which for Iago is at odds with any morally and imaginatively constructive aspiration. Othello is being purged, unpacked, disabused, like Crispinus in Jonson's *Poetaster:* so much for the so-called 'Othello music', with its 'stufft' epithets and fancy notions. And in Iago's sadistic farce the handkerchief is a key prop: it will allow us to see Othello babbling of bits of anatomy ('Noses, Eares and Lippes') before collapsing in a fit—and when Othello comes to, he immediately starts roaring at Iago for laughing at his horns (4.1.42–62). The final scene is full of strange dark undercurrents of warped feeling: we see Othello girding his 'Soule' for the 'Cause', but stopping to ogle, and even sniff, that skin which is as 'smooth as Monumentall Alablaster'. Even when Othello knows that Desdemona was innocent he can bend over her corpse, murmur 'Cold, cold, my Girle?', and then add, 'Even like thy Chastity' (5.2.278–9). To be sure, few would want to describe that grotesquely disquietingly detail, or the sniffing, as *comic*, but they contribute to the scene which Dr Johnson found too terrible to endure, by being so wrenchingly untragic.

Such details are grotesque, examples of what Rossiter calls that vision of under-Nature which 'invites artistic expression in terms of agony, distortion, clashing paradox, diabolism'. Or we might describe such details as 'tragi-comic', to direct attention to the remarkable way in which the play itself includes two versions of 'Othello'. The two versions follow from Othello's and Iago's mutually exclusive visions of the nature of Nature, and the jarring effect is that of a grotesque *Gestalt* in which images from a vicious farce are superimposed upon images from a tragedy. Within Iago's Theatre of Cruelty the self-vindicating comedy is being staged with great success; yet we are also watching a tragedy of idealism in which the process of disjunction has itself contributed to Othello's dreadful vulnerability.

Precisely because Othello has *invested* Desdemona with unique value and then seen her as the *source* of value and significance, he has provided his materialistic inquisitor with the necessary opening: Iago can make Othello doubt Desdemona by making him doubt himself, and by exploiting the idealist's sense of personal insufficiency in relation to the object of his idealism. We see Iago settling to this task in 3.3, as he makes Othello reflect on the discrepancies between his age and Desdemona's, his sootiness and her beauty, his foreign awkwardness and her confident Venetian accomplishment. Once Othello is brought to doubt Desdemona, the process of disjunction goes into reverse: we see Othello struggling to recover a sense of purpose and significance by satanising her and seeing himself as a nobly deluded pilgrim. His 'Soule' can confront a new 'Cause'. He is St George, confronting the 'cunning'st Patterne of excelling Nature' to put out its light, 'else shee'l betray more men'. The 'honourable' murder becomes an heroic, Promethean self-sacrifice: 'This sorrow's heavenly,/ It strikes, where it doth love.'

In other words, the process of disjunction is the mainspring of *both* versions of 'Othello'. If Othello did not need to endow life with value and significance, and if his attitude to sexual relations were as undemandingly Gallic and functional as Cassio's dealings with Bianca, neither the black farce nor the tragedy of idealism could get started. But the two versions provide opposed accounts of this human need to endow life with significance. In Iago's horrible comedy, the morally

17

and imaginatively constructive aspiration is the sign of an intolerably inflated, self-aggrandising self-esteem; in the tragedy of idealism, the fact that Iago's experiment *works* does not establish the truth of the nihilistically reductive diagnosis.

Othello thus provides an example of the way in which that collision between different views of Nature and Value which was internalised in Hamlet's consciousness from the first tends, in the later plays, to be externalised until that moment when it invades the protagonist's consciousness. In *Othello* we begin with representative oppositions between Iago (fair without, foul within) and Othello (fair within, foul without) and their respective attitudes to 'love and dutie', human nature and the nature of Nature; we are then gradually brought to that devastating poetic-dramatic moment when Othello's own imagination is possessed by 'uncleanly Apprehensions' and the obscenely reductive Iago-view of Nature as a merely bestial, amoral process. But then the object of Iago's dramatic experiments was never merely the destruction of two men whose success threatens his own self-esteem: the assumptive basis for that self-esteem is a nihilistically materialistic view of the 'baseness of our Natures', and his experiments are designed to expose and exhibit the monster *within*—by penetrating the 'smooth dispose' of a 'proper' Florentine finger-kisser, and the 'bumbast' of an uppity Moor.

Here both Cassio's and Othello's moral evasions become peculiarly frightening, since they may be regarded as highly suspect attempts to deny the demonstrative force of Iago's experiments. Both men try to externalise the Evil, and to deny that the monster is within. Just as Cassio speaks of the 'divel' *in* drunkenness, of an alien 'Ingredient' which will 'transforme' men 'into Beasts', Othello can see himself as a victim of the devil in jealousy while pleading that he was 'not easily jealous'; and when he can no longer externalise the Evil by satanising Desdemona he sees Iago as the 'Divell' or 'demy-Divell' who has 'ensnar'd my Soule and Body'. Iago is indeed a devil in a *metaphorical* sense; he is also an atheist, and the force of *his* reductive diagnosis of Othello's nobility is reinforced by Othello's ignoble attempts to transfer guilt. A striking classical contrast is provided by that Greek conception of *atē* which at first seems so alien to our western traditions of establishing guilt in relation to the agent's intentions or *mens rea*, and which E. R. Dodds discusses so brilliantly in the first chapter of *The Greeks and the Irrational*. In the *Iliad* Agamemnon insists that his attempt on Achilles' mistress was the result of divine possession or *atē*, as indeed it was; but he also accepts full responsibility for what he regards as *his* 'act'—the thing of darkness is acknowledged his. But Othello will not allow that his 'Monstrous Acte' was the action of a monster: rather, it was an 'unluckie' deed, committed by an 'honourable Murderer, if you will'. True, we would not expect this Christian convert to view his crime in the manner of Agamemnon; but in Act 2, when he was engaged in a *successful* struggle to 'govern' his passions, he invoked the familiar Christian conception of a stratified psyche, strung between Heaven and a non-metaphorical Hell:

> Now by Heaven,
> My blood begins my safer Guides to rule,
> And passion (having my best judgement collied)
> Assaies to leade the way . . .
> (2.3.196–9)

And that, we may notice, followed immediately upon Montano's consideration of whether 'self-charitie be sometimes a vice' and self-defence a 'sinne'. In Act 5, it would be easier to resist Iago's corrosive diagnosis of Othello's self-deceiving 'baseness' if Othello were not so ready to invoke metaphorical devils in order to deflect any sense that the monstrous act is his, and to forget the contrary force of his wife's terror on his, as well as her own, behalf:

> That death's unnaturall, that kils for loving.
> Alas, why gnaw you so your nether-lip?
> Some bloody passion shakes your very Frame . . .
> (5.1.45–7)

Bradley and Coleridge were ready to share Othello's view of himself as an 'honourable Murderer'—but the 'self-charitie' of that view depends on an unChristian readiness to suppose that the murder would have been justified if Desdemona had committed adultery!

As I have already suggested, in Act 2 we also see how Cassio manages 'self-charitie'. He at first condemns himself in a harsh way: 'I have lost the immortall part of myselfe, and what remains is bestiall' (2.3.255–6). But this is unendurable, and Cassio is soon ready to invoke the 'divell drunkennesse' and the 'divell wrath' to explain why he would 'frankly despise my selfe'. The hint of recovering self-esteem in 'frankly' provides Iago with the chink to plug: 'Come, you are too severe a Moraller', he obligingly insists—and within a few moments Cassio has persuaded himself that he owes it to himself to 'beseech the vertuous Desdemona to undertake for me'. It is this all too human process of moral evasion which prompted T. S. Eliot to observe that Othello is guilty of 'moral bovarisme' in that very speech in which other critics had seen a revival of Othello's nobility; and of course Leavis approved of this negative diagnosis. But neither Eliot nor Leavis confronts the far uglier, nihilistic explanation which Iago has already provided for such self-deceiving evasions. The 'double vision' of Othello is sustained to the end: the nobly deluded tragic hero is also, as Emilia insists, a 'Gull' and 'dolt', as ignorant as dirt. The ensuing division in our own responses could be characterised in the terms of Donne's *Satyre III*. 'Kinde pitty', of the sort which Leavis extends to Angelo but withholds from Othello, chokes our spleen; but 'brave scorn'—our sense of what is monstrous in Othello's actions and evasions—forbids our tears, or ensures that when they fall they are not easing. I submit that we find Othello's evasions harder to endure than Emma Bovary's, because our own struggling, Bradleian sense of what is 'tragic' in Othello's situation is being so ruthlessly exposed to far more corrosive doubts: sceptical and metaphysical terrors have infected the tragedy to the point where it is constantly merging with Iago's nihilistic farce, and where our own 'uncleanly Apprehensions' make Othello's putative nobility another proof of 'baseness'.

Here we should distinguish between two different objections to the terms of Leavis's quarrel with Bradley. As we have seen, Leavis's view of Othello's self-deceiving egotism corresponds with Iago's; Leavis too is nothing if not critical. Bradley's view of Othello corresponds with Othello's view of himself as 'one that lov'd not wisely, but too well'. Each critic discounts the evidence which impresses the other, so that our first objection must be that both critics obscure the way in which the play itself presents, and opposes, two versions of 'Othello'. But then both critics also see this play as being more limited than *Macbeth* or *Lear:* because they blur the poetic-dramatic opposition between mutually exclusive views of human nature and the nature of Nature, Bradley can argue that *Othello* does not 'distend' the mind; and Leavis can disregard the frightening way in which the play exposes what is problematic in that arresting sentence from 'Tragedy and the "Medium" '. In his Nobel Prize acceptance speech, Czeslaw Milosz remarked that the great poet presents a 'vision of Being'; *Othello* impales us on the contradiction between *two* radically opposed visions of Nature and Being, which is internalised in our own struggling responses long before it is internalised in Othello's consciousness, as he plummets into Iago-like prose and imagery. Our second objection must be that both critics minimise the play's sceptical and metaphysical terrors.

The first objection might fairly easily be reapplied to other plays which have provoked polarised critical debates by projecting opposed views of a character. So for some critics, like Harold Goddard, Shylock is a crypto-tragic victim, whose human potentialities are warped by Venetian intolerance and brutality. Other critics object (echoing Leavis's charge against Bradley and Coleridge) that such a view 'sentimentalises' Shylock, whom they see as the black-hearted villain of a light-hearted comedy. Since this play also provides evidence to support both extreme readings, the critics are offering to resolve or remove that very doubt which concentrates our interest in Shylock, as the calls on our imaginative sympathy pull against the various promptings to a more detached, diagnostically adverse judgement.

But then my second objection to the terms of Leavis's quarrel with Bradley cannot be reapplied to the earlier 'Venetian' play, since there is no corresponding sense that momentous metaphysical issues are being engaged. What the polarised critical debate about Shylock threatens to obscure is not a poetic-dramatic projection of of different visions of Nature and Being, but our sense of the sceptically *interrogative* relation between the two stories which Shakespeare chose to interweave—the story of the caskets, and the story of the bond. This comparison between the two 'Venetian' plays is worth pressing a little further, since it suggests one way of characterising the *contrast* between the plays written before and after *Hamlet*, while at the same time providing further evidence of the *continuity* of Shakespeare's sceptical concern with acts of valuing.

Appraisal: Venice's Jew and Belmont's Moor

There is indeed one obvious sense in which Shakespeare 'began with' a racist stereotype and black-hearted comic butt: that is what 'the Jew' is in Ser Giovanni's *Il Pecorone*, which provided the story of the bond (and the ring imbroglio) but not the story of the caskets. It is clear too that Shakespeare became more concerned to show, through a characteristic exercise of imaginative inwardness, how the Jew apprehends his own situation. Taking these two obvious points together might well suggest that the ultimate cause of the debates about Shylock, Bertram, Angelo and Isabella, and Othello is to be found in the extraordinary contrast between Shakespeare's habit of creative interiorisation and the absence, in those Italian *novelle* which furnished the main stories of *The Merchant*, *All's Well*, *Measure for Measure* and *Othello*, of any corresponding concern with psychological motivation and the inner dynamics of character and feeling. In the *novelle*, interest is concentrated on the ingenuity and élan of the plotting, and the nice brilliance of its resolution; we are concerned with the various characters' relation to an unfolding situation but not with the unfolding, or inner development, of character, and in drama a similar point might be made of Jonson's *The Alchemist* or Machiavelli's *La Mandragola*. Some of the *novelle*—like Cinthio Giraldi's version of the *Measure for Measure* story, in which the Isabella-figure is raped, and her brother beheaded—become morally repellent if we are continually imagining how a character in a given situation would think and feel; but this is how Shakespeare evidently read, and raided, these stories.

In Boccaccio's *Decameron* (which provided the original version of the *All's Well* story) there is a very typical story about two very close friends. Both are married, and one eventually makes love to the other's wife; when the cuck-olded husband discovers this he cleverly traps his friend in a chest, and still more cleverly seduces the friend's wife on top of the chest. Although we need not suppose that the trapped husband is happy about this, he does not foam at the mouth and have an epileptic fit, like Othello or the trapped husband in Strindberg's *Creditors;* on the contrary, everybody acknowledges the brilliant justice of the ruse, and the quartet of friends is soon closer than ever—as Californians might say, getting it altogether altogether. Although the situation is clearly conceived in comic, external terms, a Shakespearean version would be tragi-comic or comi-tragic, since Shake-speare would be much concerned with the feelings of the man in the chest. The bed-tricks in *All's Well* and *Measure for Measure*, and the legal trick in the trial scene of *The Merchant of Venice*, are similarly ingenious devices of the kind favoured in the Italian *novelle;* but the Shakespearean presentation makes them problematic, precisely because we follow Shakespeare in being more concerned with inner states and processes of feeling.

When even Parolles finds it in him to protest 'Who cannot be crush'd with a plot?' (*All's Well*, 4.3.302), he is not only objecting to (and reminding us of) the externality of such Italianate tricks or devices, he is wounded, and when he reappears in the next act he is evidently still bruised. In the spirited but relatively heartless world of Jonsonian humours comedy the 'gull' is exposed, discharged and forgotten; but in Shakespeare the gull's experience of exposure is something he undergoes, or suffers. Malvolio and Shylock are appar-ently discharged and forgotten; but *we* find this more unnerving than the characters who remain onstage, since their oblivious delight with the success of a ruse jars upon our sense of Malvolio's humiliation or of Shylock's agony of frustration and helplessness. To say this is not to 'sentimen-talise' these characters, although we may go on to do just that; rather, it is to recognise the complicating effect of imaginative inwardness, and one reason for not 'sentimental-ising' Othello is provided by our consciousness that he is, as Emilia insists, a 'Gull' in Iago's dirty farce. Critical debates about the bed-tricks or Portia's legal trick cannot be resolved by reminders that the situations resemble those in *novelle*, since the *novelle* do not show a correspondingly dynamic apprehension of character and feeling, and it is this imaginative empathy which complicates the equation. And of course the point about the compulsiveness of Shakespeare's habit of creative interiorisation might be extended: so, for example, the polarised debate about Hal's character as prince and king arises because it matters so much—in the plays, but not in the Chronicles—what Hal feels or is incapable of feeling. In *Henry V* we are subjected to another species of 'double vision' as we notice how the hero of Agincourt gives the order to cut the throats of the French prisoners *before* he is provided with a suitably heroic reason or excuse for such an order; the hero is celebrated by the Chorus and parodied by Pistol.

The polarised critical debate about Shylock accentuates (by trying to deny) the conflicting suggestions within the play, while leaving it uncertain how far these are under control. So, for example, some critics are moved, in 3.1, by Shylock's grief at the loss of the turquoise which Leah gave him before their marriage, others pick up the hint provided by Solario's 'I never heard a passion so confused' (2.8.12), and emphasise the mercantilism of a grief which confounds the loss of a daughter (or wife) with the loss of ducats and jewels. Although this suggests the need for a supple, tentative appraisal, both A. D. Moody and Harold Goddard argue that 3.1 shows how the Venetians' brutal mockery of Shylock's grief *drives* him into insisting on the terms of his bond. To believe that, we would need to be sure that his purpose was not malevolent from the first, yet in 1.3 Shylock's motives are uncertain enough for Antonio and Bassanio to arrive at quite different assessments: interestingly, the brutally anti-Semitic Antonio suggests that the 'Hebrew' is showing a Christian (or gentile) gentleness, while it is Bassanio—who addresses Shylock by name and invites him to dinner—who has misgivings about the 'merry' bond. It is clear that questions are being posed, but not clear that they are being answered.

Even Shylock's most famous lines pull us in contrary directions. The apparent appeal to common humanity in 'Hath not a Jew eyes?' is set within a speech which attempts to justify an appalling act of inhuman vengefulness. For some critics, like John Russell Brown, the contextual undercutting is decisive—but what of the larger context? Should we simply discount Shylock's account of Christian vengefulness? Those critics who are most determined not to 'sentimentalise' Shylock often spare the Christians any comparably rigorous scrutiny, and indulge in special pleading. Russell Brown writes that Shylock 'brings out the worst in those he tries to harm: the "good Antonio" shows unfeeling contempt' (74)— as though it were not clear that Antonio's contempt *precedes* any opportunity that Shylock has to 'harm' him. Far from disputing Shylock's charge of racist hatred, Antonio insists that he will go on kicking, spurning and voiding his rheum upon the Jew (1.3.125–6). His anti-Semitism is astonishingly virulent, even by 'Venetian' standards, and this suggests why the historicists' lengthy discussions of Elizabethan anti-Semitism or Lopez's execution are critically unhelpful: like Elizabethan anti-Semitism (which did not prevent Queen Elizabeth from employing Lopez as her physician), 'Venetian' anti-Semitism evidently admits different degrees of intensity. Bassanio is not virulent in this way; Gratiano is nearly as vicious, but this is entirely consistent with his shallow character, whereas Antonio is also conceived as being loving, generous and mysteriously melancholy. Portia's continual use of the word 'Jew' in the trial scene is coolly, deliberately offensive, but we do not suppose that she is in the habit of kicking Jews when she sees them, whereas Antonio is. Like Shylock, he calls for a complex appraisal: trying to iron out the apparent inconsistencies, in order to see the 'good Antonio' either as his friends see him or as Shylock sees him, actually diminishes his interest and that of the play.

Shylock's characterisation of the 'Christian example' assumes that the Christian practice of 'revenge' bears no relation to Christian principles:

> If a *Jew* wrong a *Christian*, what is his humility, revenge? If a *Christian* wrong a *Jew*, what should his sufferance be by Christian example, why revenge? (3.1.57–60)

This looks back to the first part of Portia's first extended speech, in which she effectively introduces herself through engaging reflections on the great difficulty of practising what one preaches:

> If to doe were as easie as to know what were good to doe, Chappels had beene Churches, and poore mens cottages Princely Pallaces: it is a good Divine that followes his owne instructions; I can easier teach twentie what were good to be done, then be one of the twentie to follow mine owne teaching . . . (1.2.11 f.)

It also looks forward, like Portia's strategically placed speech, to the trial scene, where we see the discrepancy between Portia's eloquent invocation of the highest Christian 'teaching'—

> . . . in the course of Justice, none of us
> Should see salvation: we do pray for mercie,
> And that same prayer, doth teach us all to render
> The deeds of mercie . . .
>
> (4.1.194–7)

and her insistence that 'the Jew shall have all justice', 'nothing but the penalty' (316–17). After preventing Bassanio from repaying the loan with interest, Portia insists that Shylock must not even receive that 'principall' which furnished Bassanio with his finery: 'He shall have merely justice and his bond' (334). As Shylock bitterly observes, the next legal trick which Portia employs would deprive him of everything but a life he does not want; the 'mercy' which Portia invites Antonio to 'render' allows him to resolve his own financial problems and Lorenzo's, while also removing the hated Jew from the Rialto, since he cannot continue as a usurer after a forced conversion. The Christians' knife is given a final sadistic twist when Shylock is forced to declare himself 'content' with this 'mercie', or to accept the alternatives of confiscation *and* death:

> Duke: He shall doe this, or else I doe recant
>   The pardon that I late pronounced heere.
> Portia: Art thou contented Jew? what dost thou say?
> Shylock: I am content.
>
> (387–9)

The quality of this 'mercie' could not be more strained, nor does the discrepancy between principles and practice depend on whether we regard the Jew as a comic villain or as a crypto-tragic victim. Gratiano is delighted by the *novella*-like tricks, and shows how delightful they seem to anyone who is not concerned with Portia's and Antonio's motives, Shylock's agony, and Christian principles; but Shakespeare's presentation of the *novella*-like devices might be said to vindicate Shylock's earlier account of what a Jew and 'alien' who wrongs a Christian must expect.

I suggested that the first part of Portia's first speech looks forward to this keenly interrogative subversion of the story of the bond; the continuation of this speech relates her general thoughts to the play's other story, as it becomes clear that she is actually protesting against her own father's rigidly principled high-mindedness—and here, of course, we might begin to consider what Shakespeare gains by interweaving the two stories:

> . . . the braine may devise lawes for the blood, but a hot temper leapes ore a cold decree, such a hare is madnesse the youth, to skip ore the meshes of good counsaile the cripple; but this reason is not in fashion to choose me a husband: O mee, the word choose, I may neither choose whom I would, nor refuse whom I dislike, so is the wil of a living daughter curb'd by the will of a dead father: is it not hard *Nerissa*, that I cannot choose one, nor refuse none?

The fluent, lightly rueful worldliness of this is engaging, as it opposes a living daughter's hot will and affection to 'good counsaile' that is cold, crippled and confining. A familiar comic situation is being established, with an appropriately comic, worldly attitude to that situation: Portia's happiness, like that of Jessica (or Hermia), is threatened by the rigid will of a stern *senex*. But our readiness to run with Portia's 'hare' and 'skip ore the meshes' has consequences in the bond plot as well as the caskets plot: Shakespeare is concerned with the 'Fancie' that directs a maiden's eye *and* with the principles that don't direct our lives and judgements. So far as the test of the caskets is concerned, the nature of Portia's 'will' and 'Fancie' becomes clear when this play's Moor appears, and when Portia's three references to his 'complexion' show that she is *not* one of those who choose 'not by the view'.

As soon as the Prince of Morocco's arrival is reported to Portia she comments, 'if he have the condition of a Saint, and the complexion of a divell, I had rather he should shrive me then wive me' (1.2.116–18). Such high-spirited frankness is winning, but also reminds us that Portia is no Desdemona: she cannot see her Moor's visage in his mind, nor is she disposed to reflect that

> If Vertue no delighted Beautie lacke,
> This Suitor may prove farre more Faire then Blacke.

Morocco commences his wooing with the plea, 'Mislike me not for my complexion' (2.1.1)—and has the sense to give this up, once he has seen how Portia responds with a graciously diplomatic shuffle. Her assurance that she is not *solely* led by 'nice direction of a maidens eies' does not deny that 'complexion' matters; she goes on to add, no less equivocally, that the *lottery* of her destiny 'Bars me the right of voluntarie choosing'. (Taking the point, Morocco replies, 'Even for that I thank you'!) Later, when Morocco's life is ruined, and he leaves Belmont to face that 'frost' of celibacy to which his solemn oath commits him, Portia comments with cool, careless relief:

> A gentle riddance: draw the curtaines, go:
> Let all of his complexion choose me so.
> (2.7.78–9)

Within the two plots, 'good counsaile' reminds us that 'All that glisters is not gold' (2.7.65) and that a 'goodly apple' may be 'rotten at the heart': 'O what a goodly outside falsehood hath' (1.3.96–7). But when the glistering Bassanio arrives at Belmont, bedecked in borrowed riches, Portia's response is different enough to remind me of an old Hollywood film in which a suspicious blonde asks Cary Grant whether he also loves her for her mind: 'Of course,' runs the reply, 'but one thing at a time.'

I take it that Morocco focuses an irony which is too light and deft to produce disapproval. Portia's responses are winning, not least when she is admitting how far she falls short of an 'ever virtuous' father's hopes. Moreover, she is right: the fairy-tale test *is* a lottery (2.1.15). It eventually delivers the father's wealth and his more than willing daughter into the ready arms of a charming fortune-hunter who (since we cannot suppose that Bassanio would feel bound by his oath) risks only another man's money and a dear friend's life. The solemn messages in the caskets might just as well be shuffled: Morocco shows how Portia herself chooses 'by the view', nor does she worry whether, in Bassanio's case, the glister might not be gold. Shakespeare's glamorous and worldly Venetians are as morally equivocal as the sophisticated inhabitants of Henry James' Mayfair, and Bassanio—an Elizabethan Vanderbank—takes his place in the rather long line of Shakespearean matinée idols whose glistering exterior may conceal a lack of inner substance, or something worse. Bertram is the crucial instance, but the line also includes Proteus, the Claudio of *Much Ado*, and Posthumus with his 'Italian weedes'; it should probably also include Laertes, Troylus, the Claudio of *Measure for Measure* and Cassio. These are all parts which would naturally be given to a theatrical company's equivalent for a romantic tenor; they are also parts in which the character's glamorous appeal is itself brought under scrutiny.

Such irony is entirely in keeping with the decidedly unlyrical sentiments of the lyric heard 'whilst Bassanio comments on the caskets to himselfe':

Tell me where is fancie bred,
  Or in the heart, or in the head:
  How begot, how nourished. Replie, replie.
It is engendred in the eyes,
  With gazing fed, and Fancie dies,
  In the cradle where it lies:
  Let us all ring Fancies knell . . .
(3.2.63–70)

or with Portia's own deflating realism in 5.1, when she declares that 'Nothing is good I see without respect', that the effect of a nightingale's song would be different by day, and that this enchanted night is 'but the daylight sicke'. In 2.6 the references to Cupid and love's blindness are richly ironic—although Quiller-Couch suggests in the New Cambridge edition that Shakespeare borrows from the *scène à faire* in *The Jew of Malta* (when Abigail lowers treasure from a window) without having any 'real reason': 'Jessica, already dressed for flight, might even just have walked downstairs and handed the money-bags to her lover' (xix). If Jessica had done that, one nice but cruel irony would have been lost: we have just heard Shylock telling her to 'stop my houses eares, I meane my casements', in order to protect his 'sober' house from the 'shallow fopperie' of 'Christian fooles with varnisht faces' (2.5.32–4). But we would also have lost a more complex and unsettling irony. For as Jessica rounds up her father's ducats, Leah's turquoise and other swag—all of which will be exhausted by Act 5, when these lovers prettily admit to being 'starved' for fresh supplies of 'manna' (5.1.293–4)—her no less consciously pretty prattling shows that she is entirely preoccupied with her *appearance*. She feels 'shame' and wants to be 'obscur'd'—because she is in a boy's clothes, *not* because she is stealing:

> Heere, catch this casket, it is worth the paines,
> I am glad 'tis night, you do not looke on me,
> For I am much asham'd of my exchange:
> But love is blinde, and lovers cannot see
> The pretty follies that themselves commit,
> For if they could, *Cupid* himselfe would blush
> To see me thus transformed to a boy . . .
> What, must I hold a Candle to my shames?
> They in themselves goodsooth are too too light.
> Why 'tis an office of discovery Love,
> And I should be obscur'd . . .
> I will make fast the doores and guild my selfe
> With some more ducats, and be with you straight.
>   (2.6.33 f.)

Such prettiness naturally wins the admiration of Gratiano ('Now by my hood, a gentle, and no Jew') as well as Lorenzo ('true she is, as she hath prov'd her selfe')—naturally, since Jessica's priorities so clearly coincide with theirs: fine clothes, affairs, extravagant consumption, a good time and plenty of money or 'manna', which, like the 'mercie' dispensed in the trial scene, has no heavenly origin.

  Here too, the difficulty is that of registering the irony without making it seem heavy-handed or moralistic. It is obvious enough that we would think very differently of Desdemona if she eloped with bags of swag, but to make that point of an ironic comedy would be like taking Egeus' point of view in *A Midsummer Night's Dream*. On the other hand, we need to see what this comedy is being ironic *about*, and this scene beautifully shows how Jessica's priorities are, like her 'shames', 'too too light'. *She* does not see that her image of *gilding* might introduce a relevant, Macbeth-like pun on *guilt;* or that it recalls her father's reference to the *varnished* faces of Christian fools, Portia's father's reference to *glistering*, and this play's numerous contrasts (including Lorenzo's admiring reference to the *garnish* of a boy) between more sheen and substance. Her thoughtless reference to love's blindness might prompt *us* to think, once again, of the deception in surfaces, of 'Fancie' and the imagination's shaping fantasies. One effect of these ironies is that *we* cannot be as simply indulgent or simply censorious as these characters are in judging each other; rather, we see how Kingsley Amis's remark on Jane Austen *could* be reapplied to these Venetians, who also indulge where they might censure and censure where they might indulge. The play of irony establishes parallels which the characters never suspect or detect. The high spirits of Portia's 'Let me give light, but let me not be light' (5.1.129), or of her comparison of the candle's light with the shining of 'a good deed in a naughty world' (5.1.90-1), acquire a different resonance if we are thinking of Jessica's 'too too light' or of Portia's 'I can easier teach twentie what were good to be done, then be one of the twentie to follow mine owne teaching'—just as that earlier remark has a different resonance if we are considering its relation to Portia's behaviour in the trial scene, rather than her susceptibility to the gleaming Bassanio.

Instead of accepting these lovers' valuations of each other, or endorsing that clannish version of tunnel vision which prevents Jews and Christians from recognising their common humanity, we are continually prompted to make appraisals more complex and nuanced than any the characters can manage. The interrogative relation between the play's different parts suggest why it could be described as a comedy of appraisal—that is, a comedy concerned with diverse acts of valuing. The Shylock who grieves over the loss of ducats and a daughter, and who sets a material value on a pound of flesh, confuses moral or loving appraisal with mercantile 'rating'; but are we to express or suppress a similar thought when we first hear Bassanio rating 'a Lady richly left'? Portia cannot see Morocco's visage in his mind and is not inclined to try to do so, but her appraisal of Bassanio is directed by a frankly sensual, appreciative eye, while he and her other suitors must appraise the likely force of moral truisms in a test which is a lottery. Bassanio thinks Portia worth the venture; Lorenzo is told to catch a casket worth his pains. The Law must weigh Shylock's demand for 'Justice' (and the commercial dangers in refusing it) against Antonio's right to protection from an 'alien' he has repeatedly abused; when the matter is resolved to the Venetians' satisfaction, we are left to appraise the discrepancy between Justice and Mercy. As we hear Shylock, Lorenzo and Portia returning their different verdicts on music's power to move the affections, we appraise the connection between their aesthetic judgements and their characters. Even the ring imbroglio teasingly sets a husband's obligations to a wife against obligations to a friend and patron.

Because there is no imaginative summoning of the energies of the Shakespearean *under-nature*, our sense that love is itself a highly problematic act of valuing is not a source of moral and metaphysical terror, as it is in *Othello*. Yet the play's 'romantic' elements are exposed to a markedly unromantic, sceptically interrogative scrutiny; the discrepancy between seeing with the eyes (or imagination) and seeing with the mind (or reason) links both of these plays, just as it links the earlier *A Midsummer Night's Dream* to the later *Antony and Cleopatra*. To make these connections and continuities clearer we need to return to Theseus' distinction between *apprehending* and *comprehending*, and to see how the dramatic exposure of Theseus' hubristic rationalism issues not in irrationalism but in a more radically sceptical attitude towards imagination's 'shaping phantasies'.

Apprehending and comprehending

Love is an act of valuing; each time that we recognise, or simply take for granted, that somebody we love will not have the same value for others, we are managing a subtle accommodation between public and private realms of experience. In effect, we are allowing for the process of disjunction by making a nicely flexible distinction (which has its application in aesthetics) between our sense that somebody possesses unique value for us and our expectation that other people will understand this by having similar feelings about other people. But of course those who are incapable of such feelings cannot understand them, or understand them differently, like Iago. In *Measure for Measure* Claudio gives up trying to make Lucio understand that his feelings for Julietta involve more than 'Lechery', and this play's *only* act of 'mutual', reciprocal love is regarded by Claudio's judge, by his Christian intercessor, and by his self-appointed spiritual advisor as a filthy 'vice'. In the first scene of *King Lear* Cordelia's confidence that her passionate plainness will be understood (1.1.75–7) shows a loving trustfulness which effectively tests and exposes Lear: his own capacity to love is, like Gloster's, warped by the clamorous demands of the hungry ego, and their inability to distinguish between the accents of true and simulated feeling shows how reading the language of the 'heart' requires more than those anachronistic 'spectacles'.

If our love is betrayed or rejected we are not usually able to reflect, 'If I could endow her with unique value, I can do the same with somebody else', since the peculiar, self-committing nature of the imaginatively constructive investment springs from our need to believe that we are discovering or recognising values, not inventing them. Time may 'heal' such a wound, or the dark dynamics of rejection may film it over by convincing us that the object of our love was unworthy of such a gift; or we may prefer not to rebuild our lives, since this involves rebuilding the self, and since seeing how we can survive what we regarded as an unendurable loss can be unendurably shaming. The idealistic Othello garners up his heart, then sees the object and projection of his soul's desire as the source of life's significance and value: this may be unreasonable, or logically queer, but it is natural. The materialistic Iago regards love as disguised appetite combining with self-love, 'merely a lust of the blood and a permission of the will': this may be reasonable but it is unnatural—just as it would be unnatural to have merely those feelings for our parents or our children which they prompt in other people.

When Cleopatra hymns the dead Antony she does not ask Dolabella to endorse her particular sense of Antony's value. Rather, she asks him whether *his* sense of life's possibilities would make him deny the reality of any such imaginative affirmation:

> *Cleopatra*: Thinke you there was, or might be such a man
> As this I dreampt of?
> *Dolabella*: Gentle Madam, no.
> (5.2.93–4)

Cleopatra's marvelling, ironic use of the word *dream* has already allowed for a difference between the limited, material Antony and her loving apprehension of his qualities. In this way she has both anticipated Dolabella's reply and challenged it, by asking where such dreams and potentialities of feeling come from, if they are not in Nature. Her 'dream' is the most intense actualisation of her sense not only of Antony's and indeed her own potentialities, but of the mysterious and illimitable potentialities in life itself. She is challenging Dolabella to consider whether love and the creative imagination may ever see 'further then the eye hath shown' (Sonnet 69), and whether he apprehends life, and his own life, merely as a 'limited and material something'. I take that last phrase from the passage in *War and Peace* where Prince Andrew feels 'something new and joyful' stir in his soul as Natasha sings, and where Tolstoy invites us to recognise that Andrew's experience is not, or not in any conscious or simple sense, that of falling in love: the 'chief reason' for it

> was a sudden, vivid sense of the terrible contrast between something infinitely great and illimitable within him, and that limited and material something that he, and even she, was. (Book 6, chapter 18)

By so courteously setting limits on any such experience, Dolabella's 'Gentle Madam, no' deflects the real challenge of Cleopatra's 'Thinke you there was, *or might be . . . ?*'

We are returned, but by now with an immeasurably enriched sense of what is at issue, to the dialectical framing of alternatives in the play's first scene. For Dolabella is aligning himself, however regretfully, with the Philo who urged Demetrius to 'Take but good note', to 'Looke', 'Behold and see' how the 'triple Pillar of the world' has been 'transform'd Into a Strumpets Foole' (1.1.11–13). Here Antony is indeed 'transform'd' by Philo's way of seeing him, which in turn reflects that Roman concern with 'measure' and 'temper' (Philo's words) which Dolabella shares—even though he takes a more sympathetic view of the lovers' 'dotage', and pays Cleopatra a touched, touching tribute by declaring that he feels 'the very rebound' of a 'greefe' that establishes her greatness. But not her 'measure': those who cannot control themselves cannot control others—and the reward of such control is *power*, over oneself and others. Yet in the first scene it is this Roman, power-centred view of life's significance and value which is failing to satisfy the Antony who suddenly proclaims:

> Let Rome in Tyber melt, and the wide Arch
> Of the raing'd Empire fall: Heere is my space,
> Kingdomes are clay: Our dungie earth alike
> Feeds Beast as Man; the Noblenesse of life
> Is to do thus. . . .
>
> (1.1.33–7)

Antony soon lapses back into talk of 'the love of Love, and her soft houres', and asks, 'What sport tonight?' Throughout the play, such lapses reveal the lovers in their 'limited and material' aspects. Indeed, that puts it mildly, for everything we *see* on stage—that is, everything which corresponds with the Aristotelian account of an 'action'—buttresses the 'Roman' view of the lovers; but since Aristotle does not explain (in the version of the *Poetics* we have) how a poetic drama is *articulated* by its poetry, or why the prose summary of an 'action' could not of itself induce catharsis, he provides no way of accounting for this play's extraordinarily sustained *split* between what we continually *see* and what we intermittently *hear*, in those moments when the lovers' greatest poetry actualises their sense of life's potentialities and their corresponding sense of the life-denying littleness of Roman power-values. Harold Goddard has nicely remarked that the play draws a contrast between a man who gives up an empire for a whore and a man who will whore his sister for an empire. But this play's radical scepticism impales us on the opposed terms of a more momentous contrast and judgemental dilemma. Whatever sympathy we have for Antony's intermittently challenging concern with the 'Noblenesse' in life, and with a demand for significance and value which Roman power-values cannot satisfy, we also have to *see* the greying, grizzled, barrel-chested 'old ruffian' who rails at Cleopatra or messengers in a shamingly ignoble fashion, makes catastrophic decisions which betray his loyal soldiers and break Enobarbus's heart, and botches even his own suicide; the transcendental affirmations in his dying speeches are even exposed to the ludicrous spectacle of watching the women struggle to lug off that heavy, clumsily butchered carcase. Similarly, however much we want to give our imaginative credence to those revelatory intensities in Cleopatra's speech, as they summon and concentrate our sense of life-potentialities which 'Rome' denies, Dolabella's regretfully firm 'Gentle Madam, no' is also concentrating our awareness that this 'dream' can indeed be regarded as a compensatory fantasy.

Indeed, we might say that Shakespeare has invented Enobarbus (working from the merest hint in Plutarch) in order to *project* our own judgemental dilemma onto a character whose very life depends on a comparable choice. Enobarbus's great speech on Cleopatra shows how he responds—like Antony and his great predecessors—to Cleopatra's power to provoke desire and compel the imagination; and he provides the most sensitive register of the way in which Antony's own prodigal generosity of feeling inspires loyalty and devotion, unlike Octavius's 'temper' and 'measure'. But when Enobarbus is brought to acknowledge that following Antony is self-destructive or suicidal, he goes over to the other side—and dies, apparently from the force of his own despairing conviction that life on *these* terms is not worth living, let alone saving. We see Enobarbus being pressed, like that reader whom Leavis envisages in 'Tragedy and the "Medium" ', to arrive at an answer to the question, 'In what, ultimately, does the significance of life reside?' And this returns us to what is most challenging in Antony's 'Let Rome in Tyber melt' speech, or Cleopatra's 'Thinke you there was, or might be . . . ?', or to Hamlet's question about what ultimately distinguishes the life and death of a man from that of a beast. Because the characters' answers have consequences, and because we see how Enobarbus lives, and dies from, his answers, we are reminded that taking a 'Roman' view of the lovers also has consequences—like taking Iago's views of Othello. Our own judgemental dilemma is being *framed* within the play by those dual or multiple perspectives which the play itself provides in furnishing opposed views of its *characters* and of *issues* like love and honour.

J. L. Mackie's fine books on *Ethics* is subtitled 'Inventing Right and Wrong', and its main argument commences with the flat proposition, 'There are no objective values'. If values are not objective, or supernaturally sanctioned, what follows? For many people, including most Christians and many of Shakespeare's characters and critics, the answer is only too clear: cynicism, nihilism or despair. But these are not necessary consequences; other things may follow, including different kinds of self-commitment and affirmation. Enobarbus's death is a paradoxical affirmation, like that of Axel Heyst in Conrad's *Victory*. Since Shakespeare's plays suggest that the directing intelligence at work within the Works is both more sceptical than his idealistic characters and more tentatively—sceptically—affirmative than his nihilists and dogmatic sceptics, a Shakespearean formulation of Mackie's proposition might take the following form: 'There are, or may be, no objective values, but the need to endow life with value and significance is an objective fact about human nature.'

We are (very daringly) not told *how* Enobarbus dies; he appears to die, like some North American Indians, from the intensity of his wish not to go on living. This is a paradoxical affirmation because he comes to regard that prudential decision which could have prolonged his life as a denial of those values which, for him, sustain life. Before slaughtering Duncan, Macbeth also has to deny the deepest moral and imaginative needs of his 'nature'; because he is the man he is, the result of this preliminary self-mutilation is as catastrophic as Coriolanus' attempt to deny the inner promptings of *his* nature or 'instinct':

> Ile never
> Be such a Gosling to obey instinct; but stand
> As if a man were Author of himself
> And knew no other kin. . . .
>
> (5.3.34–7)

However much we might like to, we cannot and do not suppose that the human beasts who butcher Macduff's family will suffer Macbeth's inner torments. Rather, the *measure* of their inhumanity—or that of the butchers whom Macbeth appraises in 3.1: 'in the Catalogue ye goe for men'—is their lack of those moral and imaginative needs which Macbeth himself both registers, more intensely than any other character, and denies because he can no longer give them imaginative credence. In *Troylus and Cressida* Shakespeare is directly concerned with the issue of whether values are or are not objective, but in *Measure for Measure* he is far more concerned to explore the incompatibility of Angelo's and Isabella's different absolute values, and the nature of their need for self-commitment: the non-objectivity of values is only indirectly an issue—for example, when we ponder the irreconcilability of two moral absolutists' ultimate principles, and the way in which both Claudio's judge and Claudio's sister insist that their respective principles (to which Claudio is not committed) require that Claudio must die. All these plays are very different; but all represent different creative and exploratory responses to Troylus's question—or to Mackie's proposition when it is given the interrogative form, 'If values are not objective, what follows?'

We have seen how Hector's response to Troylus's glib but potentially terrifying question is to argue that the truly judicious 'prizer' can somehow match whatever 'estimate' he is inclined to make to an 'image' of the inherent value which 'dwels' in the prized and makes it 'precious of it selfe'. But this provides no sure defence against the operations of a doting, inclineable, attributive or idolatrous will: that 'image of th'affected merit' on which judgement must rely may itself be a product of the enkindled will. As Cressida puts it, the error of our eyes *directs* our mind (5.2.108), by furnishing the 'image' of what is then taken to be an in-dwelling virtue, quality or property of the valued. By the time she says this, Troylus is also registering the dilemma:

Shall I not lye, in publishing a truth?
Sith yet there is a credence in my heart:
An esperance so obstinately strong,
That doth invert that test of eyes and eares;
As if those organs had deceptious functions,
Created onely to calumniate.

(5.2.117–22)

So is Ulysses, when he explains to Achilles in 3.3 why virtue
cannot seek remuneration for the thing it was. Instead of
arguing, dogmatically, that there are no objective values,
Ulysses argues that our minds have no reliable means of
determining the objectivity or non-objectivity of a 'virtue'—
just as Montaigne will not deny that there may be witches
or miracles, but denies that the human mind can establish the
genuineness of either phenomenon. This makes the crucial
distinction between *dogmatic* scepticism, as represented by
the terminal, materialistic nihilism of a Thersites, Iago or
Edmund, and *radical* scepticism, which turns on itself—
weighing the human need to affirm values against the
inherently problematic nature of all acts of valuing.

Shakespeare's scepticism is radical in this sense, long before
there is evidence of his reading Montaigne. Here, it is worth
looking more closely at Theseus' dogmatically sceptical
speech on reason and imagination: our sense of local and
contextual ironies modifies our understanding of Theseus's
Hector-like contrast between *apprehending* and *comprehending*. Theseus himself plainly intends to be deflating: in
his own terms, whatever is not 'out there' for reason to
contemplate, comprehend and categorise does not exist, and
the lover, lunatic and poet are united by their susceptibility
to imaginative self-delusion.

                    I never may beleeve
These anticke Fables, nor these Fairy toyes,
Lovers and mad men have such seething braines,
Such shaping phantasies, that apprehend
More then coole reason ever comprehends.
The Lunaticke, the Lover, and the Poet,
Are of imagination all compact.
One sees more divels then vaste hell can hold;
That is the mad man. The Lover, all as franticke,
Sees *Helens* beauty in a brow of *Egipt*.
The Poets eye in a fine frenzy rolling,

Doth glance from heaven to earth, from earth to heaven.
And as imagination bodies forth
The formes of things unknowne; the Poets pen
Turnes them to shapes, and gives to airy nothing
A locall habitation, and a name.
Such tricks hath strong imagination,
That if it would but apprehend some joy,
It comprehends some bringer of that joy . . .

(5.1.2–20)

Here, the last lines acknowledge that very danger which Hector's argument ignores or disregards: Theseus uses the word *comprehend* ironically, since in this case the mind's 'image' of the object it would comprehend is itself a product of 'shaping phantasies'. But Shakespeare concentrates *his* (or the play's) irony on Theseus's first, *unironic* contrast between *apprehending* and *comprehending*. Theseus would apprehend the joy of thinking himself coolly reasonable: like Hector, he assumes that he has some immunity from those 'tricks' of imagination which in-form the mind's supposedly informed sense of what is 'out there' for reason to contemplate.

The main contrast between *apprehending* and *comprehending* depends on a usage of *comprehend* which is actually rare in Shakespeare. In *Much Ado about Nothing* there is comedy at Dogberry's expense when he muddles the two words (3.3.25, 3.5.46), but this joke depends on Dogberry's mistake with *apprehend*, not on a grasp of Theseus's distinction. In *The Rape of Lucrece* there is a reference to all that 'beforehand counsel comprehends' (494) and then, more significantly, to a sin deeper than 'bottomless conceit/ Can comprehend in still imagination' (701–2); but this rather suggests that a failure to *apprehend*, in immediately sensory and emotional terms, sets a limit on comprehension. The best gloss which I know, on the way in which Theseus himself intends his contrast to work, was provided some years later in Bacon's *The Advancement of Learning*, when Bacon praises King James as a scholar-king who is 'able to compass and comprehend the greatest matters, and nevertheless to touch and apprehend the least' (2). Here, the basic contrast is clarified and supported by the complementary contrast between *touching* and *compassing*. *Comprehending* evidently involves a fuller (comprehensive) grasping of a difficult meaning or idea, while *apprehending* involves a predominantly sensory or sympathetic perception, and emphasises that kind of responsive quickness implied earlier in the *Dream:*

> Dark night, that from the eye his function takes,
> The eare more quicke of apprehension makes.
> (3.2.177–8)

As in these two examples from *Measure for Measure, apprehending* may also involve a premonitory anticipation of the way in which we will be *touched* by something which cannot yet be experienced, understood or fully grasped:

> The sense of death is most in apprehension . . .
> (3.1.79)
> A man that apprehends death no more
> but as a drunken sleepe . . .
> (4.2.149)

As Julius Caesar observes, 'Men are Flesh and Blood, and apprehensive' (3.1.67). The root idea of seizing or 'taking in' impressions is more closely associated with the danger of being 'taken in'.

Here we might well pay tribute to the divining sensitivity of Shakespeare's cultural antennae, since *The Advancement of Learning* also prepares the ground for Dryden's and Locke's view of the imagination as a 'cheat'. Bacon's discussions of 'Poesy' rework some of Sidney's arguments, while giving them a more admonitory, Theseus-like inflexion. 'Poesy', it is allowed, may 'give some shadow of satisfaction to the mind of man in those points wherein the nature of things doth deny it', and 'raise and erect the mind, by submitting the shew of things to the desire of the mind'. But 'reason doth buckle and bow the mind unto the nature of things'; it is evident that, for Bacon, reality and the 'nature of things' are matters for Reason and Judgement (82–3). Later, Bacon's suspicion of 'Feigning' emerges in his remark that poetry is 'rather a pleasure or play of imagination, than a work or duty thereof', since 'in all persuasions that are wrought by eloquence and other impression of like nature, *which do paint and disguise the true appearance of things*, the

41

chief recommendation unto Reason is from the Imagination' (121). The eventual triumph of such attitudes appears in our own assumption that the term 'thinking' applies more obviously to the activity of Hume than to that of Blake, and that it would be oddly paradoxical to describe something— say, Dolabella's answer to Cleopatra—as 'merely objective'. In other words, Bacon not only helps us to clarify Theseus' contrast between imaginative apprehension and coolly rational comprehensions; he shows how Theseus's attitude tends towards a dogmatic and positivistic scepticism.

Like Sidney and Theseus, Bacon also has an aristocratically patronising conception of a spectator's or reader's involvement with a fiction; yet it would be hard to characterise an engaged response to the final scenes of *Lear* and *The Winter's Tale*, or even *Love's Labour's Lost*, in these terms, since these scenes actually prompt thought about the difference between what we expect of a work of art and what we expect of life. But when Theseus expresses his views on art and drama, they are exposed to Hippolyta's irony—and Shakespeare's:

> *Hippolyta*: This is the silliest stuffe that ere I heard.
> *Theseus*: The best in this kind are but shadowes, and the worst are no worse, if imagination amend them.
> *Hippolyta*: It must be your imagination then, & not theirs.
> (5.1.208–12)

Theseus argues for tolerance and charity, but in a way that devalues the objects of charity: all art, including 'the best in this kind', becomes no more than an entertaining interlude and Baconian 'shadow'. Theseus's attitude towards art is, of course, consistent with his distrust of creative imagination; it is, in the favourable and unfavourable sense of the word, patronising. We are pleased when he disregards Philostrate's snobbish advice, and chooses to be the presiding patron in the final scene of festive concord, but we are also aware of Theseus as a type who would patronise the author who has created him. In a typically acute way, Hippolyta's reply exposes the unconscious self-regard behind Theseus's indulgent magnanimity. Her subtle rebuke also extends, through four centuries, to those modern critics who suppose the necessarily collaborative 'recreation' of a work of art places them on a level with its creator. A great work of art never fails us, although we may fail it; but when it 'finds' us, in Coleridge's sense, what is it finding, and revealing about our own imaginative needs? Here, as we see how Theseus's confident speech on reason and imagination is quizzed, foxed, and above all encompassed, by a magic round or dance of ironic perspectives, we are also being drawn into the dance like an audience at a masque. The terms of our own imaginative engagement with *this* shaped fantasy become mysterious: like the transported lovers in Donne's 'The Extasie', 'We see, we saw not what did move'.

Such reflexivity plays on our awareness of a consummate illusion: as Dr Johnson rightly insisted, we know that we are spectators in a theatre, watching a triumph of creative imagination that is among 'the best of its kind'. But then, within the poetic-dramatic world of the play he inhabits, Theseus is simply wrong, and Hippolyta is right to call attention to the 'strange' constancy in the lover's stories:

> But all the storie of the night told over,
> And all their minds transfigur'd so together,
> More witnesseth than fancies images,
> And growes to something of great constancie;
> But howsoever, strange, and admirable.
>
> (5.1.23–7)

Hippolyta's 'howsoever' is both wondering and sceptical, where Theseus refuses to countenance the 'strange' and suspend judgement—like the radical sceptic—at that point where certainty is unattainable. Just as he persuades the quartet of green lovers to 'follow' him in dismissing their own experience as a 'dream', he has discounted or erased whatever seems irrational in his own experience—in capturing and wooing Hippolyta, and in his relationship with Titania, the 'night'-Hippolyta. Unacknowledged memories, irrational impulses and passions surround and press upon the laboriously cleared settlement of his Reason, like the 'wood' which surrounds Athens.

Various sly ironies, large and small, point to the place of the irrational in Theseus' own life. Because he likes the 'concord' of their barks, he hunts with dogs that are too heavily dewlapped to seize the game. In Athens, his citadel

of reason and law, he supports Egeus' irrational rage, and
then withdraws his support in the 'wood'. Since he is himself
a lover, he places himself in a comically false position when
he tells his bride what lovers, lunatics and poets have in
common. But the hubristic and irrational character of
Theseus's rationalism is most obviously exposed, in symbolic
terms, by the contrast with Oberon. Although Theseus
supposes that his rational government extends through the
'wood', Oberon is the far greater power, who controls the
weather and harvests, births and the affections. Theseus will
not recognise his own subjection to mysterious life-
processes—those of falling in love, or those of the circum-
ambient universe. Indeed, precisely because he is intelligent
and articulate but tries to discount his own moments of
vision, he is in this respect more ass-like than Bottom. He
is *ensconced in seeming knowledge*, like the modern philosophers who draw Lafeu's scorn in *All's Well*:

> They say miracles are past, and we have our Philosophicall persons, to
> make moderne and familiar things supernaturall and causeless. Hence is
> it, that we make trifles of terrours, ensconcing ourselves into seeming
> knowledge, when we should submit ourselves to an unknowne feare.
>
> (2.3.1–6)

True, Theseus will not have to pay for his hubris, like his
namesakes in Euripides' *Hippolytus* or Racine's *Phèdre;* nor
is there any accompanying vision of an under-nature more
terrifying than the scattered references to nasty creatures,
ruinous harvests, malformed babies and sodden English
summers. But Puck's reflection, 'Lord, what fooles these
mortals be', acquires unexpected philosophical (and Eras-
mian) depth, when we see how that very speech in which
Theseus asserts his rational scepticism keeps seeming to
dissolve and reconstitute itself in an elaborate comedy of
ironic perspectives. The very lines in which Theseus scorns
the imagination's power to body forth unknown forms are
regularly quoted out of context, as a tribute to the imagination as a Blakean power—which reveals the world by recre-
ating it, and does indeed see further than the Baconian eye
hath shown. The lines' brimming vitality makes it natural to
kidnap them in this way, disregarding what Theseus means to
mean. But the kidnap is also justified by the larger contextual

irony, of which Theseus is wholly unaware: he cannot see how his speech bears upon this play's own existence as a miracle of language and creative imagination. Puck's epilogue has the position and air of some conventionally self-deprecating authorial bid for applause; but here too the controlled magic of the conclusion is a triumphantly para-doxical and *proud* assertion of the power of 'shaping phant-asies'. Theseus's rationalism is itself irrational; like Hector, he refuses to see how his own mind's sense of what is 'out there' for reason to contemplate is subject to imagination. His refusal to submit his blinkered, dogmatic scepticism to a radically sceptical self-scrutiny is associated with a larger denial of those life-mysteries to which he is himself subject— mysteries which may be apprehended, but not compre-hended. Although Theseus does not believe in fairies, he needs, and receives, their blessing. The basic *concetto* which opposes rational Athens to the seething underlife of the 'wood' sets reason against our sense of a mysterious and uncharted hinterland: here, as in Dr Johnson's comparison of the moralist to a taper 'by which we are led through the labyrinth of complicated passions' (*Rambler* 77), the unknown bulks larger than the known.

Harold Brooks is making a similar point when he observes, in the New Arden *Dream*, that the play's abrupt, unmotiv-ated reversals 'raise doubts about the self-consistency, even the continuous existence, of personal identity, and whether we are not, in Auden's words, "lived by powers we pretend to understand" ' (cxxxviii). But then—perhaps because he sees some danger in this line of thought, or even some horrible apparition of a Nietzsche in buskins—Brooks adds: 'They raise these doubts: they do not endorse them, as in an absurdist frame of mind a modern sceptic might.' Yet if this play does not 'endorse' such doubts, it does not resolve or dissolve them either; nor does it allow the kind of categorical clarity which appears in Brook's comment that Helena's love for Demetrius 'is not folly in itself, but only so long as Demetrius is incapable of returning it', so that once 'his imagination is directed back from Hermia to her, what was her dotage recovers the nature and status of true love' (cxxxv). The point, I take it, is that love—'doting' or 'true'—is not rational: Theseus draws so many ironies upon himself by likening the lover to the lunatic and poet, and by showing how his conventional understanding of the operations of blind Cupid is associated with a more extensively derogatory attitude towards imagination.

As Erwin Panofsky observes in *Studies in Iconology*, the nude bow-boy is never blind in Hellenistic and Roman art: his blindness was a medieval innovation, 'invented and stigmatized by moralizing mythographers', and 'puts him definitely on the wrong side of the moral world' (108–9). Shakespeare places the defects of a lover's visionary fancies in a more complex and teasing relation to the effects of imagination, which are variously described by different characters. For Theseus, the imagination 'amends' and 'apprehends'; for Bottom, it 'translates'; for Hippolyta it 'transfigures'; for Helena, it 'transposes':

> Things base and vile, holding no quantity,
> Love can transpose to forme and dignity,
> Love lookes not with the eyes, but with the minde,
> And therefore is wing'd *Cupid* painted blinde.
> Nor hath loves minde of any judgement taste . . .
>
> (1.1.232–6)

Helena recognises that just as Demetrius 'erres, doting on *Hermias* eyes' and 'will not know, what all, but he doth know', she herself errs in 'admiring of his qualities'. Yet this admitted rift between judgement and fancy is not experienced—as it is, for example, in many of the *Sonnets*—as a terrible and dislocating psychic derangement. Rather, Helena accepts this rift, as one of those life-mysteries which Theseus is intent on denying. Her love remains the most important reality in her life, and she is sad and disturbed only because Demetrius has similarly irrational feelings for another.

In commenting on Helena's lines Stephen Fender draws a helpful contrast with various medieval and Renaissance presentations of 'ymagynatif' and 'blind Cupid', to isolate what is so startlingly original in Shakespeare's development of these conventional *topoi*:

> The main point to note is that this form of love was always a 'bad' one and its blindness a distinctly pejorative attitude, stemming from a

tradition of medieval iconography which associated blindness with evil, with spiritual and physical death . . . There seems to have been no argument about possible 'good' and 'bad' meanings of blindness itself.

But in *A Midsummer Night's Dream* Shakespeare adopts this convention in which blind love is unambiguously 'bad' only to qualify it radically. Helena's moral lesson on Cupid is set in a context that gives it a possible 'good' meaning too . . .

The fact that love can change the ugly into the beautiful can be condemned or admired, according to one's point of view. Looked at in one way, it is obviously absurd, and Theseus makes it an occasion for satire . . . But from another point of view it can be seen as an act of almost divine creativity. (23–4)

Instead of appealing, like Harold Brooks, to those categories of folly and reason which the play itself is constantly threatening to dissolve, Fender here isolates what is so radically sceptical in the play's ironic subversion of Theseus's distinction between 'apprehending' and 'comprehending'. The concept of *shaping fantasy* is extended so that it does indeed include love, art and lunacy—not on Theseus's terms, but in relation to what is problematic in all acts of valuing. We are brought to ask how many of those things large or small which 'give' life value—including love and friendship, and the liking for dogs, hunting or plays—depend on that shaping fantasy which 'adds a precious seeing to the eye' (*Love's Labour's Lost*, 4.3.330).

Consequently, we might characterise the disagreement between Cleopatra and Dolabella in a way which also points to the remarkable continuities within Shakespeare's *oeuvre*: Cleopatra and Dolabella are disagreeing about the force of Theseus' distinction. In a more general sense, Shakespeare is continually inviting us to 'apprehend' and 'comprehend' his characters; so, as Wilbur Sanders observes in discussing Macbeth, we are challenged to see *with* him, not merely to 'see through' him. Shakespeare's extraordinary imaginative empathy constantly allows us to see and feel how a character—Macbeth, Shylock, Othello—apprehends his own situation; at the same time the plays frame dual or multiple perspectives both on the characters and on issues like 'love' and 'honour'. One result is that we are challenged by a distinctive and irreducible kind of moral thinking which considers people both as agents and as lives: here I am drawing, gratefully, on S. L. Goldberg's brilliant essay on

'Making Moral Sense of People', which is also much concerned with the larger significance of Cleopatra's exchange with Dolabella. As Goldberg observes:

> The deepest moral consideration of a person's actions can bring the mind to swivel around to considering him as a life—as the particular, total being, with a unique moral history, which those actions manifest and which they help to shape. Similarly, the deepest moral considerations of a unique personal life can itself bring the mind to swivel around to considering certain of his actions in the light of criteria that apply to anyone and everyone. (25)

Moreover, this challenge is extended in those plays which, like *Antony and Cleopatra*, exclude Christian perspectives, since this historical and practical necessity has a liberating effect on Shakespeare's exploration of man's moral and imaginative needs. Here, we might say, Shakespeare is at times thinking like a cultural anthropologist of genius, for whom—to borrow a phrase from Clifford Geertz—man is 'an animal suspended in webs of significance he himself has spun'. The challenge to 'apprehend' and 'comprehend' Antony's sense of the 'Noblenesse of life', or those moral imperatives which culminate in Brutus's suicide or Coriolanus's fatal affirmation, involves imagining and exploring an alien culture with its own 'webs of significance' or ensemble of symbolic systems to guide behaviour and order subjective experience. In this sense Shakespeare's approaches to 'Rome' resemble Geertz's approaches to 'Islam'.

But then I take it that this is no less true of *Macbeth* or *Lear*, *Hamlet* or *Othello*—for even where there are explicitly Christian perspectives they are dramatised. They are given to characters who have no privileged, supra-dramatic status; and they are exposed, in *Hamlet* and the plays that follow, to the terrifying imaginative summoning of the Shakespearean *under-nature*. This is why *Othello* has that metaphysical dimension which neither Leavis nor Bradley acknowledges. It is also why *Macbeth* is, no less than *Measure for Measure*, a 'play of ideas' which involves us in the distinctive and irreducible Shakespearean modes of 'dramatic thinking'.

To develop these last claims, I must first complete this preliminary survey of Shakespeare's scepticism by looking more closely at the essentially poetic-dramatic conditions of

Shakespeare's perspectivism. We may best see, I think, why Shakespeare's scepticism is so radical, and why his modes of 'dramatic thinking' are richer and more complex than those of logical, discursive thought, by considering his various approaches to Troylus' question on the one hand and his poetic-dramatic perspectivism on the other; but my argument is also intended to establish that these two aspects are strictly inseparable in Shakespeare's art and thought, so that neither can be seen as the other's cause or effect.

TWO

Framing Perspectives

Well known things and beings—or rather the ideas that represent them—
somehow change in value. They attract one another, they are connected
in ways quite different from the ordinary; they become (if you will
permit the expression) *musicalized*, resonant, and, as it were, harmon-
ically related.

Paul Valéry, 'Poetry and Abstract Thought'

Registers

Poetic drama is 'scored' like a musical composition, and the
given distribution of registers of verse and prose functions as
a constituent of meaning; we need ears to see. The allocation
of a register provides a means of characterisation and also of
appraisal, since each character's register is apprehended
within the poetic-dramatic complex of internally coherent
contrasts. That Falstaff speaks only in prose is dramatically
meaningful. The registers frame and order the endless and
chaotic range of human potentialities, and here a comparison
with other conventions is instructive. In western opera a king
is usually a bass or bass-baritone since we associate authority,
conventionally, with these vocal registers. The corresponding
convention in Shakespearean drama is that a king will speak
verse, while a base mechanic will speak low prose. In Chinese
opera the role of the man with the highest authority is
commonly given to the man with the highest voice; the
different convention makes its own sense, like the different
perspectival conventions in Chinese painting, and the tenor
emperor in Puccini's *Turandot* provides a nicely pointed
Oriental exception to the Occidental rule. By extension, it is

inconceivable in *La Traviata*, but not in life, that the formidable older Germont should have a higher vocal register than his son. Sacred music deploys these associative conventions when, as in many Bach cantatas, it is also evolving into an early form of music drama. In Bach's *Jesu, der du meine Seele* such conventions determine the apparently 'natural' way in which the downward movement of vocal registers (from soprano to bass) projects a sequence of increasingly complex psychological states. Bach is not assuming that the feelings of a bass Protestant are necessarily more profound, in the other sense, than those of a soprano or tenor. The associative conventions are metaphorical or symbolic, not literal or naturalistic; this allows us to 'see', as well as feel, the depicted emotion, as we recognise its contributive place within an internally coherent constellation of registers.

The regal command of a Shakespearean king will appear, more subtly, in his sensitive command of a range of registers: Henry V is a virtuoso in the art of adapting his register to a particular audience or occasion, while Richard II or Macbeth are not. One pressing dramatic question in *Henry IV* is how well, and in what ways, Prince Hal is *equipped* to be King: amongst other things, we appraise his stylistic registers. To bring out the general point, I want to look rather closely at two scenes which show the stylistic contrast between Hal and Hotspur, who has an energetic command of a limited range of poetic registers; these scenes show how internally coherent stylistic contrasts clarify or complicate dramatic meaning, and also show how Shakespeare exploits poetic-dramatic conventions by subverting them, just as he repeatedly subverts our generic expectations.

When Hal enters speaking prose it is a shock—if we have ears to register it and actors to preserve it. Here is the heir apparent, and he is speaking prose with a commoner: the unexpected use of a prose register seems to lend weight to that comparison the king has just drawn between the two Harries; Hal and Hotspur. And yet, as Jonas Barish shows in a fine analysis (45–7), the prince's prose is courtly, beautifully and elaboratedly cadenced. Moreover, as soon as Hal is left alone at the end of this scene he speaks verse. This suggests that verse is, after all, his conventionally 'natural' register, and that the King's judgement of his son may be over-hasty. It also suggests that Hal had *chosen* to use a prosaic register in talking with Falstaff, and his stylistic mobility might seem more assured than his father's. As the play began we heard the King pitching his style very high, as if to show that he is *not* a mere usurper and a vile politician; but then, when he finally addresses pressing pratical problems, the awkward drop to a more colloquially blunt and business-like register shows the weary but purposeful politician:

> But this our purpose is a twelvemonth old,
> And bootlesse 'tis to tell you we will go:
> Therefore we meete not now. Then let me heare . . .
> (1.1.1–33)

The last word of that long speech is 'expedience'. Hal enters in the next scene, and Hotspur in the third; we soon see that Hal is indeed a stylistic virtuoso, with a very limber command of different registers of prose and verse, whereas Hotspur's tempestuous, huffing-heroic vein is limited in range and cannot be controlled at will. Since poetic-dramatic registers correspond with ways of seeing and modes of feeling—without the registers, there is no possibility of *having* certain perceptions and feelings—this provides *one* answer to the question whether Hal is equipped to be king.

But the word 'will' might focus another kind of unease, which concerns Hal's very ability to be the lord and owner of his face and styles. The King might indeed be reassured, if he could hear his unobserved son coolly planning his own glittering 'reformation'; but if we have just relished the gusto, warmth and apparent affection which animates the prose exchanges between Falstaff and his prince, a problem is being framed, rather than resolved, by the contrast between Hal's prose and verse. As its etymology reminds us, 'ingenuousness' was traditionally considered to be both a moral and a distinctively aristocratic virtue; but this stylistic virtuoso is evidently not, and in his own view cannot afford to be, ingenuous, whereas Hotspur is, and pays the price. Here we might notice how Hal anticipates and differs from another unconventional prince, who is, for better and worse, less concerned with his princely role. Hamlet is a still more impressive stylistic virtuoso, who pitches his style to its occasion and pulls register as other princes pull rank. He dances stylistic rings around the devastated Ostric (or Osric), but addresses the players, whom he likes and trusts, in a prose that is easily familiar, even startlingly democratic. Such prosaic familiarity carries its own pointedly cutting rebuke when Hamlet challenges Rosencrantz and Guildenstern to admit why they were sent for; these are men he should be able to trust, but cannot. But if Hal's stylistic virtuosity anticipates Hamlet's there is also a significant difference: Hal is concerned with how he may 'show more goodly, and attract more eyes', and it is never his pleasure, any more than it is his duty, to reveal that within which passeth show.

Must royal duty override personal inclination and affection? The second scenes of both *Henry IV* and *Hamlet* frame that question by giving us grounds for thinking, and fearing, that it must or should. In *Hamlet* it does not: one source of our gathering unease is that the prince who has just been designated heir to the throne is so absorbed by 'that within' as to be entirely indifferent to the threatened Norwegian invasion. The usurper and vile politician who occupies the Danish throne deals very shrewdly with this national danger; Hamlet's first and last action when he ascends to the throne will be to deliver his country to the foreign prince who threatened it in the second scene (and who might have been called Coldspur). In contrast, Hal's first soliloquy reassures us by suggesting that *his* sense of duty is firm and hard; but it also makes us start reckoning the likely cost, in personal rather than national terms. Those critics who are also 'severe morallers'—and there are many of them, just as there are many 'Falstaffians'—are reluctant to acknowledge any tremor of doubt or disquiet when Falstaff appears in the soliloquy's imagery as a mere base and contagious cloud, which might have smothered, but will be made to set off, the hard glittering glory of the emergent *roi soleil*. Just as the 'morallers' justify Hal's rejection of Falstaff by reminding us, with their hero's single-minded firmness, of the king's duties, they disregard the way in which the soliloquy suggests that Hal is coldly and deliberately *using* Falstaff. Love creates obligations, but these do not press upon the soliloquising prince. Which does not mean that we are justified in flying to the other, 'Falstaffian' extreme. On the contrary, we should be noticing how and why Falstaff is confined to, and confined by, his prosaic registers. The only exception brilliantly exploits the poetic-dramatic convention: Falstaff's one momentary flutter into verse occurs in 2.4—when he is imitating a king, and challenges Hal to speak 'halfe so gravely, so majestically, both in word and matter'. Like Iago, Falstaff prides himself on truth-telling but speaks a language in which it is only possible to tell some kinds of truth. His language speaks him, and its limited registers are placed within the incomparably large range of registers within the play as a whole (or two wholes: that issue need not distract us here). Our corresponding sense that various human potentialities and aspirations are entirely beyond Falstaff's range has important consequences. It should ensure that our delighted response to Falstaff's wonderful catechism on Honour commits us no further than Gloster's response to Edgar's 'Ripeness is all': 'And *that's* true *too*', says Gloster. If we do indulge our own more bluffly reductive, jovially cynical Falstaffian selves by supposing that the catechism's truth is adequate or comprehensive then we shall have no grounds for moral disquiet when Prince John deceives the rebels—promising them a pardon if they surrender without a fight, and then ordering their execution. Conversely, if we raise a morally superior eyebrow at the catechism and shake with moral outrage at John's dishonourable, Machiavellian craft, we are refusing to think about the real and pressing conflict between princely Honour and princely Duty: if the common weal be preserved by craft, why risk it in combat—and why expose brave loyal subjects to the dangers of a battlefield? Once Hal becomes Henry V, he too has to weigh the claims of honour or affection against those of duty, necessity or 'expedience'; he gives the order to kill the French prisoners before learning of the event which then provides an 'official' justification for that order; and he gives the order which puts Bardolph's fire quite out. As a prince, Hal can show fine indifference to the public honour of killing the other Harry, while also paying a movingly private and privately honourable tribute to Hotspur's mangled corpse. But the King, whose first action is to reject Falstaff, can no longer afford such moving gestures, nor is it certain that he could still manage them. Like *Hamlet*, Shakespeare's second tetralogy challenges us to think about Honour—what it means, and what its pursuit may cost oneself or others—and to recognise that the claims of Honour are not always compatible with those of Duty, or of Love.

Neither the 'Falstaffian' critic nor the stern 'moraller' can do justice to the dynamic perspectivalism of the play's exploration of opposed claims and sanctions; both kinds of critic must short-circuit the complex energies of the second scene of *Henry IV*, in order to arrive at their respective, carefully edited and mutually exclusive views of Hal. Just how far the scene pulls us in contrary directions, which depend on the articulating function of the poetic-dramatic registers, may be seen if we reflect on the insuperable problems which would confront any translator who wants to turn the whole play into prose. Even though the second scene is largely in prose, the translator cannot reproduce the shock of Hal's prosaic entry, or the correspondingly reassuring effect of his shift into verse, or the complicated ways in which both shock and relief are qualified. Nor could he recreate that sense of Hal's stylistic range and virtuosity as something which makes us reflect that whereas Hotspur and Falstaff are confined by their registers Hal is confined by his role. If these things must disappear, or survive only in mutilated form, how much is left?

A stylistic register may provide a remarkably comprehensive index to moral, social and political attitudes. We see this when the stoic, republican Brutus addresses the Romans in prose while Antony inflames them with verse: the one man does not know or want to know how to maniupulate others, and is—like Hotspur—manipulated; the other is, like Hal, a virtuoso who manipulates others and even his own deepest, genuine emotions. In *Henry IV* the quarrel between Hotspur and Glendower shows—through a less obvious but breathtaking poetic-dramatic *coup*—just how important it is to be attuned to the far-reaching implications of a clash of registers. Shakespeare presents the conflict between two medieval rebels as a clash between two Elizabethan poetics; for any member of the first audience who kept up with the very latest poetry, this scene must have seemed astonishingly topical.

As D.W. Harding observes in *Words in Rhythm*, Glendower *sounds* like one of the Elizabethan poetic miscellanies:

> I can speake English, Lord, as well as you:
> For I was trayn'd up in the English Court,
> Where, being but young, I framed to the Harpe
> Many an English Dittie, lovely well,
> And gave the Tongue a helpfull Ornament:
> A Vertue that was never seene in you.
>
> (*1 Henry IV*, 3.1.121–6)

The Tottel who so busily corrected Wyatt's supposed irregularities for his 1557 miscellany would have approved of Glendower's sentiments and his versifying, for here, with some unobtrusive Surrey-like modulations, is that steady alternation of stressed and 'unstressed' syllables which Gascoigne desiderated in his *Certayne Notes of Instruction concerning the making of verse or ryme in English;* Gascoigne's dispiriting diagrams show how opposed he was (in theory, if not in his own best poems) to admitting the disruptive, complicating rhythms of passionate speech. Shakespeare's Welsh windbag is a Courtly Maker. 'Framed' would be enough to disgust Hotspur; his rejection of this poetic is not so much disruptive as eruptive, and unexpectedly comprehensive:

> Marry, and I am glad of it with all my heart,
> I had rather be a Kitten, and cry mew
> Then one of these same Meeter Ballad-mongers:
> I had rather heare a Brazen canstick turn'd,
> Or a dry Wheele grate on the Axle-tree,
> And that would set my teeth nothing on edge,
> Nothing so much as mincing Poetrie:
> 'Tis like the forc't gait of a shuffling Nagge.
>
> (127–35)

Unfortunately, Harding defuses Shakespeare's poetic-dramatic irony when he supposes that Hotspur's lines are not iambic but accentual. This is consistent with Harding's account of metre, and shows its central weakness: he sees the tension between metrical expectation and speech rhythms as an all-out combat, in which one party must beat the other. In this respect his assumptions are paradoxically similar to those of Tottel, or the artificial scansionists of the eighteenth century, although his own allegiance is to the speech-rhythm party. Accentual-syllabic verse differs from accentual verse in having a fixed number of syllables, and Hotspur's speech actually shows, in a very provocative way, how this affords the poet a greater control over *intonation*.

This point needs a brief explanation, if we are to see how the metrical provocation is itself a constituent of Shakespeare's poetic-dramatic meaning. So far as I can tell, the great Danish linguist Otto Jespersen was the first to recognise (in print) that cumulative stressing is unusually common in English poetry. In his 'Notes on Metre' (1900), Jespersen uses numerical notation to mark the effect:

$$1 \quad 2 \quad 3 \quad 4$$
the wretched animall heav'd forth such groans . . .

As his example from *As You Like It* conveniently reminds us, this effect is common even in Shakespeare's earlier poetry, and shows four degrees of relative stress. Since the binary scansional notation of Tudor prosodists required and recognised only two degrees of stress, it could only misrepresent the way in which a line like this actually moves by scanning it in one of two ways, both wrong:

The wretched anĭmáll heăv'd fórth such groans . . .
The wretched anĭmăll heáv'd fórth such groans . . .

The conservative and legalistic prosodist has no *principled* grounds for declaring such a line metrically irregular. As Jespersen's notation brings out, the line is iambic throughout: the stress on each even syllable is stronger than that on each preceding odd syllable. If, as binary scansionists always assumed, any line which consists of five iambs is *ipso facto* regularly iambic, an iambic pentameter will not cease to be regular if it includes two adjacent iambs in which the 'unstressed' syllable of one iamb actually receives more emphasis than the metrically stressed syllable of the preceding iamb. The apparent problem—the seeming irregularity of the 3, within a 1 2 3 4 figure—dissolves, when we recognise that metrical stress, or *ictus*, need not always coincide with phrasal stress and lexical *accent* (which is something we can look up: a dictionary us how to say dĭctionarў). But the Tudor scansionist expected the lexical accent to coincide with metrical ictus; Gascoigne perceived that the spoken language admitted the *circumflexa* or 'indifferent' accent, but did not recognise the extent to which the theoretically arbitrary preference for beginning an iambic 'foot' with a lexically unaccented syllable worked against the vital energies and cadences of English speech. Spenser's *The Shepheardes Calendar* and Sidney's *Astrophil and Stella* were in this respect landmarks: they showed how speech rhythms could be played off against metrical expectations, to the nuances of shifting emotion— and of course the younger Shakespeare followed suit, together with every other ambitious poet of his generation. But then, we allow that the line from *As you Like It* is regularly iambic, what principled grounds could there be for supposing that Hotspur's cacophonous eruption is irregular, or not iambic at all?

Here, once more, are the problematic lines from Hotspur's speech, with elisions marked in the traditional way and cumulative stresses marked in Jespersen's way:

> Marry, and I am glad of it with all my heart,
> I had rather be a kitten, and cry mew
> Then one of these same Meeter Ballad-mongers:
> I had rather heare a Brazen canstick turn'd,
> Or a dry Wheele grate on the Axle-tree. . . .

Plainly, we can *hear* that Hotspur's cumulative stressing is far more violent than that in the line from *As You Like It:* this violence is compounded by forceful, wrenching elisions and the deliberately, wittily 'grating' example of what Bysshe would call the 'gaping Hiatus'. But representing that difference in prosodic terms is another matter, and involves even Jespersen in difficulties. For to say that Hotspur's 1 2 3 4 figures are more violent because their ascents are steeper is awkwardly impressionistic: the prosodist my report on relative degrees of stress *within* a line, but since he cannot establish absolute degrees of stress he cannot compare the *gradients* of 1 2 3 4 figures in *different* lines. When Elizabethans heard Hotspur's kind of metrical *Sturm und Drang*, in Donne's poetry and in contemporary verse satire, they spoke of 'strong-lined' or 'masculine' verse, but there is no evidence that they recognised the relation between this extreme cumulative stressing and quietly modulated examples like that in the *As You Like It* line; consequently, to say that the difference is merely one of degree would be true but litigious, and misleading in literary-historical terms. I am myself persuaded, and have argued elsewhere in a discussion of Donne's *Satyre III*, that Donne could hardly have presented such a radical and consistently principled challenge to the prevailing notions of metre if he had not arrived at his own distinction between metrical ictus and lexical or phrasal stress. In that great poem—which is metrically regular throughout—the wrenching cumulative stressing provides a means of registering the stress of violent emotion, and the strain of intensely demanding mental processes. Hotspur's speeches are metrically violent in very similar ways and present another landmark, since Shakespeare had never before written speeches which are so violent in their metrical provocation—and in this particular speech the substance of Hotspur's row with Glendower about 'same Meeter' balladmongering leaves no doubt that Shakespeare's contrast between two Elizabethan poetics was deliberate.

If we are to see why Hotspur sounds so unlike his namesake in *Richard II*, and why his aggressively 'masculine' and 'strong-lined' stylistic register represents—explicitly and implicitly—a nexus of related literary, moral and sociopolitical attitudes, the most helpful comparison is with Donne's other satires and with the 'new satire' of the 'wits' who were usually products of the Universities or of the Inns of Court. The 'new satire' was vehemently anti-Court in its iconoclastic disrespect for the values and proprieties of the Queen's elderly, starchy Establishment; and it was anticourtly, in its contempt for mellifluous musicality. As Joseph Hall affirms with proud satisfaction in *Virgidemiae* (1597), such satire could not 'but be unpleasing to the unskilful and overmusical ear'. 'Unskilful' and 'overmusical': the provocative collocation explains why Hotspur's skilful unmusicality could not but sound like a cacophonous din to Glendower's conventionally musical ear, just as Glendower's canorous courtliness seems to Hotspur preposterously and infuriatingly remote from that real, rude world in which he, like the Angry Young Satirists of the 1590s, makes his stand. In

Donne's first satire (c.1593) and in the very first speech we hear from Hotspur in *Henry IV*, the one kind of revolution implies another: anti-courtliness is implicit in the fierce cumulative stressing, and explicit in the vehemently satirical portrait of a scented courtly popinjay, who would, like Glendower, regard versifying as a necessary courtly accomplishment like riding or dancing. In Everard Guilpin's fifth satire, which was published in 1598 and shows that Guilpin had read one of the circulating copies of Donne's first satire, the 'harmony/ And diapason of harsh barbary' heard in his 'peopled streets' include a squeaking cartwheel and a rumbling tumbril, just as Hotspur's streetwise imagery and noises include grating wheels and mewing kittens.

That Glendower should sound like an old guard Tudor 'maker' nicely brings out the dramatic irony of this rebel's regressive nostalgia for that Ricardian court which Bolingbroke shattered: the elderly Welshman likes courts and expects deference. But he is now driven to keep strange company, as appears in his collision with a chauvinistic, intransigent young Northerner who despises courtly southern softness, shows his seniors no more respect than he thinks their merit deserves, and is, like the Edmund of *Lear*, impatient of astrological claptrap and old men's quaint follies. The stylistic contrast leaves us in no doubt that if the rebels were successful, and Mortimer replaced Henry, the new court would also have its problems since the world has moved on; but it also establishes another, more complex and far-reaching irony. For within the play's constellation of stylistic registers, it is evident that those registers which are associated with Glendower, Hotspur and indeed Falstaff are all, in their very different ways, *confining;* their heated, humour-driven excesses are opposed not merely to each other, but also to Hal's calculatingly flexible self-control, and stylistic control. When Hotspur sneers that the 'humorous' Welshman is 'a good musician', his wife pointedly comments:

> Then should you be nothing but Musicall,
> For you are altogether govern'd by humours.
> (3.1.233–6)

Lady Percy is observing, shrewdly, that both Hotspur and

Glendower are so controlled by their 'humours' as to be like opposite sides of the same coin; and Hotspur and Falstaff present another such *coincidentia oppositorum*. Falstaff's prosaic catechism on Honour and Hotspur's poetically hectic determination to 'plucke bright Honor from the pale-fac'd Moone' represent opposite ends of a spectrum, so far as Honour is concerned; but they are also seen as *complementary* manifestations of a 'humorous' or psychological imbalance. In the play's second and third scenes the repeated references to the sun and the moon show this: both Hotspur and Falstaff are associated with the moon—and with an evasion of the more demanding daylight realities which the sun-prince confronts and evokes when he firmly distinguishes 'work' from 'sport' and 'playing holidaies'. Hotspur and Falstaff are both on holiday, in moral terms; and Hal opposes to their stylistic (and moral) imbalance his own temperate and flexible measure, or *sophrosyne*. One effect of the stylistic contrasts is to oppose the excessiveness which is confining, and ultimately disabling, to that self-aware flexibility through which Hal controls himself and events.

In saying that I shall seem to have wandered into, or even taken up residence in, the camp of the critical 'morallers'. But the stylistic contrasts are also pulling in another, contrary direction. The extraordinary rhythmic verve and emotional-vitality of Hotspur's speech to Glendower or of his earlier description of the scented popinjay is something we relish all the more keenly after hearing this:

> I know you all, and will a-while uphold
> The unyoak'd humor of your idlenesse:
> Yet heerein will I imitate the Sunne,
> Who doth permit the base contagious cloudes
> To smother up his Beauty from the world,
> That when he please againe to be himselfe,
> Being wanted, he may be more wondred at,
> By breaking through the foule and ugly mists
> Of vapours, that did seeme to strangle him.
> If all the yeare were playing holidaies,
> To sport, would be as tedious as to worke;
> But when they seldome come, they wisht-for come,
> And nothing pleaseth but rare accidents.
> So when this loose behaviour I throw off,
> And pay the debt I never promised;

By how much better then my word I am,
By so much shall I falsifie mens hopes,
And like bright Metall on a sullen ground:
My reformation glittering o're my fault,
Shall shew more goodly, and attract more eyes,
Than that which hath no foyle to set it off . . .
                    (1.2. 188–208)

To be sure, the references to unyoked humours and holidays establish the perspective of the 'morallers'; but Hal's verse also provides an opposed perspective, by giving us a strong and disquieting sense of what it means to be *yoked*. In one of several swipes at Puritan jargon, Falstaff had assured Hal that "tis no sin for a man to labour in his vocation'; now we hear Hal labouring in his.

In metrical terms Hal's lines are unarresting. Their endstopped, accretive regularity is never threatened or enriched by the disruptive rhythms and energies of passionate speech; Hal's trisyllabic 'promised' is as formal and inelastic as Glendower's bisyllabic 'framèd'. Within the play's constellation of registers there is a pointed contrast with the eruptive vitality of Hotspur's verse on the one hand, and with the livelier rhythms of Hal's richly cadenced 'holiday' prose on the other. The soliloquy's conventional, ponderously developed imagery reinforces these contrasts. If we apply Keat's 'poetical thermometer' to this emergent sun it seems chillier than Hotspur's 'pale-fac'd moon', and very much less warm and beneficent than that 'blessed Sunne' which Hal had likened to 'a faire hot Wench in Flame-coloured Taffeta'. This wintry sun needs cloud and soil to set it off, just as the 'glittering' of 'bright metall on a sullen ground' is cold and hard. And, despite the strong-minded purposefulness of the speech's logical and syntactic constructions ('Yet heerein will I . . .', 'By how much . . . By so much . . .'), the logical premises are unconsciously betraying. As he asserts that the enjoyment of holidays depends on their infrequency Hal admits that 'worke'—of the sort for which he is preparing— *is* 'tedious'; 'nothing pleaseth but rare accidents' is a sad, revealing remark, which invites pity even as Hal anticipates admiration. At this point in the play we are only in a position to make the contrast with the warmth and gusto of Hal's holiday prose; but that prepares us for the next scene—which introduces Hotspur and shows how *his* warmth is humanly engaging, personally disabling, and politically dangerous.

When that scene begins, Shakespeare characteristically fuels our disquiet about Hal's 'measure' while seeming to turn to other matters. The King's first words have an apparently accidental relevance to the soliloquy we have just heard: 'My blood hath beene too cold and temperate,/ Unapt to stirre'. We are then introduced to Hotspur, whose blood 'more stirres/ To rowze a Lyon, then to start a Hare', and who resolves to 'ease my heart,/ Although it be with hazard of my head'. This provides yet another perspective on the soliloquy in which Hal had calculated effects and hazarded the heart, not the head. Moreover, Hotspur has hitherto been fighting rebels; but now, far from being impressed or cowed by Henry's determination to display 'Majestie'—which is just what Hal is also planning to do, in time—Hotspur is alienated by the 'bare and rotten policy' of a 'King of Smiles' who does not ever feel, let alone yield to, the holiness of the heart's affections. Hotspur hates the King for his personal inauthenticity and 'half-fac'd fellowship'. To be sure, we see how Hotspur's inability to control his feelings makes him all too easy to manipulate—but is it obviously better to be a manipulator, like that *prince* of smiles who proposes first to enjoy and then exploit his own half-faced fellowship with Falstaff? And when Hotspur expresses his disgust with candy deals of courtesy, can we coolly discount the spontaneous vitality of that complex, celebrated image—a vitality which Hal rivals only in his holiday prose? The driven, compulsive energy of Hotspur's 'strong-lined' verse points to a disability (and suggests that Shakespeare, like Ben Jonson, was suspicious of such metrical extremities); but it also provides a telling contrast with Hal's strong-willed but cold and metrically sluggish soliloquising.

The powerfully interrogative nature of Shakespeare's scepticism appears in this dynamic clash of different perspectives, which produces in us the sense of being pulled in different, and even contrary directions. Both the 'moraller' and the 'Falstaffian' are testifying to this experience when they work so hard to deny it, and try to *reduce* the drama's powerfully conflicting effects to critical order. Precisely because the dramatic issues are framed in pressingly urgent, contradictory ways, critical attempts to extrapolate a single view are as understandable as they are reprehensible. The particular examples I have taken also suggest how the allocation of a particular register of verse or prose may of itself prompt contrary responses and valuations. The contrast between Hal's prose and verse establishes his complexity and inner division with more psychological delicacy and moral insight than any documentary transcript of a real prince's speech and behaviour could ever provide: his stylistic range and problematic self-control show that he is indeed a formidably well-equipped prince, while also implanting doubts about the dehumanising effect of a 'measure' which may (to borrow from Burns) harden all within and petrify the feeling. And this contrast is subtly extended, reinforced and enriched by the further contrast with Hotspur, whose 'strong-lined' verse both confines and distinguishes him, prompting discrepant valuations of *his* character and of the very different human potentialities he represents.

In arguing that metrical characteristics—in this case, Hotspur's Donne-like cumulative stresses—are a constiutent of dramatic meaning, I am not assuming (as Gerard Manley Hopkins assumed) that they are expressive in themselves, before they have been attached to dramatic and conceptual references. Alexander Pope was properly cautious in maintaining that the sound of verse must *seem* an echo to the sense (*An Essay on Criticism:* 365), for, as Dr Johnson remarks in *Rambler:* 94, the same metrical rhythms may suit the triumphs of a battle or of a honeymoon. Shakespeare's decision to make the Hotspur of *Henry IV* sound like Donne, and the 1590s satirists, and very unlike the Hotspur of *Richard II*, should rather be seen as an inspired and brilliantly provocative *conceit*. A musical analogy is provided by Peter Maxwell Davies' decision, when he was composing the *Vesalii Icones*, to represent Christ's flagellation with a Victorian hymn tune. But because the Hotspur-music comes to be associated with, and symbolically representative of, those human potentialities and modes of feeling which he alone represents within the play, his death acquires a corresponding symbolic significance: it represents a defeat of human potentialities, like the death of Miss Birdseye in Henry James' *The Bostonians*, or the death of Viscount Falkland in Clarendon's *History of the Great Rebellion*. Similarly, Falstaff's death signifies that certain human potentialities have atrophied, or been amputated, within the body of the commonwealth. Falstaff speaks only prose, like Thersites in *Troylus and Cressida;* but he also speaks prose of magnificent richness and variety, unlike Thersites, and this too has a controlling, conventionally encoded significance within the play's internally coherent complex of poetic-dramatic registers. But here we need to consider some of the other ways in which Shakespeare's poetic-dramatic procedures create the illusion that a play's poetic-dramatic 'world' is all-encompassing, a seemingly inclusive 'mirror' of that world we all inhabit.

Framing: the play's 'world'

The end of drama is, and always was, to hold up a mirror to nature: so Hamlet confidently informs the players. For Oscar Wilde, this was Hamlet's attempt to convince everybody that he was totally insane. Wilde's joke is very good: like his argument that nature imitates art, it has a serious point to make about the mirror analogy. But then Wilde had to ignore Hamlet's 'as 'twere'—which makes Shakespeare's joke even better, and more profound. Before we hear Hamlet's speech on the need for naturalism we heard the kind of dramatic verse which *he* thinks most 'excellent', 'honest' and 'wholesome': for Hamlet, the speech on rugged Pyrrhus is an Arnoldian touchstone, which he has almost by heart, and the Player's recitation has to be broken off when the prince turns colour and begins to weep. Far from being natural, or naturalistic, the speech on rugged Pyrrhus is as stiffly conventional as *Gorboduc* (the play which Sidney so praised), and is 'o'ersized' with its own 'coagulated gore'. In remembering how the speech 'pleas'd not the Million' but satisfied the discerning few, Hamlet even allows himself a little Arnoldian (or Sidneian) self-congratulation. Here the joke is not that the speech is bad, but that for a late Elizabethan audience it would have recalled the kind of declamatory verse which *had* thrilled and perhaps still thrilled the 'Groundlings', but which, to the discerning, now seemed *passé* and unnatural. Yet the speech finds Hamlet, and nearly unmans him: he is responsive to conventions which were losing their power in the period which separates the so-called *Ur-Hamlet* from *Hamlet*. The mirrors which art holds up to nature are themselves subject to fashion and change. Racine's audiences responded to—and probably imitated—the signal of intense distress when an actress lifted her arm up to, but never indecently beyond, her shoulders. By first inviting his audience to compare their own responses to the Player's speech with Hamlet's incapacitating distress, and then giving Hamlet his assured speech on the *constant* end of drama, Shakespeare passes his own consummately ironic comment on Hamlet's 'mirror'.

But then how are we to account for the impression that the poetic-dramatic world of each Shakespearean play seems both distinct and inclusively representative? *Richard II* and *Henry IV* belong to the same tetralogy; yet it is also common for critics to assign *Richard II* to that 'lyrical group' of plays which also includes *Love's Labour's Lost*, *Romeo and Juliet* and *A Midsummer Night's Dream*, and to suggest that both parts of *Henry IV* show the 'harder texture' of the later, 'non-lyrical' group which also includes *The Merchant of Venice* and *The Merry Wives of Windsor*. So, in his Introduction to the New Arden edition of the *Dream* (from which these quotations are taken), Harold Brooks goes on to remark that the 'only' passage of comparable 'lyricism' in the later 'group' of plays is 'the scene of music, moonlight and star-light at the final return to Belmont' (xiii). It hardly seems controversial to suggest that *Henry IV* and *The Merchant of Venice* treat aspects of human experience which cannot be subdued to a lyrical treatment; moreover, the 'world' of the *Dream* is plainly less panoramic than that of *Henry IV*, as its characterisation is less complex, its verse more stylised. Given this, and the sad fact that most aspects of human experience are not obviously lyrical, we might therefore expect to have some strong, limiting sense of how much of life the *Dream* leaves out; yet in the *Dream*, as in the other so-called 'lyrical' plays, the poetic-dramatic world seems distinct, varied and inclusive. The concept of internal coherence is important here—as appears, somewhat unexpectedly, if we ask whether the general agreement that Mendelssohn's overture for *A Midsummer Night's Dream* is wonderfully 'Shakespearean' makes any kind of sense.

The most familiar kind of explanation offers to match the overture's four main episodes with different parts of Shakespeare's play; but such an explanation rests on an exceedingly naive notion of 'representation'. So, we are usually told that the first musical episode (bars 8—66) portrays or represents the moonlit murmurings of the enchanted fairy world, which is then contrasted with the splendours of Theseus' court and wedding celebrations (Section A); the third episode (Section B) portrays the palpitating quartet of youthful lovers, and this in turn gives way to the hard-handed mechanicals' rustically earthbound dance, complete with drones and some ophicleidal brays to represent Bottom's transformation into an ass (section C). Then, rather unaccountably, all of these episodes, including Theseus's wedding march and Bottom's transformation, are reshuffled and repeated in a different sequence. If we want to play this matching game, is there any compelling *musical* reason why we should not play it differently? We might suppose, for example, that the first episode presents the gossamer fleetness of Peasblossom and the *child* fairies, who are then sent packing by the arrival of the superb Oberon's court; that the third section presents Titania and her tender fascination with the Indian boy; and that the fourth section presents the Till Eulenspiegel-like pranking of Puck, the earthily vigorous lob from country folklore.

Indeed, this alternative 'programme' would have one considerable advantage: it would suppose that Mendelssohn was sensitive enough to respond to the sharply differentiated levels of Shakespeare's fairy realm, instead of taking a partial and disappointingly wispy view of it, and that Mendelssohn chose to concentrate on representing that fairy realm, instead of making a far more arbitrary selection of different fragments of the play. But of course, both programmes are distracting since there is no clear sense in which we could or should be *thinking* about the play while listening to the overture. (An old joke: '*Think* of the Parthenon. Good. Now count the pillars.') Although it may be argued that music is like a 'language' in having a syntax of structural progressions and a grammar of tonal relationships, it has no lexicon, no readily ascertainable vocabulary of conceptual references. Even that association between the ophicleidal bray and Bottom as ass is imitative and extra-musical: we might doubt whether it would have been made if Mendelssohn had given his overture a different title, just as we may doubt whether it would then have occurred to Donald Tovey to describe the melody of the third episode as 'schoolgirlish'. Thomas Mann's *Doktor Faustus* brilliantly exposes and exploits this gulf between musical and verbal language, when accounts of real master-pieces like Beethoven's last piano sonata are followed by comparably searching accounts of Adrian Leverkuhn's music: we imagine that we know what Leverkuhn's music is like, but it does not exist.

It is far more instructive to see how Mendelssohn's contrasted musical episodes are integrated—held together by what post-Schenkerian 'functional analysts' call a 'dynamic *Grundgestalt*', or underlying, unifying principle. In *Style and Idea*, Arnold Schoenberg observes that the 'real' composer 'does not compose merely one or two themes, but a whole piece': the 'form of its outline, characteristics of tempo, dynamics, their contrasts and deviations—all these are there at once, though in embryonic state'(165). And the progression of chords which launches Mendelssohn's overture is in this sense 'embryonic': beginning in E major, it eventually issues into E minor—and at once we hear the rapid, scudding pianissimo figure which is the basis of the first episode. This figure descends from E in the melodic minor (E,D,C,B), and the episode triumphantly reasserts the major key in its variation on this tetrachordal descent (E, D#, C#, B). To reinforce this impression of unity in diversity—an impression which we register intuitively, and which analysis merely confirms—the third episode brings another variation of this figure within the key of B major, the dominant, while the fourth episode brings yet another transformation of the figure, with further dynamic, thematic and tonal contrasts. Since the third episode is also soft, but less ethereal than the first, while the fourth episode is also disruptive, but less rudely festive than the second, there is a complementary and dynamic—as well as a thematic and tonal—relationship between the sequence of episodes; this, I suspect, is why the authors of programme notes suppose that Mendelssohn moves from the fairy world to the human world. But since the music itself cannot provide conceptual references it can neither portray nor explain: in Schopenhauerean terms, it *inhabits* Oberon's pre-conceptual realm of the Will, and can enter Theseus's realm only when accompanied by the word.

My alternative 'programme' is as good (and bad!) as the conventional one. But opposing these two programmes directs attention to something very important in Shakespeare's play, which the subtle interrelationships in Mendelssohn's overture might be said to transpose. Shakespeare's carefully differentiated stylistic registers articulate two complementary hierarchies within the 'wood' and Athens. Theseus is lord of one realm, Oberon of the other; doubling their roles makes excellent dramatic, psychological and symbolic sense, because they are the respective representatives of reason and of those life mysteries which reason cannot encompass or control. The hubristically rationalistic Theseus disregards the greater power of Oberon, which can determine the success of harvests or births; the fact that in another time (or realm) Theseus had relations with Titania, and Oberon with Hippolyta, underlines the irony that these seemingly opposed realms are properly interdependent and need to be integrated, brought into harmony with each other. The relationship between Athens, the walled city of reason, and the darkly mysterious natural world of 'wood', where lovers become 'wood' (or mad) might be compared with that of the mental 'clearing' and the surrounding 'forest' in Ted Hughes' poem 'The Thought Fox' or with Hawthorne's *The Scarlet Letter*.

Each realm has its own hierarchy of differentiated registers, with counterparts in the other realm. This is why the closely integrated poetic-dramatic world seems so inclusive, so coherent internally—even though it is predominantly lyrical, unlike our or Shakespeare's world. True, when we compare the so-called 'lyrical' and 'unlyrical' groups we may want to observe that the later plays admit more of those multifarious, disruptive and discordant elements of reality which cannot be subdued to lyricism. And yet, in their very different ways, *Love's Labour's Lost*, *Romeo and Juliet*, *Richard II* and the *Dream* create the illusion of a self-sufficient, internally coherent world; each presents an 'orchestrated' interplay of

constellating registers, characters and images; each admits
what might be called representative dissonances, through
which the play appears to acknowledge more of human
experience than it is directly concerned to explore. The
Dream includes the harshly dissonant violence of Egeus; it
glances at the all too real miseries caused by failed harvests
or births that go wrong—just as *Richard II* furnishes telling
glimpses of the ordinary folk whose lives are ruined by a
Richard or a Bolingbroke. *Love's Labour's Lost* opens with
the courtiers' attempt to exclude those realities which invade
the play at the end, and include the everyday horrors of
death, poverty and incurable illness. Romeo's ardently lyrical
intensities must make their way not only against the psycho-
pathic Tybalt, but also against the ribald, complex energies
of Mercutio and the *terre-à-terre* vitality of the Nurse;
various minor touches, like the lovely 'inset' on the apoth-
ecary's shop, remind us of the bustling realities of a larger,
mundane and unlyrical world—which is in this way included,
though not explored, within the poetic-dramatic world.

Such considerations also suggest why, although Shakespeare had the foresight to bring on a figure called 'Hotspur'
in *Richard II*, this figure could never sound like his namesake
in *Henry IV*. The 'Hotspur-music' is nowhere heard, nor
could it be (even if we thought that Shakespeare could write
such verse when he wrote *Richard II*): such distinctive strains
could only disrupt, or more likely destroy, the more lightly
orchestrated, binary contrast between Richard's equivocally
poetic lyricism and Bolingbroke's unpoetically pragmatic
realism. Here is that paradox over which so many nineteenth-
century critics tumbled, when discussing the wonderful 'gall-
eries' of characters in Shakespeare, Dickens or Tolstoy, as
though it hardly mattered which work a character appeared
in. On the contrary, the more rich and complex the embodied
life of a character in a poetic drama seems the more likely it
is to depend on those internal contrasts and connections
established within the particular poetic-dramatic 'world'; this
is true, in different ways, of novels and music dramas. That
sum of poetic-dramatic impressions which we call 'Hotspur'
could not have existed in the earlier play, just as the Shakespearean Falstaff can take lodgings in Windsor but cannot exist
there. So, for example, Shakespeare's intransigently chauvin-

istic Northerner exists in and through the poetic-dramatic contrast with the other Harry; and the exploration of different kinds of 'honour' and of 'Englishness' which that contrast affords is mythopeic as well as 'historical'—and not historical at all, if we remember that the historical Hotspur was older than Henry IV.

In all these very different poetic dramas, or for that matter in the Bach cantata I mentioned earlier, our impression of inclusiveness depends upon the symbolic registers. Because the symbolic representations are not confiningly naturalistic, their references can become external and internal, social and psychological. Bach's *Jesu, der du meine Seele* does in one sense 'mirror' the variety of devotional responses within a German Protestant community, and of course its performance assembles a smaller community including soloists and instrumentalists, choir and congregation; at the same time it presents a community of *shared* human potentialities, of feelings which frequently succeed each other or coexist within each of us as individuals, and are plainly not peculiar to (say) sopranos or basses. Similarly, the constellating registers in *A Midsummer Night's Dream* project a diverse but ultimately harmonious community, while at the same time providing a complex, dynamic metaphor for conflicting conscious and unconscious impulses which need to be integrated within each individual psyche.

So, while *Henry IV* presents a seemingly panoramic picture of a disharmonious commonwealth, the play is bringing us to acknowledge, within the ebb and flow of our own sympathetic responses, the tensions between our own diverse impulses and inner needs. Indeed, the imagery of *Henry IV* persistently develops the analogy between the individual body and the body of the commonwealth: just as we can recognise the psychological felicitousness of the *Dream's* poetic-dramatic contrast between Athens and the 'wood'—in modern shorthand, the conscious and the unconscious—we can recognise what is implied, in moral and psychological terms, by those ominous encounters in the second part of *Henry IV* between Falstaff and the grave Lord Chief Justice. The battle of Shrewsbury similarly corresponds with that inner, psychic arena within which the claims of principles like heroism and honour contend against amoral and self-serving Falstaffian instinct: this is why it makes immediate sense to speak of our own 'Falstaffian' selves. By projecting, and challenging us to recognise and appraise, representative human potentialities, the play involves us in a critical and exploratory process of *thinking* which is unlike the step-by-step process of logical, discursive thought. That a Falstaff or a Thersites speaks only prose is, as I have argued, a constituent of meaning in what may be called 'poetic-dramatic thinking'; but it will not settle, and indeed aggravates, the exploratory questioning of concepts like honour and chivalry—and we have seen how this is also true of the poetic-dramatic contrasts between, say, Hal's verse and prose, and Hotspur's very different heroic registers. Here, it is very important that my use of terms like 'registers' or 'constellating' should not be taken to suggest something static, with a fixed significance: a poetic drama unfolds in time, like a sonata, and the processes of 'poetic-dramatic thinking' depend upon this dynamic process of unfolding. The experience of being pulled in different and sometimes contrary directions is a direct result of the way in which the play frames its different perspectives on characters and issues. In *Henry IV* this poetic-dramatic projection and exploration of competing human potentialities repeatedly suggests that one impulse can be satisfied only at the expense of another, so that the 'integration' of a commonwealth or of the individual 'self' entails sacrifices and amputations. Here the contrast with the *Dream* is striking: that play also provides a teasing *image* of our world and inner make-up, since the seemingly inclusive, internally coherent 'world' of the play engages our sense of interrelationships which are both communal and psychological; but here the 'festive', integrating outcome is less equivocal.

In emphasising those ways in which the play's world becomes an 'image' of our own, but as a metaphor not as a 'mirror', I am wanting to recover something like the older sense of the term *concetto*. Alma Altizer directs attention to the needed distinction when she remarks that in Michelangelo's poetry the term *concetto* 'retains the connotation of "thought" or "idea", but it means a thinking in forms or images, rather than an idea arrived at by a critical or analytic process of logic or reason'; and she observes that Battaglia's

Grande Dizionario della lingua italiana shows that *concetto* is not used to indicate a rhetorical figure until Tasso, in the mid-sixteenth century. The English word 'conceit', in its rhetorical sense, derives from the *later* meaning of the Italian 'concetto'; the increasingly narrow definition of terms like *concetto*, *ingeno* or *agudeza* reinforced 'the split between thought and imagination, making thought ever more analytic and increasingly dissociated from that "faculty to intuit . . . and to apprehend things directly" which was once the definition of "ingegno" ' (x). A 'conceit' in the later, narrower sense, is an 'ingenious or witty imaginative-conceptual figure'; a *concetto*, in the older, richer sense, is 'an imaginative-intuitive figure that brings together seemingly disparate images or ideas' in 'an act of intuition, a direct apprehension of underlying forms of experience' (x-xi). In seventeenth-century poetry the distinction might be illustrated by comparing almost any poem by Cleveland with, say, Marvell's 'The Coronet'. Marvell's poem is—as Altizer observes of Michelangelo's 'Non pur d'argento o d'oro'—'entirely structured upon a single extremely complex insight or "concetto" '(2). And of course I am wanting to emphasise the ways in which the poetic-dramatic 'world' of a Shakespearean drama is also in this sense a *concetto*—a still more complex, dynamically articulated 'image' of our world.

Altizer's distinction should help us to avoid some familiar but still troubling dangers. Since the pioneering studies of Shakespeare's imagery by Caroline Spurgeon and Wolfgang Clemen, the term 'imagery' has too frequently been used as a kind of rhetorical Gladstone-bag or tropic hold-all, without regard for whether we should be speaking of metaphor or synecdoche. Doubtless the term 'image', with its often unwanted implication that something is to be *visualised*, should be used with more circumspection. But then our sense of the seemingly inclusive, internally coherent 'world' of the play is also established through imagery; and sometimes what are not, in their local context and in the strict sense, 'images' at all none the less contribute to our sense of the play as an integrated, 'imaginative-intuitive' *concetto*. I hope it is not merely some kamikaze instinct which makes me want to illustrate this point with two examples—from *Hamlet* and

Troylus and Cressida—which editors have often thought in need of emendation.

In *Troylus and Cressida*, Agamemnon's disgusted reference to Thersites' *Masticke Jawes* has provoked a stream of speculative commentary. The context is important: just before Ulysses delivers his speech on degree he asks for permission to speak—and this clearly calls for some response, if only a nod or 'Speake on'. No response is indicated in the 1609 Quarto, but in the Folio text we hear Agamemnon thrown into a little fluttered ecstasy of anticipation:

> Speake Prince of *Ithaca*, and be't of lesse expect:
> That matter needlesse of importlesse burthen
> Divide thy lips; then we are confident
> When ranke *Thersites* opes his Masticke Jawes,
> We shall heare Musick, Wit, and Oracle.
>
> (1.3.70–4)

We have in fact just heard a deal of 'matter needlesse' from Ulysses himself, whose request to speak was so stuffed with obsequious compliments it took up sixteen lines. But, as we now gather, this is exactly what Agamemnon regards as 'Music, Wit, and Oracle'. Precisely because he knows he can count on Ulysses to start prating of heavenly axles and the like, Agamemnon can even bring himself to remember the 'ranke' Thersites, whose analogies are invariably filthy, not flatteringly cosmic, and (as Nestor peevishly puts it) 'match us in comparisons with dirt'.

Remoteness and grandeur are the stylistic registers Agamemnon prefers, and his own metaphors usually race to establish a distance between tenor and vehicle that can buttress self-esteem by deflecting unpleasant actualities. Throughout the policy debate he is obsessed by rank and status, since the prolonged failure to take Troy has threatened his own position; and here, when Ulysses' shameless massage so tickles him, his attempt at a regally magnanimous response is merely flatulent and self-betraying. Part of the point of the speech is its pointless redundance; its syntax is convoluted, its sense constipated, and even its sound—with the awkward cluster of echoing '-lesse' words—is muffled and clumsy.

As various editors point out, *Masticke* appears to be associated with *masticate;* somewhat less obviously with *mastix* (as in *Histriomastix:* Thersites is a scourging satirist and railer); and even with *mastiff.* Such associations are more telling if we remember that dogs and cynics are etymologically related in the Greek *kunikos:* that is a point to which I must return in Chapter 4, but here, where Agamemnon's speech so pointedly speaks him, we need to pay particular attention to the association of *Masticke* with *ranke.* The rank Thersites is a dirty eater, indeed a dirt-eater, since he likes to chew on filth—whereas the 'Musick, Wit, and Oracle' of the well-born, well-bred Ulysses barely *divides his lips.* Agamemnon's obsession with status and degree appears in that metaphorical association between nice speech and nice (table) manners. The same obsession makes his use of the word *ranke* so telling. Here we might remember Nietzsche's discussion, in *The Genealogy of Morals,* of the relationship between the class term *schlecht* and the ethical term *schlicht,* since Agamemnon's disgust with Thersites' 'matter' is inseparable from his distaste for what Clarendon would call a dirty fellow of no name—a bastard, who would level all distinction.

In this connection it matters that Thersites speaks only in prose (save for one 'close') while Agamemnon, Ulysses and Nestor speak in verse, and—as though through some infection—Achilles speaks prose with Thersites in 2.3, 3.3 and 5.1. Being confined to prose implies another kind of rankness; but here the play releases another unsettling irony. Thersites' prose 'places' him within the internally coherent constellation of registers and images, in just such a way as to lend support to those assumptions which inform Agamemnon's use of the word *ranke.* But Ulysses' manipulative *poetic* 'Musick, Wit, and Oracle' is rendered suspect both by its own excesses and by Agamemnon's anxious self-regard. The truth may be as prosaic, and filthy, as Thersites, in which case the conventions of poetic drama (and that kind of *Stiltrennung* which Agamemnon expects and demands) are themselves rendered suspect: verse would be no more than another means of concealing those base drives and appetites which 'really' direct behaviour, while truth requires ugly prose. Here, once again, we see how the allocation of particular stylistic registers of prose and verse may accentuate, without resolving, a problem—since the latter possibility would make poetic drama itself a self-consuming artefact. Finally, in noticing how Agamemnon's speech characterises both the speaker and the play's world, we may notice how the idea of Thersites as a dirty eater associates with the play's innumerable references to appetite—for example, in Ulysses' subsequent vision of a world without degree in which universal appetite finally eats up itself, or in Pandarus's trivialisation of love as appetite, or in the play's four uses of the word *distaste* (a word Shakespeare only uses elsewhere on two occasions). To claim each of these instances as examples of 'imagery' would be rash; but they all contribute to the characterisation of a poetic-dramatic world in which imagery of appetite is part of the play's central nervous system.

My other example concerns Claudius's reference to Hamlet's *browes* in the following lines, which various editors have also wanted to emend:

> The termes of our estate may not endure
> Hazerd so neer's as doth hourely grow
> Out of his browes.
>
> (3.3.5–7)

Dr Johnson observed of this, in his characteristically engaging way: 'I take *browes* of the quartos to be, properly read, *frows*, which, I think, is a provincial word for *perverse humours*, which not being understood was changed to "lunacies" [in the Folio]. But of this I am not confident.' Dover Wilson argues, very much more confidently, in his epoch-making edition of *Hamlet*, that *browes* should be emended to *brawls*, and refers the reader to his supplementary volumes on *The Manuscript of Shakespeare's 'Hamlet'*. There, he dismisses *browes* as 'absurd' (9) and a 'nonsense word' (10); some 300 pages later he suggests that *browes*, 'though nonsense, at least gives us what the Q2 compositor, far too engrossed in the letters of his copy to be bothering about the sense of what he read, thought he saw before him as he set up his type . . . My own guess, for what it is worth, is "brawles", which would make "browes" a combined a:o and l:e error' (324). Oddly, the vigorously defended emendation does not appear in the text itself.

Which is just as well. To begin with, there is no real difficulty in seeing why Hamlet's brows alarm the king. He is referring to Hamlet's menacing facial expressions, which convey a threat to his person and the hazard to this throne. In other words, *browes* is synecdochal. Having just emerged from the Mousetrap scene, Claudius has every reason to feel *brow-beaten;* and, as the NED reminds us, early usages of that word always associate the brow in question with the beater, not that of the beaten party. Synecdochal references to brows are common enough in Shakespeare. Sometimes they are straightforward and function as oblique stage directions, as in *2 Henry VI* when Eleanor asks, 'Why doth the Great Duke Humfrey knit his brows . . . ?' (1.2.3); sometimes they figure in complex, compound metaphors, as in *1 Henry IV* when Hotspur bitterly complains of the king that

> By this Face,
> This seeming brow of Justice, did he win
> The hearts of all . . .
>
> (4.3.82–4)

That Dover Wilson thought *browes* absurd is puzzling, but one possible explanation is suggested by the contrast Alastair Fowler draws, in *Conceitful Thought*, between Elizabethan and so-called Metaphysical conceits. Fowler's thesis—which is startling in outline but impressively substantiated in his analyses—is that the Metaphysical conceit is, typically, simpler than the Elizabethan conceit in one crucial respect:

> If we were to construct a model Metaphysical conceit, we would not specify complexity of comparison. The specification would be a single tenor and a single vehicle, related by a single system of analogies. Whether the grounds of similarity are numerous or the comparison oilstone down to one Clevelandish catachresis; whether the things compared are briefly mentioned or unpacked into many items and aspects on each side, wittily interconnected by puns, ambiguities and other word-plays: at all events an overall simplicity of tropic structure prevails. (105–6)

As Fowler puts it, 'Such metaphors can, as it were, be solved'—whereas the relationship between tenor and vehicle in Elizabethan conceits or metaphors is often 'mixed' and 'multiple', and even produced compound metaphors in which it is impossible to say which is the tenor and which the vehicle.

In Claudius's speech both Hamlet's hostility and the danger it represents are, as it seems to the King, increasing by the hour; but whereas the hostility is represented synecdochally in *browes*, the increase in danger is represented metaphorically as something that 'doth hourely grow' (like a stag's menacing horns) *on* those same brows. In each case a synecdoche figures within a metaphor. Moreover, the very first sentence we hear from Claudius in the play includes another synecdochal *brow:*

> Though yet of *Hamlet* our deare brothers death
> The memorie be greene, and that it us befitted
> To beare our harts in griefe, and our whole Kingdome
> To be contracted in one browe of woe . . .
>
> (1.2.1–4)

In this carefully prepared speech Claudius pays tribute, as he must, to a man whose death he cannot sincerely mourn; his concern is with propriety, bearing and befitting expressions of sorrow. We then hear Hamlet insisting in his own first long speech that the trappings and suits of woe cannot 'alone' denote *him* truly: they are only authenticated by 'that within'—which, paradoxically, 'passeth show', since the 'dejected haviour of the visage' is something which can be acted or dissimulated.

That contrast recurs in the innumerable metaphors contrasting that within with outward show—images of make-up and painting, of seeming health and inner corruption, of devotion's visage sugaring over the devil, and so on. For the same reason it would not do for Hamlet's father to have been stabbed or stifled: the curious poisoning leads to an eruption from within, as the King's smooth body is suddenly crusted by lazar-like sores. And of course the same contrast characterises the play's two mighty opposites. Both the range of Hamlet's imagery and the intensity with which it is actualised in his poetry are prodigious; in sharp contrast, Claudius's images are seldom realised with any imaginative intensity and are drawn from a revealingly narrow range of interests and experience. Here we might compare Macbeth. The *intensity* of his imaginative apprehensions, as he struggles to fathom and suppress his deepest imaginative impulses and inner needs, recalls Hamlet; yet the *range* of his imagery might rather recall Claudius: drawn from hunting, fighting and half-remembered scraps of a nursery education, it suggests intellectual interests as restricted as those of any Scottish lord.

The lines which Dover Wilson wanted to emend figure within these more extended poetic-dramatic contrasts. In particular, we may notice that Claudius, unlike Hamlet, both trusts his sense of what is signified by outward appearances (those frowning brows) and acts promptly in consequence (by arranging to send Hamlet to England). We might indeed feel squeamish about citing either of Claudius' references to brows as 'images'—as appears quickly enough, if we try to imagine Hamlet's brows sprouting menace, or a kingdom contracting into a brow which itself contracts in grief; but in each case the metaphors characterise Claudius and figure within those constellating images which distinguish this play's poetic-dramatic world.

I have attended to these examples so closely because they show how imagery (in the loose or inclusive sense) contributes to the internal coherence of the play's 'world' while also reminding us that that 'world' is itself a *concetto*. They also show Shakespeare thinking *through* images, and *through* the non-realistic conventions of poetic drama—conventions which in this respect have less in common with prose drama than with music drama. For we need not necessarily suppose that Shakespeare consciously determined that Falstaff should speak only in prose or that Macbeth's images should be limited in range but not in intensity, just as it would be silly to imagine Mozart or Wagner making consciously determined decisions, in each instance, about how to represent character in rhythmic, harmonic and melodic terms. But to say that is not to suggest that the meanings which emerge from the processes of 'imaginative-intuitive', 'poetic-dramatic thinking' are not (as Stanley Cavell would say) very well *meant*. Nor is the experience of being pulled in contrary directions evidence that the plays are (as Dr Johnson and Wittgenstein would have it) confused or irresponsible in their relation to life and the 'real' world: on the contrary, their sceptical reflexivity, which I must next consider, reminds us no less tirelessly than Nietzsche himself that we interpret the world as we interpret a text.

Reflexivity: the two worlds

In *The Merchant of Venice*, as in *A Midsummer Night's Dream*, the main action is virtually complete by the end of the fourth act. In the *Dream*, there is then a dazzlingly unexpected and expansive development of the opposition between Reason and Imagination, but in the final act of *Merchant* the play seems rather to contract—into that 'scene of music, moonlight and starlight' which Harold Brooks singled out as an isolated 'passage' of pure 'lyricism'. Because this shift or modulation is in itself startling, the spectator is all the more likely to ask, like a Schoenbergian 'functional analyst', whether and how it is integrated within a unitive design. For four acts we have been concerned with problems which also have a distressing reality in the world we know; moreover, although Portia's trick is offered as a resolution of the most pressing problem, this, and the Christians' subsequent treatment of Shylock, is unlikely to steady our hitherto turbulent responses. And yet, in the 'lyrical' scene that follows, the play appears to be behaving as though we had all the while been watching some innocent entertainment which is safely and soothingly removed from the strains and perplexities of the world as we know it. Such serenity seems unsettling and provocative: all's well that ends well—*isn't* it? Indeed, this very effect may seem to launch a reflective irony, if we are attending to the overall design or composition. For the elaborately orchestrated lyricism is being offered to us in just such a way as to call attention to its contrivance and conventionality: it reminds us, quizzically, that we are watching a play, in which the conventions of comedy require some contrived closure even where life affords no ready resolutions.

Like Theseus' speech on the lunatic, lover *and poet*, Lorenzo's mellifluous tribute to music and poetry also releases reflexive ironies of which the speaker is altogether unaware. For we can hardly 'marke' this 'sweete musique' without pondering the nature of the spell cast by *this* poet's 'feigning':

Jessica: I am never merry when I heare sweete musique.
Lorenzo: The reason is, your spirits are attentive:

> For doe but note a wilde and wanton heard
> Or race of youthful and unhandled colts,
> Fetching mad bounds, bellowing and neighing loud,
> Which is the hot condition of their bloud,
> If they but heare perchance a trumpet sound,
> Or any ayre of musicke touch their eares,
> You shall perceive them make a mutuall stand,
> Their savage eyes turn'd to a modest gaze,
> By the sweet power of musicke: therefore the Poet
> Did faine that *Orpheus* drew trees, stones, and floods.
> Since naught so stockish, hard, and full of rage,
> But musicke for a time doth change his nature,
> The man that hath no musicke in himselfe,
> Nor is not moved with concord of sweet sounds,
> Is fit for treasons, strategems, and spoyles,
> The motions of his spirit are dull as night,
> And his affections darke as *Erebus*,
> Let no such man be trusted: marke the musicke.

The poet feigns and can, like Orpheus, change natures—but only 'for a time', and not *all* natures. Shylock is stockish, hard, full of rage, with a spirit impervious to music (2.5.27 f.); his nature has just been broken, not changed. Lorenzo is happy to think that the man who hath no music *in* himself and is therefore not moved with concord should not be trusted, but here another irony flickers into sight, even as this romantic *spinto* tenor delivers his carefully placed aria. Should we too be beguiled, and forget that this man, who so lightly tells us who should not be trusted, has shown his fitness for strategems and spoils? Lorenzo's happiness depends on his successful ransacking of another man's daughter and treasure chests; he is still more delighted later in the scene, when Portia's Law brings new supplies of 'manna', and it turns out that the lovers who sold Leah's turquoise for a monkey have already exhausted their present funds.

I take it that Shakespeare expects our minds, as well as our 'spirits', to be 'attentive', and that Lorenzo's very assertion of sweet concord alerts us to underlying dissonances which are more like Dowland's 'jarring, jarring sounds'. Instead of simply surrendering to the spell cast by Fancy's beguiling nocturne, or gazing at these not very innocent lovers through suddenly dewy eyes as though this scene really has little to do with the rest of the play, we might rather notice how

Lorenzo's hymn to music and the affections asks to be set against Shylock's own unmusical, sardonic verdict:

> Affection,
> Master of passion, swayes it to the moode
> Of what it likes or loaths . . .

Or against the decidedly unlyrical sentiments of the lyric in Act 3:

> Tell me where is fancie bred,
> In the heart, or in the head:
> How begot, how nourished. Replie, replie.
> It is engendred in the eyes,
> With gazing fed, and Fancy dies . . .

Or against that cool observation which the Belmont *Nachtmusik* draws from Portia:

> Nothing is good I see without respect,
> Methinks it sounds much sweeter then by day?

'In such a night,' sing the self-delighting lovers; and their vision of the floor of heaven, 'thicke enlayed with pattens of bright gold', is 'engendred in the eyes' and in their mutual happiness. Once again Portia's words call attention to the precarious and subjective nature of such enchantment:

> This night methinkes is but the daylight sicke,
> It lookes a little paler, 'tis a day,
> Such as the day is, when the Sun is hid.

And of course, we cannot examine this night sky for ourselves, to resolve this discrepancy of vision and 'moode': Portia's words also remind us that the spell is a magical but equivocal product of the poet's 'feigning'.

Local reflexivity of this kind is of course very common in Shakespeare. We may recall Hamlet's reference to a 'distracted globe' which is at once his head, the play's world, our world, and the absorbed Globe audience; or Cleopatra's fear that she will be mimicked by a squeaking boy actor; or the related kinds of dramatic joke which ensue when a boy actor is playing a woman who is pretending to be a man; or the prologues of *Henry V* and *Troylus;* or the epilogues delivered by Puck, Rosalind and Prospero. The conditions of Elizabethan staging—unlike those of nineteenth-century naturalism, with its 'fourth wall'—encouraged the dramatist to test and celebrate his audience's imaginative agility. The daring, joyous readiness to remind us that we are being delighted or moved by an illusion strikingly demonstrates the power of illusion, to which Lorenzo is also consciously and unconsciously testifying: the miracle is all the more triumphant for being a trick which is being proved upon our own responsive pulses.

But Portia's disenchanting observations about music and the night, of crows and nightingales, also help to establish a more sustained structural reflexivity. She is speaking within the play as a character, and is entirely oblivious to the way in which her words reflect on the play and its concern with the operations of Fancy; in this sense she becomes the vehicle of a complex irony, in which the dramatist and his audience exchange significant glances. Similarly, although the reflexivity of Hamlet's reference to the 'distracted globe' could be seen as an isolated flare-up, the play abounds in metaphors involving acting: even as we are immersed in the play's action, we are invited to reflect on what the play is doing, and how it is doing it. When we first see and hear Hamlet we see a man who is isolated by, and ill at ease in, his role and costume as mourner; and we hear an *actor* reflecting, in tones of feigned desperation, on the impossibility of expressing that real inward grief which passeth show. Yet the authenticating grief 'within' cannot be authenticated, and of course the actor playing Hamlet playing the authentic mourner must feign emotion, like the actor playing the actor who so moves Hamlet with his speech on Hecuba. The end of this play, like that of *The Spanish Tragedy*, leaves the stage littered with corpses, and in this respect the play seems to be satisfying conventional expectations about how a revenge tragedy will end, just as the final Belmont scene *seemed* to be working towards a conventional happy ending. But Hamlet's revenge, unlike Hieronimo's, is unplanned and fortuitous, the result of an accident or series of accidents; and what is an accident within the play's world is also the play's carefully engineered climax.

The effectiveness of this *coup* derives partly from the impossibility of presenting a true accident in a contrived work of art: as soon as we look for the accident's significance and meaning, we are of course considering it as something contrived and *meant*. One impressive fictional example is provided by 'Mark Rutherford' in *The Revolution in Tanner's Lane*: the accidental death of the Major, who had promised to be the major character, produces an unforgettable shock—which inevitably prompts the reader to begin asking what reason the author had for *engineering* the 'accident'. Shakespeare frequently uses accidents to explore the tension between unshaped reality and its apparent reflection in a work of art, and to set two kinds of expectation against each other: what we expect from a 'comedy' or 'tragedy' is unexpectedly exposed to our sense of what we must also expect in the real world.

In the final scene of *Love's Labour's Lost* the masquers' various entries are followed by the unexpected appearance of a character who has no place in their entertainment, but an important role in Shakespeare's. Monsieur Marcade's dismal news abruptly shatters the courtly 'merriment' and the lovers' hopes, and the subversion of our own conventional expectations is teasingly reflected in Berowne's consternation as he observes that 'the Scene begins to cloud'. But although the death of the princess's father is a grotesquely untimely accident for the characters and a surprise for us, we have also been waiting to see the play's title explained, and expecting some kind of unpleasant irruption ever since Berowne warned the courtly academy that it was showing scant regard for 'necessities'. When Berowne goes on to complain that Jack is not getting his Jill, that this wooing 'doth not end like an old play', and that the tasks set by the ladies will take 'too long for our play', he is of course complaining that 'life' is more bruising than works of art and that this is not how things happen in plays: the reflexive irony suggests why, in *this* play, the songs of Apollo give way to the harsh words of Mercury, and the wintry owl supplants spring's cuckoo. And that conclusion is itself the result of a still more intricate reflexive irony, and seeming accident. Armado begs to be allowed to present what 'should have followed in the end of our shew', and the King agrees, prompted by kindness rather than interest: through a superb act of appropriation, the end of the courtly entertainment—which is now bereft of its point and function within the play's world—becomes the marvellously pointed conclusion of Shakespeare's play.

It would seem a very large leap from Berowne's complaint to Kent's agonised question in *King Lear:* 'Is this the promis'd end?' But then Cordelia's death is also an elaborately contrived accident, as appears when we consider the intolerable screwing up of tension between Edmund's first hint that he may be 'mov'd' to 'do good'—

> This speech of yours hath mov'd me,
> And shall perchance do good, but speake you on,
> You looke as you had something more to say . . .
> (5.3.199–201)

and his eventual revelation, so many lines later, of what more *he* had to say:

> I pant for life: some good I meane to do
> Despight of mine owne Nature. Quickly send,
> (Be briefe in't) to'th'Castle, for my Writ
> Is on the life of *Lear*, and on *Cordelia:*
> Nay, send in time. . . .
>
> (5.3.243–7)

The word 'perchance' suggests with what artful purpose the dramatist is turning the screw—as does any invitation to the loquacious Edgar to speak on. The reiterated emphasis on the need to 'be briefe' and 'send in time', and the quite extraordinary dithering over who has the 'Office' and what 'token of repreeve' should be given to the Captain, further underline the way in which, within the play's world, Cordelia's death is a grotesque, meaningless accident which might have been, and nearly was, avoided.

But then Cordelia's death is so peculiarly shocking for the spectator because he is aware—as no character within the play can be—that it is also the result of a deliberate and carefully executed artistic decision. The dramatist has determined that she shall die, and die like this, so that Kent's 'Is this the promis'd end?' has one meaning within the play, and another meaning in relation to our sense that this accident is contrived and *meant*. Similarly, Edmund's 'perchance' makes circumstantial sense within the action, but is also an excruciatingly insouciant reminder that we are being confronted with yet another elaborately engineered accident—in a play where nothing, not even the catastrophe, 'comes pat'. We feel with and also for Lear when he asks—or howls—a question which we may all expect to ask in life, as well as of this work of art:

> Why should a Dog, a Horse, a Rat have life
> And thou no breath at all?
>
> (5.3.306–7)

But as spectators we were not able to feel with and for Lear *in the same way*, when he voiced a no less heartrendingly natural feeling:

> This feather stirs, she lives: if it be so,
> It is a chance which do's redeeme all sorrowes
> That ever I have felt . . .
>
> (5.3.265–7)

We are of course still immersed in the action, and understand why Lear begs for that redeeming 'chance' and feels that to have this prayer answered would seem, as it were, to make things right. But we, as spectators, are wishing that the *dramatist* would *make* things less wrong. This makes it impossible for us to join with Lear in supposing that a *chance*, which would certainly mitigate his sorrows, could ever *redeem* them. Bradley's supposition that *we* would feel better, if we only agree that Lear dies in the happy delusion that Cordelia still lives, by chance, ignores the cruelly disillusioning effect of the reflexive irony. We are being reminded—as we were, far more happily, in *Love's Labour's Lost*—that life does not imitate art.

Here *The Winter's Tale* provides a telling contrast, by reminding us that Hermione's survival is neither less fortuitous nor less contrived than Cordelia's death. Even as the triumphant Paulina insists on the miraculous nature of the spectacle which *she* has contrived, the reflexive irony establishes that this redeeming chance is a trick of art—of Shakespeare's art, as well as Paulina's:

> That she is living,
> Were it but told you, should be hooted at
> Like an old tale; but it appears she lives . . .
> (5.3.115–17)

Like Theseus or Lorenzo, Berowne or Portia, Kent or Lear himself, Paulina is entirely unaware that what she says within the play provides a complex and disconcerting comment on what the play is doing: 'appears' works at two levels, like Edmund's 'perchance'. We do not 'hoot', but by reflecting on its own resemblance to 'an old tale' Shakespeare's *Tale* challenges us to reflect on our deeper reasons for not hooting. In one sense this increases the distance between the spectator and the play, by fracturing the illusion; but it would be misleading to see this as a Shakespearean equivalent to Brecht's 'V-effect', for we are also drawn into, and included in, an irony which depends both on our presence and on the continuing power of the illusion. We find ourselves contemplating a play which appears to exist in some realm between our world and the world of artless old tales.

The question, 'Why does Cordelia die?', is rightly regarded as fundamental in *Lear*-criticism; I submit that this is because, even while we register our horror at an obscene accident, we are aware that this is something which the dramatist is very deliberately doing *to us*. We are doubly violated. It helps us not a jot to reflect that Cordelia dies 'because she is strangled', or 'because it just happens, "perchance", that help comes too late'—although this is the only kind of answer which is furnished within the play's action. Nor can our pain be alleviated by the other obvious answer, which presents itself as soon as we begin to reflect on the play's complex relations with the real world: 'in real life, such things happen'. The triteness of either kind of answer aggravates our distress at an ending which requires both kinds of answer; I take it that my own suggestions are uncomfortably close to platitudes *because* we are being impaled on a contradiction which is all the more horrible for being so simple and elementary. We *know* that we cannot expect life to display the order, meaning and significance which we *expect* from great works of art; consequently, we also know that it cannot be a serious or sufficient objection to *Lear* as a work of art to protest that it shows life as it sometimes is, not as it should be. Dr Johnson continued to be profoundly troubled by this dilemma long after he had recorded his approval of Nahum Tate's revised ending, in which Cordelia survives and marries Edgar.

That, some will say, is a fate worse than death. But then Edgar also focuses thoroughly disconcerting reflexive ironies. Those who find him 'insufferable' because of his moralising all too frequently write as though 'Poor Tom' were an independent character; yet in assuming that role the high-born, privileged and legitimate Edgar shows just that *moral* awareness of the bare forked animal's plight which Lear himself must learn. Like Paulina, Edgar rouses indignation as a self-appointed spiritual midwife who protracts torture for the good of the tortured—but then, as Stephen Booth points out (1983: 57), 'When Edgar at last does reveal his identity, the news kills Gloucester instantly.' In more general terms, we repeatedly see characters struggling to discover significance or meaning in their own or others' agony, and invoking the gods or astrology when they are confronted with more than they can confront or endure; and, as William Elton so systematically demonstrates in *King Lear and the Gods*, they invoke a representative variety of *incompatible* attitudes and beliefs. This is critically most disconcerting, because the characters prefigure our own divergent attempts to discover—or impose—meaning. Kent anticipates nihilistic or existentialist readings when he prepares to quit a world in which all is cheerless, dark and deadly; in Edgar's case—and not least in that comfortless gesture towards formal closure which is offered by his, and the play's, last words—we contemplate that very human longing for some 'redeeming' revelation or assurance of order and meaning which reappears in the various Christian readings of *Lear*.

Like Enobarbus, Edgar is the register within the drama of those judgemental difficulties which are also troubling the audience as the play unfolds: he is both a participant in a stubbornly unconventional 'tragedy', and a surrogate critic or commentator, who is continually struggling to make sense of, or impose sense on, arbitrary and contingent horrors. As Stephen Booth remarks: 'In Edgar's desperate attempts to classify and file human experience, Shakespeare tantalises us with the comfort to be had from ideologically Procrustean beds to which he refuses to tailor his matter' (47–8). But then this very *refusal* to 'tailor' is itself tailored, and a crucial part of this play's 'matter'. Today, reflexivity is frequently associated with forms of artistic and critical narcissism, and a self-regarding, self-defeating insistence on the autonomy of the work of art. The reflexivity in the final scene of *Lear* concentrates a moral challenge: it is Shakespeare's means of establishing, in dramatic terms, that important and subtle critical distinction which Booth makes, between our sense of 'an encompassing order in the *work*' and our sense of the absence of any comparable order in the *world* the work 'describes' (27). The perplexity which we feel in contemplating the play's world, and various characters' different attempts to make sense of their world, is disconcertingly extreme but still more disconcertingly familiar.

And by making Cordelia's death a conspicuously contrived matter of 'chance' the play is also anticipating, and undercutting, the arguments of critics like Jan Kott, who see Cordelia's death as a (congenially) despairing and even nihilistic gesture on the part of the dramatist. For the very fact that she might just as easily have survived, within the play's world, means that the accident of her death neither necessitates nor legitimises a nihilistic view of existence: if she had survived, Kent's view of life would have been different, but Kott's would not.

Nor can the accident of her death invalidate our earlier responses to everything that has moved us so deeply—in the reconciliation scene, as in all those other scattered, precious moments of tenderness and simple solicitude when characters care for each other or poignantly invoke a 'Grace' which exists in the *Lear*-world only as it is actualised in their own responses and needs. Such references reveal what poetry can reveal—not the assurances of divine Revelation, but those struggling human potentialities which affect us all the more deeply in this play because they are left so terribly exposed. To be sure, the play's deliberate accident deprives us, pointedly, of that satisfaction which Wilde's Miss Prism expects of fiction: 'The good ended happily, and the bad unhappily. That is what Fiction means.' And this throws us back on our responses, which are all we have, but not nothing. The play's ultimate horrors do not obscure, but rather accentuate, our sense that there *is* a vital difference between Cordelia and her sisters, or our sense that a momentous advance was taking place when Lear's sudden registering of the misery felt by the Fool who loves him prompted that great, inundating swell of compassion for all the world's poor naked wretches. Far from being rendered meaningless by the horrible ending, such responses are the measure of that horror. What they affirm is proved upon our pulses, and incompatible with nihilism; the resulting moral challenge is that of having to recognise that no contrived happy ending could give such responses more or less meaning than they already have.

This was not Dr Johnson's view. And yet, paradoxically, his grounds for preferring Tate's revised ending (which, we should remember, held the stage for well over a century) show how deeply he responded to the *exemplary* force of Shakespeare's ending. In his Preface, Johnson enters a general complaint about Shakespeare's failure to 'make the world better':

> he makes no just distribution of good or evil, nor is always careful to shew in the virtuous a disapprobation of the wicked; he carries his persons indifferently through right and wrong, and at the close dismisses them without further care, and leaves their examples to operate by chance. This fault the barbarity of his age cannot extenuate; for it is always a writer's duty to make the world better, and justice is a virtue independent on time or place. (66)

Yet Johnson also commends Shakespeare for 'exhibiting the real state of sublunary nature, which partakes of good and evil, joy and sorrow, mingled with endless variety of proportion and innumerable modes of combination' (62). There is a contradiction here, which reappears when Johnson considers the final scene of *Lear* as a supreme instance of this failure, and explains why 'I was many years ago so shocked by Cordelia's death, that I know not whether I ever endured to read again the last scenes of the play until I undertook to revise them as an editor':

> Shakespeare has suffered the virtue of Cordelia to perish in a just cause, contrary to the natural ideas of justice, to the hope of the reader, and, what is yet more strange, to the faith of the chronicles. . . . A play in which the wicked prosper, and the virtuous miscarry, may doubtless be

good, because it is a just representation of the common events of human life: but since all reasonable human beings naturally love justice, I cannot easily be persuaded, that the observation of justice makes a play worse; or, that if other excellencies are equal, the audience will not always rise better pleased, from the final triumph of persecuted virtue. (126)

This does not explain, directly, why Johnson finds *this* death so unendurable; but he is evidently well aware of, and deeply troubled by, the general discrepancy between his wish for a 'just representation' of what life (real sublunary nature) is like, and his requirement that the artist 'make the world better' by imposing a more just distribution of good and evil than life itself affords. He is responding, perhaps more intensely than any of the critics who admire and defend the last scene of *Lear*, to the issue which that scene makes so pressing.

For Sidney, it was indeed the 'peculiar' commendation of Poetry that it allowed men to see virtue exalted and vice punished:

For indeede Poetrie ever setteth vertue so out in her best cullours, making Fortune her wel-wayting hand-mayd, that one must needs be enamored of her. Well may you see *Ulisses* in a storme, and in other hard plights; but they are but exercises of patience and magnanimitie, to make them shine the more in the neere-following prosperitie. And of the contrarie part, if evill men come to the stage, they ever goe out (as the Tragedie Writer answered to one that misliked the shew of such persons) so manacled as they little animate folkes to followe then. But the Historian, being captived to the trueth of a foolish world, is many times a terror from well dooing, and an incouragement to unbrideled wickednes. (170)

The poet's advantage over the historian is that the latter is tied 'not to what shoulde bee but to what is' (164) and is 'bound to tell things as things were' (168). Precisely because the poet is not tied to the truth, he can more easily win 'the mind from wickednese to vertue: even as the childe is often brought to take most wholsom things by hiding them in such other as have a pleasant tast' (172). And similarly, because men are childish in the best things, the poet enjoys an advantage over the philosopher who 'teacheth obscurely, so as the learned onely can understande him; that is to say, he teacheth them that are already taught'—whereas 'the Poet is the foode for the tenderest stomacks' and can 'make many, more beastly then Beasts, begin to heare the sound of vertue' (167).

In this happy flow of conventional argument, the social and ideological correlative of Sidney's ostentatious idealism is aristocratic condescension. Here we might recall H. A. Mason's patient and elaborate demolition of Sidney's claims to critical originality, and of the 'noble lie' in his idealisation of the courtier; or Stephen Greenblatt's brilliant exposure, in 'Murdering Peasants', of the obsessive concern with status in Sidney's *Arcadia*. Behind the representative dicta I have quoted is the assumption that an audience is childish, and more in need of milk than meat—and in those passages from *The Advancement of Learning* which I quoted in Chapter 1, Bacon's underlying assumption is similar, with the important difference that *he* prefers meat to milk. His discussion of 'Poesie' as 'FAINED HISTORY' reworks Sidney: poetry can 'raise and erect the Minde, by submitting the shewes of things to the desires of the Minde' and giving some 'shadowe of satisfaction to the minde of Man in those points wherein the Nature of Things doth denie it.' But then, although Bacon allows the consolatory and edifying value of such shadowy satisfactions, his first concern is with that judgement, and reason, which 'can buckle and bowe the Mind unto the Nature of things'. Neither Sidney nor Bacon can help us with *Lear*, but between them they frame that problem which so disturbs Dr Johnson.

For Johnson also wants art to be truthful. The final scene of *Lear* presents him with a nearly intolerable critical dilemma because it buckles the mind unto the nature of things *and* refuses to provide a shadowy satisfaction. Moreover, since what is an accident within the play's world is also conspicuously contrived and very evidently *meant*, it confronts Johnson with a form of truthfulness which he cannot accommodate: he sees clearly enough that virtue is not regularly rewarded, but does not see how Shakespeare's dramatic perspectivism—his habitual 'framing' of dual or multiple perspectives on characters and issues—is more morally instructive than any invocation of a supra-dramatic Order. Just as Shakespeare exposes the terrible gap between what must be expected of life at its worst and what we customarily expect a work of art to do or not to do, he

exposes the gap between different characters' intensely apprehended need for values like 'justice' and the apparent absence
or invisibility of any corresponding Order and Justice in the
play's world. The responses of an Edgar, Cordelia or Kent
are the expressions or manifestations of their respective lives
or ways of being: the play throws us back on our own
responses by challenging us to appraise such representative
potentialities without any reassuring invocation of a supra-
dramatic Truth and without any final triumph of persecuted
virtue.

But then, as we have already seen, Shakespeare's predilec-
tion for elaborately reflexive closures is apparent in plays like
A Midsummer Night's Dream and *Love's Labour's Lost*,
where he is largely or entirely responsible for his own plotting. In plays like *The Merchant of Venice* or *Measure for
Measure* Shakespeare deliberately produces problems by
yoking together what were originally independent stories—
the stories of the bond and the caskets; the Claudio-story
and the Mariana-story (which derives, like Mariana's name,
from the story in Boccaccio which Shakespeare first used in
All's Well)—and then exposing the *apparent* resolution which
is offered within the play to our sense of the play as a
contrived fiction. And in *The Winter's Tale*, as in *Lear*,
the reflexivity is produced by deliberate departures from the
source material: Cordelia does not die in the pre-Shakespearean versions, nor does the main source for *The Winter's
Tale* include a statue scene.

The Winter's Tale suggests what all of these examples have
in common, when Paulina shows Leontes the 'statue' and
tells him to prepare to see life 'lively mock'd' (5.3.19). A
moment later the astonished Leontes declares that 'we are
mocked with Art'—as of course 'we' are, when Paulina's
reference to 'old tales' calls attention to Shakespeare's
contrivance. Where *Lear* refuses to finish like a fiction, *The
Winter's Tale* pointedly reminds us that it is a fiction. The
ending of *Lear* is a radical and exemplary subversion of
Sidney's idea of what tragedy, and works of art in general,
should do—not merely because it ends horribly, but because
it reminds us that it could easily have ended happily. But the
ending of *The Winter's Tale* is, in its different and complementary way, also subversive: Fortune, Sidney's well-

waiting handmaid, puts in an appearance on this occasion, but is accompanied by the reminders that the kind of thing which happens in old tales and *is* happening in this *Tale* usually draws hoots for being so unlifelike. The illusion is not fractured in any final or Brechtian sense; rather, we become aware of our participant roles, find ourselves considering the nature of our own involvement with the 'feigning', and find that the play we are watching is watching us. The effect is 'witty' in that sense which Eliot elaborates in his essay on Marvell, and which admits painful variants: implicit in the experience which the given closure provides is a sense of other possible kinds of experience and closure. Our sense that the given ending is the result of a deliberate artistic choice reinforces our impression of the play as a sustained conceit or *concetto*, in which the internally coherent poetic-dramatic world provides a grim or teasing reflexion of the world we all inhabit. In opposing the 'feigned' to the 'true' or 'real', neither Sidney nor Bacon allows for the effect—or possibility—of Shakespearean reflexivity; yet, by continually challenging our awareness of our own moral and imaginative needs, this reflexivity embodies a far more profound—and sceptical—awareness of the complex, interdependent relations between Art and Life.

THREE

Hamlet and the Art of Grafting

> We are to think, apparently, that Shakespeare wrote a play which was
> extremely successful at the time (none more so, to judge by the refer-
> ences) and continued to hold the stage, and yet that nearly two hundred
> years had to go by before anyone had even a glimmering of what it was
> about. This is a good story, but it is rather too magical.
>
> William Empson, '*Hamlet* When New'

The problem of the problem

I take it that Empson is right: because it took so long for
Hamlet to seem in any serious sense a 'problem' we must
confront the problem of the problem. One bibliography of
Hamlet criticism records that 2167 items of one kind or
another appeared between 1877 and 1935; since later critics
have not been more reticent there have been several critical
studies of *Hamlet* criticism, notably those by Morris Weitz
and Paul Gottschalk. In the case of *King Lear* there is at least
a received reading to think from or against: as A. L. French
observes, testily, it was adumbrated by Dowden, reached full
explicitness in Bradley, is developed by Traversi, Danby,
Heilman, L. C. Knights, G. I. Duthie and Kenneth Muir,
and is 'generally associated with a sort of unctuous religiosity
which I, for one, find most distasteful in itself as well as
absurdly inappropriate to the spirit of Shakespeare's play'
(144). There is also, as I shall argue, a received reading of
Macbeth, in which critics repeatedly make just that 'interpretative leap' to an externalised moral and spiritual Order which
the play—terrifyingly—refuses to make. Yet in the case of
Hamlet the staggering proliferation of conflicting, utterly

incompatible readings makes it desperately hard even to agree on what the critically relevant *questions* are.

Eighteenth-century critics barely discussed that 'melancholy' which figures so prominently in almost any Romantic account of the play that one can think of. Even if we were so perverse as to want to read Hamlet as though Goethe and Mackenzie, Turgenev and Freud had never existed we still could not do so, any more than we can see what our grandparents saw in photographs of our parents as children—the intervening writers have shaped the sensibilities we bring to *Hamlet*. Trying, like Stoll, Schücking or Lily Campbell, to cut out the intervening commentary by seeing the play in strictly 'Elizabethan' terms is *un*historical as well as aesthetically impossible: the Elizabethan audience was no monolithic entity, and, as Empson drily observes, in the sixteenth and seventeenth centuries, as in our own, men killed each other because they thought differently about matters large and small. The *Scrutiny* critics lambasted Bradley for reading plays as though they were novels, but the essays by Leavis and others on 'The Novel as Dramatic Poem' shows that *their* idea of how the greatest novelists should be read actually corresponds with their view of Shakespeare. Two familiar examples may suggest a yet more unnerving general reflection: that the most vital and original thinking about *Hamlet* has tended to appear in those very interpretations that seem off-beat, maverick, partial and perverse. And the examples will also help me to formulate what I take to be the two crucial questions we must ask about this play.

Ernest Jones's notorious psychoanalytical account explains Hamlet's unconscious repugnance for his task in terms of the so-called Oedipal process. After assuming the existence, and universality, of this process, Jones argues that Hamlet's Oedipal feelings are reactivated by Claudius's crime: 'through Claudius Hamlet has vicariously accomplished the Oedipal feat of murdering his father and marrying his mother', and the supposedly 'unconscious' disturbance that follows *explains* Hamlet's near-paralysis. Jones does not explain how a marriage may be 'vicarious', or why all of Hamlet's references to his father are loving—save by his argument that Shakespeare himself was suffering from a repressed but reactivated Oedipal process that made *him* 'unconscious of what the play projects'. It readily follows that any reader who is unable to accept so many assumptions about Hamlet's, Shakespeare's and the universal human condition must be similarly disabled: arguments of this kind are satisfying, and bad, precisely because they discount contrary evidence and are not open to refutation.

Yet Jones made a crucial contribution to our thinking about *Hamlet:* as A. J. A. Waldock points out in his book on the play, earlier critics had never attended so closely to the play's 'sexual quality'. Hamlet's nausea in the first soliloquy is markedly sexual, like his appalled and appalling fascination with what goes on in an 'unseamed bed', with his mother's 'honying and making love/ Over the nasty Stye'; a woman is involved—Ophelia, Gertrude, 'Hecuba'—each time he loses control; and later critics have repeatedly recognised that these things are there in the text. Where and how far we go in pursuing them is another matter, but we are forever indebted to Jones for making us look and see.

Similarly, we might argue that every chapter of Wilson Knight's *The Wheel of Fire* is perverse and unacceptable, but contains insights so vital that in comparison, sober and judicious critics appear to be marking time. Knight argues that *Hamlet* is centred on a metaphoric conflict between life and death, good and evil, health and disease—all familiar enough, save that for Knight it is Hamlet who represents death, evil and disease: 'Except for the original murder of Hamlet's father, the *Hamlet* universe is one of health and robust life, good nature, humour, romantic strength, and welfare; against this background is the figure of Hamlet pale with the consciousness of death' (32). 'He is the ambassador of death amid life'; the Court and Claudius symbolise humanity—'with all its failings it is true'—but whereas they have failings, Hamlet is radically sick. Knight does not explain what distinguishes sickness from mere, ordinary human failings like murder or incest, and of course the obvious objection to his extended metaphor is (as Francis Fergusson and others have complained) that it is the wrong way round. Hamlet is (or at any rate was) healthy, while the Court's 'life' is founded on deception, intrigue, murder and (less clearly, I think) incest. And, even if we feel that Wilson Knight or D. H. Lawrence (whose somewhat similar view of 'Amleto' appears in *Twilight in Italy*) have some excuse to find Hamlet repellent, he plainly cannot be regarded only as a symbol of death: there is more, indeed rather a lot, to him: he likes plays, for instance, just as Mark Antony likes fishing.

Yet if we glance back, and across the Channel, we find that there was a long preparation for what looks at first like a sudden reversal of the accepted English wisdom about Hamlet. In France at the beginning of the nineteenth century, Châteaubriand was alarmed by the new 'leaning towards Shakespeare': 'In the English, it is simply ignorance; in us, it is depravity'—of a kind which not even Ophelia's 'ravishing ideality' could excuse. Yet the great master of the unideal ravishing or *fiasco* gave his characteristically candid testimony on the spreading of this rot: by the age of nineteen, Stendhal confesses, he spent 'more time thinking about *Hamlet* and *Le Misanthrope* than about real life'; and by the 1830s Hamlet had possessed Paris and obsessed artists as unalike as Musset, Delacroix and Berlioz. The reaction—not only to *Hamlet*, but to the native traditions—followed. By 1871 Taine could describe the history of Hamlet as 'the story of a moral poisoning', and by the end of the century Hamlet was being transformed into a peculiarly French, *fin-de-siècle* dandy, who seemed to have studied Schopenhauer and Villiers de l'Isle Adam in Wittenberg. Mallarmé is fascinated by the way in which Hamlet makes the real world of Elsinore seem unreal, and 'effaces the too clearly defined beings about him by the disquieting or funereal invasion of his presence', moving through his play as 'the dark presence of the doubter'. Laforgue's Hamlet is an artist beset by 'universal nausea': his sterile promontory has a geographical location and psychological landmark in the artist-hero's lonely tower, which has at its base all the rotting refuse from the palace greenhouses (rather as if Shakespeare's Hamlet had to super-vise the palace laundry), and Ophelia is a little 'upstart' who writes her letters on heavy, expensive paper, so that when our neurasthenic hero tears them up his delicate fingertips smart.

In Germany, we need only compare Schlegel's early 'Etwas über William Shakespeare, bei Gelegenheit Wilhelm Meisters' (1796: this essay still awaits an English translation) with the

1808 Vienna lectures to see how his Hamlet is becoming more crooked and dangerous, less like Goethe's and perhaps more like Goethe. And Turgenev was evidently influenced by Schlegel in his magnificent essay on 'Hamlet and Don Quixote' (1860), where he writes of Hamlet's 'sickly inanition': 'What does Hamlet represent?—Analysis, first of all, and egotism . . . Hamlet embodies the doctrine of negation'. Here too there was a movement away from the early Romantic Hamlet of Mackenzie and Goethe—from the Werther-like Man of Feeling who only lacks the strength of nerve which forms a hero. Rebecca West pleaded in vain with her Yugoslav friends that the Hamlet they described was more like Goncharov's Oblomov—and just how much *Hamlet* mattered as an influence on Russian literature is very pregnantly suggested by a note in Grigori Kozintsev's diary, which was printed in *Shakespeare: Time and Conscience*: 'Hamlet is Lermontovian in the "Mousetrap" scene, and Pushkinian at the end' (267). In Russia Hamlet was assimilated to the idea of the 'superfluous man', was associated with Onegin and Pechorin, with Turgenev's 'Hamlet of the Schigrov District' and Saltykov-Schedrin's 'Hamlet of Krutogor Province'. By the 1880s the changing view of Hamlet was informed—as in France and Germany—by changing views of the native tradition: Chekhov's Ivanov is disgusted with himself for becoming 'a sort of Hamlet, a Manfred'. By the 1890s Mikhailovski took a morally muscular view of Hamlet as 'an idler and a milquetoast, and from this angle, idlers and milquetoasts can recognise themselves in him'. Oddly enough, the wheel would come full circle in Soviet Russia when the nobly introspective Prince finally reappears transformed into the Christ-like, self-sacrificing hero of Pasternak's various versions of *Hamlet* and his poems which refer to Hamlet. Such a transformation could be managed only by glossing over or omitting uncongenial Shakespearean matter, especially those frightening images of internal corruption and the hints that Hamlet's mind *has* been 'tainted' by things rank and gross in nature.

This is a mere sampling, culled from LeWinter's *Shakespeare in Europe*, Eleanor Rowe's *Hamlet: A Window on Russia*, and the works already mentioned; and plainly the net could be cast wider. But it is not a very long step from

Turgenev's embodiment of 'negation' or Mallarmé's dark presence of the doubter to Wilson Knight and Lawrence: it seems longer than it should because the English criticism in the century that separates Coleridge from Bradley and Wilson Knight is so settled in its assumptions, dull and provincial. Disconcertingly, different ages seem to be reading different texts of *Hamlet*, and indeed the history of *Hamlet* criticism is a very pungent reminder that there are no purely literary values. Goethe's Werther and Mackenzie's Man of Feeling have something in common with each other, which reappears in their creators' influential readings of *Hamlet* (Mackenzie's essay was published in 1780, before *Wilhelm Meisters Lehrjahre*). But, strikingly, Hamlet has never suffered an eclipse—unlike Werther or the Man of Feeling, who both caused a sensation and a splash of suicides but became less interesting to succeeding generations. That *Hamlet* has—without interruption, although in very different ways—compelled and inspired the western imagination for nearly four centuries is surely a most important fact about the play. To my mind, this suggests why it will not do to 'explain' Hamlet's melancholy with reference to Timothy Bright or Burton, unless we are also remembering that it is expressed in poetry no age is willing to forget. Similarly, everything that *Hamlet* does not have in common with so-called revenge plays—which did not even interest English audiences for many years—must be vastly more important than any connections.

This brings me to my two leading questions. The first must surely be, *What kind of play could so enthral the western imagination?*, and must no less surely receive the kind of humbled answer that begins, 'This truly miraculous achievement . . .'. But then we have also to ask a second, sourer question: *How could any work have seemed to submit to so many divergent and incompatible readings, without being in itself flawed and obscure?* The second question might be restated as a condition: there can be no convincing reading of *Hamlet* which does not also explain or suggest why it has been so long in coming. Most critics make some approach, however indirect, to the first question and disregard the second; but the nights are drawing in, and it seems ever harder to set out as though it were dawn. At any rate, I must start setting out my own reasons for thinking that being unable to understand *Hamlet* is not part of the irreversible doom of man. Since *Hamlet* criticism is what it is, the reader may still find himself echoing that legendary remark which confronted a luckless student: 'This is both good and original: unfortunately, the good parts are not original and the original parts are not good.'

Hamlet without the prince

I doubt whether we can tackle the second question without adopting something like Empson's strategy of thinking about the play's first audience. This need not lead to silly speculations. We know from those references which survive from the late 1580s and early 1590s that the old, pre-Shakespearean play had been a roaring success and that intellectuals were rather sniffy about it. We know there was a Ghost; that Hamlet was mad or pretended to be, like Kyd's Hieronymo; that he bellowed 'Revenge' in a way that came to seem funny; we may be sure that the finale was bloody. One early reference plays on Kyd's name; if, as is thought likely, Kyd was the author of the old play, it is also likely that it had included a play-within-a-play like that in *The Spanish Tragedy:* the device worked very well and, as Empson puts it, Kyd 'had a powerful but narrow, one might say miserly, theatrical talent, likely to repeat a success.' That Shakespeare, at the height of his powers and success, had chosen to redress this somewhat tarnished popular success must have aroused a stir of curious anticipation like that which would follow, today, if it were announced that Ingmar Bergman was remaking *High Noon* or that Samuel Beckett was revamping Agatha Christie's *The Mousetrap*. Our hypothetical spectator—who did exist, and about whom I shall try not to speculate—would have watched the new play while remembering the earlier play, as we remember *Hamlet* in watching *Rosencrantz and Guildenstern are Dead*.

It is worth remarking that we do not know where our spectator would have been. The Bad Quarto tells us that *Hamlet* was performed at the Universities, and several scholars and critics (notably J. B. Nosworthy) have found this suggestive. The circumstances of a special performance—a gala, given by wandering players like those in the play, in a University building with interior lighting—would allow for a longer play than was the rule at the Globe; and *Hamlet* is very long. It is also packed with students: Hamlet, Horatio, Rosencrantz, Guildenstern—and even Laertes if we think, like Nosworthy, that Laertes leaves for the University of Paris; and Laertes' father blethers happily about drama in his Varsity days. And of course *Hamlet* is a markedly intellectual play; its nearest rivals in this respect—*Troylus* and *Measure*—belong to the same period; that *Troylus* seems never to have had a public staging in Shakespeare's lifetime has encouraged many scholars to suppose that it was staged in the Inns of Court.

Nor do we *know* whether the early play was anything like as taut and exciting as *Hamlet*, which is, even if we consider it merely as a scenario or melodrama, superb 'theatre'; this seems to me unlikely, but Empson thinks that Shakespeare could have kept Kyd's structure. Several critics have remarked on the way the play is stunningly constructed as a series of tense and exciting movements; this is worth emphasising, since it is not uncommon for critics to underestimate the importance of the 'action' in their concern with the prince.

The atmosphere of foreboding is marvellously conveyed in the first scene: a king dead, his country rearming; a prince not on the throne; raw-nerved soldiers, tired and apprehensive as they keep their midnight watch. As this first movement develops in the second scene we take in the relations of the two chief families while observing the initial opposition between Hamlet and Claudius, the mighty opposites. And these early scenes reverberate against each other, as has been well brought out in Emrys Jones' and David Rose's discussions of their scenic form: a stepfather advises his stepson; Polonius advises his son—who is, unlike Hamlet, allowed to leave Denmark, and would be alive at the end of the play if he had kept his father's fussy but shrewd advice; a dead father advises his son.

In the second movement tension mounts with the postponement of a direct clash between the mighty opposites; we see Hamlet and Claudius circling each other, intriguing, manoeuvring for advantage. So, for example, Hamlet quickly establishes that Rosencrantz and Guildenstern have been sent to spy on him; since they naturally keep this from Claudius, Hamlet could exploit his advantage—but throws it away in the nunnery scene when he starts snarling about one marriage he will not tolerate. Much of the suspense depends on our knowing what Hamlet or Claudius don't know. The third movement brings what Dover Wilson liked to call the 'climax'—that is, the stage in a Shakespeare play when the action reaches a high point, that will determine the eventual outcome. At last we have the direct confrontation, in the Mousetrap scene—but then, in an excitingly unexpected way, the 'climax' is spread to the scene where Hamlet confronts his mother. Once again he loses the initiative: by publicly threatening the King in the one scene and killing Polonius in the other, Hamlet allows Claudius to dispose of him, and his departure marks the brief anticlimactic period that is characteristic of Shakespeare's dramatic structures. Then, after this momentary relaxation or *Luftpause*, there is a rapid revival and increase of tension when Hamlet returns to Denmark and steps into a grave: by the end, Denmark's two main families are entirely destroyed and the country itself is delivered to Fortinbras.

Plainly, this kind of résumé is anything but inward, but then my purpose is to recall the play's external strengths in order to establish what I take to be a crucial contrast. The scenario owes something, perhaps a great deal, to the old play—and yet, even though the phrase 'Hamlet without the prince' is now a synonym for something absurd and unimaginable (like omelettes without eggs), this is precisely what the old play must have offered. 'Must have' may suggest that I am now speculating, but the prince who dominates Shakespeare's play was and probably still is the most complex character ever to have appeared on an English stage, and such astonishing originality is the prerogative of genius. Nobody has ever suggested that Kyd or any other candidate for the authorship of the old play had that kind of genius, or that the old 'Hamlet'—who bellowed 'Revenge' and made intellectuals snicker—was the model for that prince who has compelled the western imagination for four centuries. It follows that Shakespeare was grafting *his* prince onto the old play, and that Hamlet's psychological complexity, the inwardness of the dramatic conception, the tenor, authority and searing power of his pessimistic scepticism, were all *new*. Indeed, if our hypothetical spectator had not read Montaigne in French—for Florio's translation had yet to be published—these things would have seemed all the more unprecedented.

This of course suggests one answer to my first question. What would have astonished our hypothetical spectator and has never lost its hold on the imagination of audiences—in Schlegel's Germany or Pasternak's Russia—is the intensely inward and original rendering, *in* Hamlet's tortured consciousness, of that momentous Renaissance conflict between different conceptions of the nature of Nature, of human nature and human potentialities, and of Value which I discussed in Chapter 1. Since western man has never ceased to feel the consequences of these cataclysmic cultural developments, such an answer seems intrinsically more plausible, more likely to account for the play's continuing and extensive appeal, than, say, ingenious arguments about the duality of the revenger as agent and victim. In emphasising those perceptions which *Hamlet* has in common with Montaigne's great 'Apology', rather than those things which Hamlet has in common with Kyd's Hieronimo, such an answer would also help to explain why writers like Wilson Knight, Taine, Turgenev or Mallarmé saw Hamlet as a negative portent, associated with death, negation and corrosive doubt. And yet this also suggests something deficient or incomplete in such an answer: those problems which could never be resolved by killing Claudius—the problems that are still with us—would seem to have only a circumstantial connection with the father's death and the mother's remarriage. In sharp contrast, that 'duality of the revenger' theory which Nigel Alexander outlined in *Poison, Play and Duel* and which Harold Jenkins elaborates in the New Arden *Hamlet*, would seem to stand in a nearer relation to the play's 'action'; in this case the difficulty is rather that of explaining why the play which Jenkins explains seems so unlike, and so much smaller than, the play which obsessed Goethe and Schlegel, Turgenev and Pasternak. To put this in different terms, which remind us that the play is a 'graft': what seems obscure is the *connection* between the 'action' which is partially or largely inherited from the old play and the new play's prince and central nervous system.

If we are trying, as I think we should, to weigh what would have startled and impressed an audience which remembered the old play and those things which have compelled the western imagination ever since, we must also attach some weight to another kind of 'appeal', which is closely connected with the play's extraordinary theatricality. In turning through Mander and Mitchenson's useful compilation, *Hamlet through the Ages*, it is indeed fascinating to see how the changing images of Hamlet accommodate and reflect changing notions of what is 'attractive'—from the Coleridgean Kean to Forbes Robertson's clean-cut manly hero, from Sarah Bernhardt's Proustian matinée idol to Mikhail Chekhov's passionately soulful Slav. Much of the comedy in Lawrence's account of Hamlet in *Twilight in Italy* derives from the unfortunate actor's inability to conform with prevailing notions of the attractive hero, which soon launches Lawrence into his argument that Hamlet really is not attractive in any deeper sense. Even provocatively unattractive recent Hamlets, like those of David Warner or Nicol Williamson, reflected the prevailing attraction to Angry Young Men and 'anti-heroes', which had its parallel in the images of fashion magazines. This suggests that some image of the beautiful young man, suffering the slings and arrows of fortune like a St Sebastian idealisation of our suffering selves, exerts a potent and insidious appeal. And throughout *Hamlet* Shakespeare's prince is the constant focus of attention: even when he is not on stage the other characters are discussing him and worrying about him. Hamlet is overwhelmingly *present* to us, whether or not we find this presence agreeable.

This helps us to account for the Pirandellian effect that strikes so many readers: Hamlet seems to be a 'real' man who finds himself trapped in a play and forced to perform, or act. Even when he is obscure or inconsequential—as when he says, 'I, but while the grasse growes, the Proverbe is something musty'—we are less likely to think that Shakespeare is nodding than we are to reflect on the verisimilitude of such incoherence. Mallarmé was responding to this effect when he wrote that Hamlet 'effaces the too clearly defined beings about him' and makes the real world of Elsinore seem unreal; so was Victor Hugo, when he remarked that Hamlet seems like a somnambulist. But here we might once again consider the kind of surprise this held for our hypothetical spectator who *knew* the old play and was curious to see what kind of facelift Shakespeare had given to a protagonist whose melodramatic bellows of 'Revenge' were recalled in street jokes like the catch-phrases of a modern television series. For our spectator, the immediately interesting issue in the second scene would be not whether Shakespeare *makes* Hamlet theatrical, but what he does with the original Hamlet's melodramatic theatricality.

His prince does indeed make a highly theatrical entry. As Dover Wilson showed, the second Quarto stage entry at the beginning of this scene shows that Hamlet is subverting the new King's first Council meeting from the start. Instead of entering with the King and Queen, he is drooping behind like Apemantus, tetchily detached from, and contemptuous of, the routines of Court. After some cryptic comments in which he seems to speak for his own satisfaction or relief, Hamlet delivers his first speech—and reflects on that ostentation which has isolated him from the glittering court:

> Seemes Maddam, nay it is, I know not seemes,
> Tis not alone my incky cloake good mother
> Nor customary suites of solembe blacke
> Nor windie suspiration of forst breath
> No, nor the fruitfull river in the eye,
> Nor the dejected havior of the visage
> Together with all formes, moodes, shapes of griefe
> That can denote me truely, these indeede seeme,
> For they are actions that a man might play
> But I have that within which passes showe
> These but the trappings and the suites of woe.
>
> (1.2.76–86; Q2)

This prompts Howard Jacobson to comment, in *Shakespeare's Magnanimity:*

> the inevitable question is: why, in that case, the ostentation of the trappings? A sharper mother than Gertrude might have put that brutally. As it is Gertrude doesn't put it at all, and we, I think, should put it gently. (28)

A. L. French is not inclined to put this gently, and writes that such 'artificiality' and 'conceitedness' could not be the result of 'mere inadvertence' on Shakespeare's part:

> Hamlet's winds and rivers don't invoke the natural world or point the inwardness of his suffering; rather, they recall the conventionally literary world of Petrarchan poetic diction. There is, one feels, a certain unreality in his grief, a certain kind of histrionic self-regard. (45)

Yet Hamlet does *not* say that his inky cloak and 'customary' signs of grief do not denote him truly; if he said that, Jacobson's *riposte* would be deserved. What he says is that the 'trappings' cannot *alone* denote him truly, although he feels obliged to wear them. He is painfully aware of what may be taken for ostentation—of what *has* already seemed like the melodramatic theatricality of his predecessor in the old play: but he intercepts criticism by insisting that there is no way of showing grief that cannot be dissimulated, and no way of making visible that authenticating inner grief which passeth show. He is objecting—in a way that launches the elaborately reflexive ironies I discussed in Chapter 2—to the impossible part he must play, and one wants to ask the hostile critics what Hamlet could do instead. To appear as a mourner at a coronation, wedding and Council meeting cannot but seem like an ostentatious gesture—but should he therefore dress gaily, and play the game? I take it that our worries about Hamlet's behaviour in this scene are of a different kind.

Similarly, it seems that there is nothing that Claudius could do or say, or not do and not say, in this scene, which would forestall his determined critics—but why are they so determined, if we do not yet know that Claudius is a murderer? One paradox in this scene is that we find ourselves watching the villain struggle, rather manfully, to say and do the right thing, while the hero is spitefully intent on disruption: the main business of the Council meeting could hardly be more urgent, but Hamlet is entirely indifferent to the threat of invasion. We discover that Claudius has already dealt with this danger, very shrewdly, and we see him trying to be the magnanimous ruler—and solicitous father. His first speech is obviously prepared, for the no less obvious reason that it is working through the Council agenda: that he begins by paying tribute to King Hamlet shows that this is the first Council meeting; he then reports the emergency and his responses, before considering the less urgent item. Plainly he cannot feel deep grief over a calamity from which he gained a much desired wife and throne; no less plainly, he is expected to pay a preliminary tribute to his predecessor, just as the present British Prime Minister was expected to commend an outgoing Prime Minister whose policies she deplored: public office calls for some ceremonious insincerities.

It is axiomatic in dramatic criticism that we should keep close to the dramatic process of unfolding, without assuming in Act 1 what a play does not tell us until Act 3. None the less, critics are apt to pounce on Claudius from the first, as the villain of this piece, even while they pay lip-service to this fundamental principle. So, for example, L. C. Knights argues that 'even before we know that Claudius is a murderer, it is clear on his first appearance that we are intended to register something repulsive'; after quoting Claudius's first seven lines, Knights remarks that we must all 'react to those unctuous verse rhythms with some such comment as "Slimy beast!"' (1960: 41–2). But that comment is one we might rather reserve for Hamlet's apology to Laertes in Act 5. The stylistic crash in Claudius's reference to 'one Auspicious, and one Dropping eye' is very obvious in the Folio, and only a little softer in the second Quarto's 'an auspicious, and a dropping eye', but how much follows from this? Claudius is addressing a crisis not a convention of literary critics, and perhaps only literary critics would attach so much more importance to a lack of rhetorical finesse than to the efficient diplomacy which has saved Denmark from war. We might be more concerned by Hamlet's lack of concern over the threat of invasion—which suggests that the dangers of excessive grief may be national as well as spiritual, and that it is a good thing for Denmark that Claudius is on the throne. Ironically, Claudius simply assumes that discretion should fight with nature in his first, carefully rehearsed speech, and is then forced by an immediate and unexpected emergency to develop this difficult theme in an entirely unrehearsed speech to his new stepson.

Shakespeare's consummate mastery of scenic form appears in these subtly counterpointed contrasts, which introduce the play's two 'mighty opposites'. Claudius's first speech shows him struggling in an effortful but creditable way to do those things which a good king should do: apart from the rhetorical lapses in his tribute to the dead king (which at least does not pretend that his grief is unmixed with delight), we might notice how his elaborately effusive encouragement to Laertes is overdone, and suggests a chairman who has not yet mastered the knack of seeming caressingly and magnanimously informal while pressing on through the less pressing parts of an agenda. In sharp contrast with the King's attempts to *stage* himself as a good king, Hamlet refuses to behave as a prince should behave; his anguished reflections on how he must stage himself—in giving private grief absolute priority—insist on the gulf between appearance or 'show' and inwardly apprehended reality. This presents Claudius with an unexpected and trying test of his ability to respond as a wise king *and* as a loving stepfather: with more than regal patience he chooses to ignore what is bloody-minded in Hamlet's behaviour and tries, instead, to address Hamlet's misery. Given the demanding circumstances, his impromptu speech is far from unimpressive: we see him struggling to be solicitous and tender, and to suppress his exasperation at having to instruct an intellectual stepson on what an unschooled understanding knows to be 'as common/ As any the most vulgar thing'. And when Hamlet responds to this with a brutally deliberate snub, by speaking only to his mother, Claudius tries to deflect, or ignore, that, and commends what is patently not, so far as he is concerned, 'a loving and a faire reply'.

If we are seeing Claudius from the first as a slimy 'Belial', like Knights, or as Bradley's (and Hamlet's) drunken bloat king, we will miss the disconcertingly subtle and worldly, even Chaucerian, ironies of Shakespeare's characterisation. Despite his contrary protestation, I cannot but believe that Knights subjects Claudius's first speech to a blast of unworldly, inflexibly high-minded censure *because* he knows that Claudius is a murderer. Wilson Knight provides a sharp and telling critical contrast by going to the other extreme: when, as we have seen, he commends this king and Court for robust health and sanity *he* is responding like someone who genuinely does not know that Claudius is a murderer.

Nor is it clear that Claudius's solicitousness is not genuinely kindly and perceptive. Why are the King and Queen so anxious that Hamlet should not leave Denmark? The question is the more pressing if we are allowing ourselves to remember that Claudius is a murderer and that Hamlet has no means of knowing this. Claudius has nothing to fear from Hamlet—but Hamlet's own behaviour suggests why there is a reason to fear *for* him: if that thought has not occurred to us already it should occur a moment later, when the King and Court leave and Hamlet's first soliloquy confirms that he has been considering 'self-slaughter'.

Indeed we observe how Claudius's bewilderment and irritation grows through the first half of the play, until the emotional release of that moment in 3.3 when he at last announces, in flatly final terms, 'I like him not'. Here we might notice how a great critic plays fast and loose with the text, on what is not a complicated interpretative problem but an ascertainable matter of fact. The text tells us that Claudius resolves to send Hamlet to England to collect a 'neglected Tribute' (3.1.169–70), immediately after hearing Hamlet swear that of those 'that are married alreadie, all but one shall live'; then that Claudius decides to do this 'forthwith', after he and the Court have watched a play in which a nephew kills his royal uncle (3.1.1–7); and finally that Claudius decides to have Hamlet killed in England, after Hamlet has butchered Polonius (4.3.58–68). There is no textual authority for Bradley's assurance that Claudius is already planning his second murder in 3.3, when he is at prayer (1965: 138–9); and yet, as A. L. French points out, other critics, including Morris Weitz and W. W. Robson, treat this unwarranted assumption as fact (77–8). This might be compared with the way in which it is frequently supposed that Gertrude summons Hamlet to her bedroom *because* of the Mousetrap: in his recent book on *Hamlet*, Andrew Gurr speaks of the Queen's being finally stirred to action (50). Yet if the Queen entertained any suspicion that her second husband had killed her first husband, her first words to Hamlet ('*Hamlet*, thou hast they father much offended') would be both amazingly self-possessed and morally monstrous. And of course Gertrude is merely carrying out the plan which was suggested by Polonius and approved by Claudius *before* the Mouse-trap:

> my Lord, doe as you please,
> But if you hold it fit, after the play,
> Let his Queene-mother all alone intreate him
> To show his griefe, let her be round with him,
> And Ile be plac'd (so please you) in the eare
> Of all their conference. If she find him not,
> To England send him: or confine him where
> Your wisedome best shall thinke.
>
> (3.1.180–7)

Just as the critics are unwilling to suppose that Claudius first plans to send Hamlet to England in the hope that 'seas, and countries different' will improve his health, they are unwilling to suppose that the only effect the Mouse-trap has on Gertrude is to confirm that Hamlet is now not only off his head but dangerous. But the text runs differently, subverting and complicating that simple outline which the critics would prefer; and Claudius's solicitousness on Hamlet's behalf is gradually eroded by his recognition that to let Hamlet's madness range is becoming more and more dangerous.

A. L. French is pointing towards the basic difficulty when he remarks that the fact that we do not *know* that Claudius is a murderer until the 'revelation' in 3.3 leaves us wondering 'why Shakespeare has hitherto thrown us off the scent by making him considerate and affable' (75); and yet French himself is not taking the full measure of the difficulty. In fact, because *Hamlet* is a national classic, we do all know that Claudius is a murderer, just as we all know that Oedipus killed his father. The problem is what we are to do with knowledge which the play itself takes so long to confirm. And here we are let down very badly by that fundamental principle that we should not assume in Act 1 what we only learn in Act 3 and should rather be trying to put ourselves in the position of a first audience.

For our hypothetical spectator would also have known—from the old play which had been such a popular success and was not then very old—who killed King Hamlet. Instead of being thrown 'off the track', in French's sense, his interest would have been concentrated on the new play's deliberate and intriguing departures from the familiar track. He would have been surprised when the second scene worked against his expectations by contrasting the villain's good qualities with the hero's questionable qualities. As Empson observes, the first audience could not have known that it was watching our national classic: there was rather a danger that Hamlet's melodramatic entry would provoke a laugh of recognition and memories of his ranting predecessor—but Hamlet's first speech is brilliantly calculated to exploit such potentially disruptive memories. When Hamlet begins to protest against the role he is being forced to play, what I have called the 'Pirandellian effect' would be accentuated by memories of the old play: this overwhelmingly original prince has been grafted onto, and is indeed trapped within, a framework provided by what had been 'Hamlet without the prince'.

All of this makes for an exceedingly uncomfortable paradox. We have no access to that old play on which Shakespeare was working brilliant variations; yet the principled modern critic who tries not to assume what he has not yet been told is in a position as ludicrous as that of a critic who tries to suppress all knowledge of *Hamlet* while watching *Rosencrantz and Guildenstern are Dead*.

Coming of age in Shakespeare's Denmark

I have so far been trying to limit myself to that internal evidence which Shakespeare's play provides, and to the surviving scraps of reliable information about the old play. I have certainly been less speculative than those critics who assume that when *Hamlet* was first staged there was already a distinct genre of so-called 'revenge drama' which Elizabethan critics irritatingly forget to mention.

At this point the temptation to speculate is actually very strong, and, although I think we should continue to resist it, it is worth recalling a few of those questions which the new play poses but refuses to answer, and which knowledge of the old play might have clarified. Why, for example, does Shakespeare's Hamlet send Claudius that extraordinary letter, begging leave to see his kingly eyes and promising to ask for a royal pardon (4.2.42–7)? It is hard to suppose that Hamlet is prosecuting some devious plan, when the Hamlet of Act 5 is so resigned and fatalistic, and appears to have no plan of any kind. He drifts into the obviously suspicious fencing match, ignoring Horatio's warning. For all that the text tells us, even the change of swords is an accident, while Hamlet's decision to kill Claudius is a sudden, furious and impulsive act of retribution which avenges his mother's accidental death rather than his father's murder.

It would obviously be helpful to know how the old play had presented the Queen. The new play does not make clear whether her relationship with Claudius changes significantly after the promises she makes to Hamlet in the bedroom scene. Nor do we ever know how guilty she was, since we do not know whether she was adulterous before her first husband's death, or what we are to make of the fact that, apart from Hamlet and the Ghost, nobody worries about the issue of incest. In the terms of Elizabethan law her second marriage was technically incestuous; but, although modern Scottish laws on incest are still based on *Leviticus* and until recently made no distinction between sleeping with a brother and sleeping with a brother-in-law, most modern Scots would doubtless think the distinction important, and we have no right to assume that an Elizabethan audience's thought about such matters could never be more intelligent than the law.

That last problem is compounded by an internal twist within the new play. Claudius expresses his love for Gertrude rather movingly on more than one occasion, and it is presumably for her sake that he protects Hamlet's reputation even after the killing of Polonius; there is no obvious warrant for Hamlet's assumption, in the bedroom scene, that their relationship is merely lustful. In sharp contrast, the Ghost's dreadful image of lust preying on garbage (1.5.53–7) does not convey *love* for Gertrude. If anything, it suggests that the purgatorial fires are failing in their intended effect, since he casts himself in the metaphorical role of a 'radiant Angell', and speaks with far more obvious interest and passion of 'my smooth body' and of the 'naturall gifts' which should have made the marital bed 'celestiall'. And although the Ghost insists that Gertrude must be spared and left to feel the pricks and stings of conscience, it is Claudius, not Gertrude, who appears as the desperately suffering sinner.

Kind, stable Horatio has nothing to say to Hamlet's grumbles about incest, and lets us down on two other occasions where we might long for more clarity and the opportunity to make a detailed comparison with the old play. His remarks after the Mouse-trap are ambiguous: 'Half a share' seems to be an embarrassed joke, prevaricating over the fact that what he has seen has not been enough to convince him of Claudius' guilt (3.2.273). And when Hamlet gloatingly explains that Rosencrantz and Guildenstern have gone to their deaths with no 'shriving time alow'd', Horatio's subdued response prompts Hamlet's indignant (and untruthful) protest: 'Why man they did make love to this employment' (5.2.56–7). Horatio's stoicism is something of a puzzle, since it is not clear whether it should reflect on Hamlet's wickedness: some of Hamlet's speeches are critical of Christian-Stoic fortitude, and there is an awkward gap, which might be variously explained, between Hamlet's painful sense of the need to 'be' and do, and his professed admiration for the friend who refuses to be passion's slave.

These are all cases where we might regret the disappearance of the old play, and its rediscovery would of course help us to trace the Shakespearean variations. It is possible that the Player's speech on Hecuba is itself a very good in-joke, recalling the play which Shakespeare has made new: it is equally possible that it is not, and the dangers of speculation are more obvious than the temptations. On the other hand, if we agree that members of the first audience would have known something of the old play, it is clear that they would have been curious to see what Shakespeare had done with the inherited 'big moments': the appearance of the Ghost, mad Hamlet, Hamlet bellowing for revenge, the play within a play (probably), and the final bloodbath. These are preserved in the new play, but take complicated, ambivalent forms. The Ghost is an original and disturbing figure, for we are forced—for the first time in English drama, unless we think that this may have been a feature of the old play—to consider his moral nature, and whether he is a 'Spirit of health, or Goblin damn'd'. As for mad Hamlet, Shakespeare's prince resolves to adopt madness as a cover, but it is not clear when he is feigning and when he is out of control: there is, as Claudius and Polonius quickly recognise, often reason in his madness, while the soliloquy on Fortinbras shows (as I argued in Chapter 1) how much madness there is in Hamlet's reason and how that madness is related, in Shakespeare's play, to problems which could not be resolved by killing Claudius. This play's Denmark has come of age, in that the new prince is intensely troubled by those moral, metaphysical and cultural strains which made Donne write of the new philosophy calling all in doubt. Here it is impossible to suppose that the earlier play had been so resonant and challenging; and in general terms Shakespeare appears to be recalling the old play in some respects while introducing unexpected profundities, twists and complications. What then should we make of the Mouse-trap, and should we join with the New Arden editor in simply and confidently dismissing those 'notorious' doubts which have troubled critics like W. W. Greg, W. W. Robson and A. L. French?

Hamlet's reasons for devising the Mouse-trap are clearly stated, both at the end of Act 2 and in his brief exchange with Horatio when he tells him what to watch for:

> . . . Observe my Uncle, if his occulted guilt
> Does not it selfe unkennill in one speech,
> It is a damned ghost that we have seene,
> And my imaginations are as foule
> As *Vulcans* stithy; give him heedfull note,
> For I mine eyes will rivet to his face,
> And after we will both our judgements joyne
> In censure of his seeming.
>
> (3.2.78–85)

Despite Hamlet's confidence that the grounds for 'censure' will appear as more than foul imaginings, he is scrupulously recognising the need to establish *two* things: his uncle's guilt, and the Ghost's provenance. Horatio watches and is, as we have seen, far less convinced than Hamlet that either of these things has been established. One difficulty is obvious: even if the King were as innocent as a lamb he would have every reason to terminate this performance. The play's subject—the killing of a king by his *nephew* (not brother)—is all the more grossly provocative for being accompanied by Hamlet's commentary and his attempts to wound and humiliate the Queen; her 'the Lady doth protest too much mee thinks' is an impressively cool deflation, entirely beyond the range of Bradley's 'sheep in the sun' Gertrude. It is quite naturally assumed that Hamlet is publicly threatening his royal uncle; as Claudius observes in the next scene, to 'let his madnesse range' is clearly no longer 'safe', after this astonishing performance.

We shall of course learn—or have it finally confirmed—that Claudius is a murderer when we hear him at prayer. But Hamlet does not hear the prayer, and has no reason for feeling confirmed in his suspicion, unless we infer that the King must have betrayed his guilt before then. It is true, and important, that the printed text of a drama is at best an imperfect record, and may exclude significant stage business; but to suppose that Claudius betrays his guilt while watching the play creates more difficulties than it resolves. The Court shows no sign of suspecting that Claudius has killed the King. If there were the merest suspicion of this, the diffident and deferential Rosencrantz and Guildenstern would never dare to babble to Claudius about 'the cesse of Majestie' in the next scene: they clearly think that Hamlet is the (potential) king-killer. So does Polonius, to judge from his reference to Hamlet's 'prancks', which have become 'too broad to beare with' (3.4.2). And so does Gertrude, who was in a position to observe the King very closely: if her first complaint to Hamlet is crafty simulation we must think her a very nasty piece of work indeed, but critics dodge this problem.

It would be remarkable if Shakespeare had included so many suggestions that the Mouse-trap aborts, while making its success depend on a precarious and intricate piece of stage business which the text does not record. There could be no revealing exchange of glances, for instance, since Claudius would then know that Hamlet suspects him, and it is clear that Claudius does not know this. In the prayer scene he assumes that nobody, apart from God, knows of his crime. He refers to shuffling successfully in this world and speaks of *retaining* 'th' offence': this is why he cannot fully repent, yet he could not hope to retain 'My Crowne, mine owne

Ambition, and my Queene' if he knew, or feared, that he had just betrayed his guilt in public—and Shakespearean characters do not lie in soliloquies, although they may, like Macbeth, deceive themselves. Not even Horatio, who was so carefully briefed, is convinced that Claudius has revealed his guilt, and the conclusion seems unavoidable: he has not, so that we must explain not how he has but why Hamlet thinks he has. The speech in which Hamlet briefed Horatio provides that explanation: his imagination *is*, as he fears, as foul as Vulcan's stithy. Here is the most devastating twist of all: that Hamlet's foul imaginings are also correct. And here we may remember that Hamlet suspected Claudius even before he saw the Ghost, and greeted the Ghost's revelations with the exclamation, 'O my propheticke soule!' Such a reading is consonant with the view that Hamlet's once noble mind is 'tainted' and 'o'erthrown': he realises that he should test both the Ghost and Claudius, but will not see that the test has been a lamentable failure.

Let us consider the Ghost more carefully. It is generally agreed, now, that we can no longer accept Bradley's view of the Ghost as a nobly suffering apparition of great moral majesty, a representative of the hidden ultimate power of divine justice. Moral majesty is precisely what the Ghost lacks since, as Dover Wilson and Eleanor Prosser have shown, Shakespeare raises so many doubts about the Ghost's provenance. The Ghost's injunctions are contrary to the Scriptures; he starts like a guilty thing when the cock crows; in the notoriously difficult cellarage scene he behaves like a stage devil, and Hamlet addresses him as one—as 'boy', 'truepenny', 'old Mole', 'worthy Pioner'. Indeed, the question is not so much whether the Ghost is divine or infernal, 'wicked or charitable', 'a Spirit of Health, or Goblin damn'd'—for if those are the only alternatives there is far more evidence of his infernal origin; rather, the dramatic question is whether we conclude, very quickly, that 'this fellowe in the Sellerige' is an instrument of darkness, or whether Shakespeare somehow manages to make us share Hamlet's own doubts.

Protestantism had of course dispensed with Purgatory, as a Roman invention; Eleanor Prosser's *Hamlet and Revenge* collects a large body of evidence to show how Elizabethans

117

were 'bombarded' with reminders that souls could not return since they were justified by faith alone and proceeded directly to Heaven or the other place. But it is hard to see why the sustained bombardment could ever have been thought necessary, unless people 'needed' it—because their ideas about the after-life were far more confused and jumbled with scraps of folklore and Catholicism than some tidy-minded historians care to suspect. This casts doubt on the historical plausibility of Prosser's contention that the same Elizabethans would have been quick to see that the Ghost is an instrument of darkness sent to ensnare Hamlet when his melancholy has made him deeply vulnerable and indeed suicidal. And there is a complementary critical objection to Prosser's thesis, since it reduces the whole scope and interest of the play if we suppose that the Ghost is, from the first, clearly infernal. The sceptical pessimism that invades and corrodes Hamlet's mind, and which he expresses in poetry no age has been willing to forget, would be placed as 'sinful' for dogmatic, *a priori* reasons, before it could take hold of the imagination. The play would shrink into a period piece showing how immoderate grief is as wicked and dangerous as Claudius suggests, and showing how melancholy is a weapon taken into Satan's hand. Prosser's answer to the second of the two questions which I suggested any convincing reading of *Hamlet* must address would deprive us of any plausible and satisfying answer to the first of these questions.

Hamlet himself sees from the first that the Ghost *may* be an instrument of darkness sent to ensnare his soul, and the doubts which appear in his first words to the Ghost are the best possible reason for not rushing, thoughtlessly, to his revenge:

> Angels and Ministers of grace defend us:
> Be thou a spirit of health, or goblin damn'd,
> Bring with thee ayres from heaven, or blasts from hell,
> Be thy intents wicked, or charitable,
> Thou com'st in such a questionable shape. . . .
>
> (1.4.39–43)

Horatio is more certain that the apparition is infernal and may yet 'assume some other horrible forme' to 'deprive your soveraigntie of reason' and 'draw you into madness'

(1.4.72–4). I take it that we follow Hamlet in believing that there are more things in heaven and earth than are dreamt of in Horatio's philosophy, and in being suspicious about the Ghost but *not sure*. Since the grounds for suspicion and the dangers this may represent for Hamlet are both being emphasised from the first, we should also be noticing those moments when Hamlet is tempted to believe the Ghost on insufficient grounds. 'O my propheticke soule' reveals Hamlet's inclination to believe in the truth of a foul imagining, and it never occurs to him that the Ghost may be both infernal *and* telling the truth (Hamlet has not seen *Macbeth*). The rogue and peasant slave shows Hamlet first yielding to, and then resisting, this dangerous inclination to believe the Ghost on insufficient 'grounds'. He declares, quite illogically, that he is 'prompted' to revenge by 'Heaven' *and* 'Hell'; and then he picks himself up, forcing himself to remember that

> The spirit that I have seene
> May be a devle, and the devle hath power
> T'assume a pleasing shape, yea, and perhaps,
> Out of my weakenes, and my melancholy,
> As he is very potent with such spirits,
> Abuses me to damne me; Ile have grounds. . . .
> (2.2.594–9)

The Mouse-trap is to provide the 'grounds', but we have already seen how confident Hamlet is, when he briefs Horatio, that the 'grounds' for censure *will* appear. As the play is being performed he anticipates the result again, and jeopardises the test with an insulting choric commentary which would prompt an innocent king to terminate this performance. And when the Mouse-trap aborts, Hamlet refuses to see what has happened—yielding at last to the temptation, and the foul imaginings, which he has known he should resist.

Why is Hamlet so determined to insult and compromise the King, even in the second scene, before he has any knowledge of the Ghost, and any grounds for suspicion? What leads Hamlet himself to concede the likelihood that his 'propheticke soul' was giving credence to 'imaginations are as foule/ As *Vulcans* stithy'? Here, I suggest, we need to give more weight to that 'sexual quality' in the play which, as Waldock remarked, has gone on interesting critics ever since Jones developed his discredited thesis. And instead of supposing, like Jones, that Hamlet's situation is like that of Oedipus, when the obvious classical analogy is with Orestes, we should notice how Hamlet is disposed from the first to loathe the man who has replaced an idealised, deeply loved father in his mother's bed.

I suggested earlier that the old play was 'Hamlet without the prince', and that Shakespeare's Denmark 'comes of age' when he grafts onto the old play's framework a prince who is overwhelmingly modern and representative in his tortured sense of the insecurities engendered by the 'new Philosophy'. I also suggested that, although this provides one answer to my first question by explaining Hamlet's continuing appeal, the answer seems insufficient in another sense. For it would then seem that Shakespeare is exploiting the inherited situation: the death of Hamlet's father and his mother's remarriage provide a sufficient *occasion* for a mental disturbance which Shakespeare renders with unprecedented profundity—but then Hamlet's most profoundly representative problems could never be resolved by killing the King. Moreover, this kind of answer to the first question does not engage with the play that was interesting Ernest Jones or D. H. Lawrence; it does not explain that 'erotic' appeal which made Mackenzie speak of Hamlet's 'overwhelming charm' and has tempted innumerable readers to see Hamlet as an idealised projection of their suffering adolescent selves. Growing up—'coming of age' in the other sense, which concerns individual rather than cultural development—involves coming to terms with one's own sexuality and also with one's middle-aged parents' sexuality. Here too Hamlet's problems cannot be resolved by killing a man whom his mother plainly loves, or by seeing that love as a perverse and obscene lust, or by hysterical outbursts of sex-nausea. But here the specific occasion for Hamlet's more inclusive disturbance matters very much: the death of the idealised father and the remarriage of a mother whose sexuality Hamlet cannot accept provides a sufficient explanation for Hamlet's fatal inclination to believe the worst of Claudius before he has 'grounds', and for the foul imaginings which distort his impressions not only of the loathed Claudius, but of his mother, Polonius, and even Ophelia. Hamlet's disturbance is sexual as well as moral and metaphysical. His mind is 'orethrowne'—to use the word Ophelia uses in contrasting the Hamlet we see with the humanistic paragon she remembers and loves—not only by its intense registering of the kinds of 'problem' which are also treated in Montaigne's 'Apology' for Sebonde, but by an extreme form of a developmental crisis which we must all live through.

Grafting problems

When Mozart was considering his handling of the oracle in *Idomeneo* he remarked to his father that the longer a supernatural being is on stage the more critical our inspection of it becomes: 'If the speech of the Ghost in *Hamlet* were not so long, it would be far more effective.' This is not a damaging criticism of *Hamlet* if we suppose that we are indeed encouraged to inspect the Ghost very closely; but that inspection reveals a more pressing problem, in the discrepancy between those ultimate sanctions which the Ghost invokes. The Ghost sets Hamlet two tasks, not one. He must kill Claudius; this is, at best, the Old Testament of revenge at its most primitive and barbaric. But Hamlet is also told that he must not 'taint' his mind, and must leave his mother 'to heaven' and to those thorns that in her bosom lodge to prick and sting her: this invokes the New Testament ethic, with its emphasis on inner repentance and its absolute prohibition of revenge. Here Hamlet never asks the obviously pressing question, although his failure to ask it in simple, direct terms is not conspicuous while he is recognising that the Ghost may be of infernal origin.

Let us approach the problem from another direction. The idea that even the best of men must burn in hellish or purgatorial fires if he has the bad luck to die unaneled and unanointed is itself barbaric; yet this is the reason for those torments which the Ghost says he cannot divulge, and then divulges. Divine justice would appear to have the morals of a fruit machine; but for much of the play this barbaric idea seems to function as a premise. It reappears as Hamlet's reason for not slaughtering the King while he is at prayer (3.3.73–94); there the moral barbarism of the premise is accentuated by the irony that it is Claudius, not Gertrude, who feels the stinging thorns of conscience and acknowledges the Christian demand for what he cannot manage—a radically inward and comprehensive repentance. And the barbaric premise reappears when Hamlet gloatingly reflects that Rosencrantz and Guildenstern were unshriven. But the premise is *apparently* forgotten at the end of the play, when Horatio imagines flights of angels singing the unaneled, unshriven Hamlet to his rest. And it is *certainly* forgotten in the play's most famous soliloquy, when Hamlet speculates on whether death may be followed by anything more, and even describes death as the undiscovered country from which *no* traveller returns (3.1.79–80). In his *Mélanges littéraires* (1802) Châteaubriand remarked on the considerable problem this presents:

> I always ask myself how the philosophic Prince of Denmark could entertain the doubts which he expresses on the subject of a future state. After his conversation with the 'poor ghost' of the King, his father, ought not his doubts to have been at an end? (LeWinter: 72)

It is true that the needs of a play sometimes require that we do not press its premises too hard. It would be fatuous to suppose that *Hamlet* will tell us whether Shakespeare accepted or rejected Protestant teaching on purgatory, for example. But in a great play we expect the premises to withstand a little pressure—and all the more when the play is one which most critics and readers have felt engages with life's ultimate issues. It is true that a play may enlist our sympathies in internally choherent ways, which allow us to forget or disregard divine prohibitions: we respond differently to the suicides in *Romeo and Juliet* and *Julius Caesar*, and nobody ever seems to be shocked when Macduff takes his revenge on Macbeth. And it is true that a character's incoherence about religious matters need not suggest that the play is confused. Hamlet's allusion to the 'Everlasting', his appeal to 'Angels and Ministers of grace', or his references to 'Heaven' are at odds with doubts about what follows death, but this is dramatically intelligible—consistent with our impression that these are the natural reflexes of the mind which Ophelia recalls, and which has now been shattered but not altogether shattered: his earlier, habitual beliefs still reappear, like his logical and analytical habits. Yet a fundamental difficulty remains.

However disturbed and 'orethrowne' Hamlet's mind is, it is still obviously subtle and powerful. And yet, although he addresses the western imagination with such unprecedented forcefulness, he cannot address his own dramatic situation with as much intellectual acuity as we might confidently expect from a Banquo. He never asks the obviously pressing question about the ethics of revenge. In his Montaignian aspects he speculates, profoundly, on man's place in what may be an unaccommodated universe; but he never asks questions about the moral nature of a deity who will fry his father for allowing himself to be murdered before he had engaged a priest. Here an appropriate contrast would be with Laertes' finest moment, when he scorns the 'churlish Priest' who refused to enlarge his sister's obsequies—or with the moral revulsion which would follow any suggestion, in *Macbeth*, that the murdered Duncan is bound for the flames. But Hamlet cannot be permitted to ask such questions, because the play's inherited framework—which deploys supernatural interventions as plot mechanisms—would begin to disintegrate. And the questions which Hamlet cannot ask are the very questions which bear most obviously on what, in his particular situation, he must do or must not do.

This suggests an answer to the second of the two questions which I suggested any new reading of *Hamlet* should address. It is not surprising that the innumerable critics who feel, quite rightly, that Shakespeare's play engages profound questions about life none the less keep running down different blind alleys. There was a limit to the miracles which Shakespeare could work with the old play; nor could he skirt this difficulty by leaving out his play's more inward moral resonances (beginning with that injunction to leave Gertrude to heaven and her conscience), since there would then be no place for his unprecedentedly inward, intellectual prince. *Hamlet* is the 'graft' which could not take, since it could only take if Shakespeare had been content to write an inferior play.

It will be apparent to anybody acquainted with J. M. Robertson's *The Problem of Hamlet* (1919) that I have arrived, though by a very different route, at conclusions similar to his. My reasons for not mentioning his name before might, if quartered, show 'but one part wisdom,/ And ever three parts coward', for Robertson unfortunately harnessed his reading to an extraordinary series of speculations on the nature and content of the old play, and on the provenance of the bad Quarto. His speculative arguments were eventually keelhauled by another Scot, G. I. Duthie, and now, if we may judge from a book like Weitz's *Hamlet and the Philosophy of Literary Criticism*, there is a general feeling that Robertson was dealt with and duly dispatched. Now he is read, if at all, by those with an interest in T. S. Eliot's essay on *Hamlet*, which owes still more to Robertson than to Stoll. But then—with respect to Weitz, who is a philosopher as well as a critic—in logic a conclusion may be valid without being true, and may be true even though the establishing argument is invalid. Robertson's taste for ingeniously speculative reconstructions cannot be defended; despite the date of his book, we might borrow a phrase from Thomas Mann and describe its *method* as 'bad nineteenth century'. But in criticism this is not necessarily—and in logic, it is necessarily not—a reason for dismissing his conclusions.

These might be summarily presented in quotations which offer to answer my two basic questions. What is it that has made *Hamlet* compel the western imagination for four centuries?—

> Utter sickness of heart, revealing itself in pessimism, is again and again dramatically obtruded as if to set us feeling that for a heart so crushed revenge is *no remedy*. And this implicit pessimism is Shakespeare's personal contribution; his verdict on the situation set out by the play. (73–4)

How could this play have seemed to submit so many divergent and incompatible readings, if it is not in itself flawed?

> The ultimate fact is that Shakespeare *could not* make a psychological or otherwise consistent play out of a plot which retained a strictly barbaric action while the hero was transformed into a supersubtle Elizabethan. (74)

Robertson sees that the second question must be asked, and that its answer is to be sought in the new play's relationship to the play on which it was working such brilliant variations. This, I have argued, can be established from the play we have and from the little we know about the play we have lost, without recourse to further speculation.

It will be clear that I do not think Robertson's answer to the first question sufficient; and I hope it is clear that it would be absurd to suggest that the most important critical conclusion about Shakespeare's miraculous achievement should be diagnostic. Indeed, both Robertson and Eliot went some way—though not nearly far enough—to qualify their accounts of the play's 'artistic failure'. Some supreme works of the human spirit admit flaws: it should not seem shocking to suggest that *Hamlet* calls, like *War and Peace* or *Die Zauberflöte*, for some sifting and disentangling. It remains a momentous achievement, both in itself and within the *oeuvre*, where it represents Shakespeare's first attempt to explore, in a wholly serious and sustained manner, the consequences of the collision between different accounts of Nature and Value. And if we judge this play to be a 'failure', God help the successes.

FOUR

The Genealogy of Ideals:
Troylus and Cressida

The Motives of the best Actions will not bear too strict an Enquiry. It is allow'd, that the Cause of Most Actions, good or bad, may be resolved into the Love of ourselves: But the Self-Love of some Men inclines them to please others; and the Self-Love of others is wholly employ'd in pleasing themselves. This makes the great Distinction between Virtue and Vice.

Swift, *Thoughts on Various Subjects*

Would anyone care to learn something about the way in which ideals are manufactured?

Nietzsche, *The Genealogy of Morals*

Unpacking motives

Nothing but self-love, declares Swift; nothing but lechery, says Thersites, whose unvarying view of human motives is terminally reductive, sclerotically dogmatic. For Thersites, everything 'comes down to' lust, bloodlust, the lust for power. Understanding any ideal or value *means* seeing through it, 'resolving' it in Swift's sense, and discrediting it through a levellingly reductive account of its origin and provenance—of what Nietzsche would call its *genealogy*, and Pandarus at one point calls its *generation*:

Paris: He eates nothing but doves love, and that breeds hot bloud, and hot bloud begets hot thoughts, and hot thoughts beget hot deedes, and hot deedes is love.
Pandarus: Is this the generation of love?

Troylus's would-be Petrarchan verse flights are for Pandarus merely pretty, titillating foreplay, and prompt comments like

126

'go to' or 'rub on'; for Thersites, Troylus's theme of honour and renown is a blowsy high-class 'Whore' or 'placket'; for Achilles, Hector's chivalrous challenge is self-advertising 'trash'. The play repeatedly presents rival genealogies.

So, in this play, stylistic dissonances regularly betray more than a want of style: they point to some 'genealogical' tension, focus a misgiving. The strict enquiry into motive is launched when the very first sentence commits a kind of stylistic *hara-kiri:*

> In Troy there lyes the Scene: From Iles of Greece
> The Princes Orgillous, their high blood chaf'd
> Have to the Port of Athens sent their shippes
> Fraught with the ministers and instruments
> Of cruell warre: Sixty and nine that wore
> Their Crownets Regall, from th'Athenian bay
> Put forth toward Phrygia, and their vow is made
> To ransack Troy, within whose strong emures
> The ravish'd *Helen, Menelaus Queene,*
> With wanton *Paris* sleepes, and that's the Quarrell.

In one sense we were prepared for that startling, stately belly-flop: for from the first the massively constructed sentence insidiously undermines its seemingly grand and imposing effects. 'Orgillous' is a word which was becoming *passé* in Skelton's lifetime; it sounds grandly remote, but then, like Harold Wilson's revival of the old word *governance*, its imposing sound is rather too obviously meant to sound imposing. And since the word means 'haughty, proud, swelling', it is a grand or magniloquent term for emotions which may be 'high' or very mean. The orgulous princes' 'high' motive for going to war evidently had little or nothing to do with reason: the word 'blood' suggests passion, and 'chaf'd' suggests that the high hot passion in question here may be some irritable tantrum or princely paddy. The play on *ransacked* and *ravished* is no less disquieting. The words were interchangeable in Elizabethan usage, so that there is nothing odd about the later description of Helen as a 'ransack'd Queene' (2.2.150). Here, giving the words the same position in adjacent lines suggests that there is little to choose between the impetuous chafed motives of Greeks and Trojans: Helen has been ransacked so Troy must be ravished, in a genocidal tit-for-tat. One kind of lustful act begets another, and the false notes in this preliminary, awkwardly high-flown fanfare alert us to the alternative, unheroic genealogy.

Talking big is often counter productive, of course; any false note or too conspicuous effortfulness may suggest that what is being dignified is in reality trivial or vicious. The 'arm'd' Prologue is here supplying the first examples of this play's most characteristic ironic strategy: the signalled inflation invites us to deflate, to scrutinise and unpack some meaner reality. If the actor chooses to lean on the seemingly accidental false notes the invitation will be all the more pressing. But such underlining is not essential, for as soon as this flawed grand style is exposed to a mundane reality and a correspondingly low or mean colloquial register the whole precarious edifice crashes to the ground: Helen is sleeping with wanton Paris, her husband's horn-mad, and *that's* the quarrel.

But the Grand Style revives at once, like Pope's Sir Plume, and achieves a momentary, curiously Miltonic, grandeur:

> To Tenedos they come,
> And the deepe-drawing Barke do there disgorge
> Their warlike frautage: now on Dardan Plaines
> The fresh and yet unbruised Greeks do pitch
> Their brave Pavillions . . .

(11–15)

As poetic narrative this is both compressed and spacious: the use of the historic present tense actualises the remote, legendary events while also summoning our sense of the wan perspectives time and distance afford. The *deep-drawing* is almost simultaneous with the *disgorging* of Greeks who are *now* pitching their brave pavilions. But that *now* is also opposed to the raspingly Miltonic *yet* in 'yet unbruised', which bruises everything around it: that 'fresh', 'brave' ardour is being evoked in a vivid flashback from a standpoint which is not fresh but stale, disillusioned, potentially derisive. And now all of our suspended uneasiness over the cause of this catastrophic 'Quarrell' is refuelled, as the Prologue goes on to speak of 'Expectation tickling skittish spirits'.

For that calls into play jarringly different senses of the word *spirit*—a word to watch in this play. The epic or heroic sense would correspond with the thirteenth sense recorded in the *New English Dictionary*: 'Mettle; vigour of mind; ardour; courage; disposition or readiness to assert oneself or to hold one's own'. And the *Dictionary* provides a useful touchstone when it cites Vernon's description of Hal at Shrewsbury, in the first part of *Henry IV*: 'All furnisht, all in Armes,..As full of spirit as the Moneth of May' (4.1.101 f.). For Vernon, Prince Hal clearly *is* the epitome of chivalry. Are we to suppose that the armed Prologue is attempting, but failing to achieve and sustain, some similarly lofty tribute to the Greeks' and Trojans' ardent, gamesome mettle? Or is he leaning on his words in a deliberately sarcastic fashion? I doubt whether the most determined interpreter could altogether eliminate the unheroic implications of those references to *tickling* and *skittishness*, which suggest inflammable hotheads—Hotspurs, not Hals—and so release the pejorative senses the word *spirit* may have. These are many, and include the clinical senses in humours psychology. Most pressing, perhaps, is the twelfth sense recorded in the *Dictionary*— 'The emotional part of man as the seat of hostile or angry feeling'—and illustrated by a quotation from *Timon of Athens*: 'And not to swell our Spirit, He shall be executed presently' (3.5.104–5). And the ambiguity is troubling and significant, precisely because it precipitates and crystallises opposed *genealogical* possibilities which will continue to trouble us in the scenes that follow.

In the so-called Trojan debate, for example. Here Hector argues that Helen should be returned, according to those 'Morall Lawes' which (he says) exist

> in each well-ordred nation,
> To curbe those raging appetites that are
> Most disobedient and refracturie . . .
> (2.2.180–2)

Troylus protests that such 'cramm'd reason' makes 'Livers pale, and lustyhood deject', and by the end of the scene Hector himself is suddenly commending what he had before condemned—praising his 'spritely brethren' and contrasting 'our' fiery spirits with the 'drowsie spirits' of 'dull and factious' Greeks. In doing this, Hector never meets his own objection that honour cannot be obtained by achieving 'bad successe in a bad cause'. Rather, the word 'spirit' is being employed as a dignifying euphemism for what those 'Morall Lawes' regard as raging, disobedient and refractory *appetite*. There is the alternative, corrective genealogy: spirit is lustihood erect, and ready to expend itself in any waste of shame.

Troylus is wanting to escape the force of that corrective account when he insists,

> Were it not glory that we more affected,
> Then the performance of our heaving spleenes,
> I would not wish a drop of Trojan blood
> Spent more in her defence . . .
>
> (2.2.195–8)

But that is conspicuously at odds with his own earlier protest:

> Fools on both sides, *Helen* must needs be faire,
> When with your bloud you daily paint her thus.
> I cannot fight upon this Argument:
> It is too starv'd a subject for my Sword . . .
>
> (1.1. 89–92)

This is the 'paint' which Thersites strips in insisting, 'all the argument is a Cuckold and a Whore' (2.3. 68); and Troylus's cosmetic imagery makes Hector's point, that Helen is 'not worth what she doth cost/ The keeping' (2.2.51–2). And the references to 'heaving spleenes' and 'lustyhood' show how, as Arnold Stein observes in a brilliant essay, the strain in Troylus's continual efforts to 'spiritualize the sensual' actually suggests some 'imminent threat that the spiritual will become sensualized' (1969: 149). The perceived discrepancies lend credibility to that reductive view which Troylus is wanting to discount: it seems that the 'spirit' in question *is* material rather than spiritual, and proceeds from the humorous imbalance generated by an inflamed liver and heaving spleen, by what Hector has called 'the hot passion of distemp'red blood'. In other words, the so-called debate extends the ironic strategy first deployed in the Prologue, and deepens our doubts about the relation between 'spirits' and 'high blood chaf'd': once again, an inconsistent or flawed assertion of some 'high' motive makes the low, reductive genealogy all the more plausible.

In the Prologue's sardonic conclusion an aggressive indifference to the war and ethical issues is extended to the play and its aesthetic effect on an audience:

> Like, or finde fault, do as your pleasures are,
> Now good, or bad, 'tis but the chance of Warre.
> (30–1)

Here the 'chance of Warre' becomes a metaphor for the audience's reception of a work of art, as the Prologue expresses his lack of confidence in 'Authors pen, or Actors voyce' and in the audience itself. Whatever may be 'good' or 'bad', in the war or in the play, spectators will think whatever it pleases them to think. This approach to Troylus's great question, 'What's aught, but as 'tis valew'd?', combines moral and aesthetic challenges in that insouciant 'Like, or finde fault'—for if values are not objective, part of the world's fabric or furniture, how could judgements of 'good' or 'bad' refer beyond 'chance' and the 'pleasures'—or as Swift would say, 'Self-Love'—of the play's self-appointed judges?

Indeed, it would be very strange if our valuations of the play's characters and issues were nowhere touched and threatened by its mordant enquiry into the nature of valuing. The Prologue's 'Like, or finde fault' seems menacingly prophetic when we notice how many critics have fallen in, then fallen out—disagreeing about *which* characters invite approbation and sympathy, but rarely asking how the play is *designed* to frame and generate such disagreements. So, for example, Frank Kermode refers to Hector as the 'noblest of heroes', whereas Joyce Carol Oates finds it entirely consistent with Hector's character that he can slaughter a stranger for his armour, so long as nobody else is watching. George Wilson Knight is moved by the 'admirable philosophy' of Agamemnon, whom Michael Long finds a portentous windbag. Una Ellis-Fermor declares that Troylus is 'an honest but confused idealist', whereas O. J. Campbell thinks him a decadent sexual gourmet. Numerous critics tell us that Ulysses is Shakespeare's spokesman, and suppose that he believes what he says in the oration on Degree; and numerous critics tell us that Ulysses is an unprincipled manipulator who believes what he says in his oration on Time, which is quite incompatible with any belief in Degree. Everybody agrees that Helen is a worthless chit; but even that becomes problematic, if we then ask whether she is *objectively* worthless, and whether we can, after all, distinguish with Kantian firmness between her *Würde*, or intrinsic 'worthiness', and her *Preis*, or 'worth' as determined by subjective demand.

Another curious problem appears when we find critics placing their trust in those very distinctions and concepts—like 'idealism', 'chivalry', 'honour'—which the play is rendering problematic. So, in taking issue with O. J. Campbell, Kenneth Muir insists that 'if' Troylus 'is satirized it is not as lecher but as an idealist', but this revamps Troylus's suspect claim to be motivated by a concern with 'Honor' and 'glory', not by a heaving spleen; the contrary view that idealism in love *is* lechery in fancy dress is represented implicitly by Pandarus and explicitly by Thersites. The point is not that Muir's distinction is insupportable, but that it is under attack within the play itself. Similarly, Ellis-Fermor's view of Troylus as an 'honest but confused idealist' might make us ask what an unconfused idealist would look and sound like, in this play's world. We need to see how this play makes such valuations problematic by design.

Hector's *volte-face*

Since it will be most helpful to consider a complicated example closely, let us take up that problem which once prompted A. P. Rossiter to argue, in a letter to the *Times Literary Supplement* (8 May 1948) that the text is at fault:

> It concerns the last 25 lines of Act II, Scene 2, where Hector makes an abrupt *volte-face* to join the opposition to his own motion that Helen be returned to the Greeks. Imediately before this switch he had dealt with Paris and Troilus, the misguided men of blood (or passion) in the most measured and weighty terms, appealing—like Ulysses in the Greek War-Council—to Natural Law itself. But as our texts stand, he crosses the floor in the very climax of his argument, without reason of his own or persuasion from the other side, whose 'reasons' he has, in fact, treated

with contempt. Until I had seen the play twice, I supposed that this *volte-face* might be plausibly smoothed over by making Hector speak like a man who knows the right course but feels all the time that 'the sense of the meeting' is against him; so that he gives in, rather as he does in Chaucer over the exchange of Cressida, because 'substaunce of the parlement it wolde.' Now, however, I believe that the change is too sudden to make sense in playing or reading; and since Hector is no weathercock—is, indeed, by no means deformed, defiled, or degraded with all the other 'heroes of antiquity'—it is tempting to suppose that the text is at fault.

Rossiter then argued for a textual arrangement, to remove 'the reader's difficulties with Hector's "character" of Shakespeare's intention in what is incontestably an important scene.' Fortunately, he had thought better of the rearrangement by the time he wrote the brilliant chapter on *Troylus* in *Angel with Horns;* yet he remained committed to what is by now the generally accepted notion, that Hector changes his mind, not merely his position in a debate.

This is curious, for the dramatic sequence suggests that the inconsistency occurs not at the end but at the beginning of 2.2, when Hector so unexpectedly steps forward as the suddenly sober champion of reason, morality and Natural Law. His challenge has already committed him, and Troy, to a course of action which his subsequent argument in 2.2 would exclude. Far from wanting to end the war, Hector's concern had been to end the 'dull and long-continued truce' (1.3.261). Far from being sober, the affected courtliness of the challenge verged on the ludicrous, and was dismissed by Achilles as so much 'trash' (2.1.122). And in issuing the challenge without consultation Hector has shown his indifference to family councils and policy debates; like Ulysses, the other suspect champion of Natural Law, he never doubts who is the 'natural' leader. In short, nothing has prepared us for Hector's argument that Helen should be returned; and there is a complementary surprise when Hector's chief adversary in the debate turns out to be Troylus—who had previously been maintaining (and in soliloquy) that only 'Fools' would 'fight upon this argument'. The so-called *volte-face*, when Hector suddenly commends his 'spritely brethren' and at last tells them of his 'roisting' challenge, shows a return to the challenge's diction and sentiment. Why should we not say that Hector is once again speaking *in* character?

One answer to that is that our doubts about what is 'in' or 'out of' character are not confined to this scene. Every scene in which Hector appears (and also two extended reports of his behaviour) includes some seeming inconsistency, and insinuates doubts about what motives really direct Hector's behaviour. In other words, the dramatic strategy again parallels that observed in the Prologue and 2.2. A typical example is provided by the report in 1.2, which describes Hector as the peerless hero whose 'patience/ Is as a virtue fixed', but also reveals that Hector has been chiding his wife and striking his armourer: this is chivalry? In the next scene that irony is given a further twist when the tetchy husband poses as Love's self-appointed champion, who 'hath a Lady, wiser, fairer, truer,/ Then ever Greeke did compasse in his armes'.

When Hector at last faces Love's Greek champion (appointed in a rigged lottery!) his wish to seem the pattern of chivalry is not in doubt; but his behaviour is, in chivalric terms, unorthodox. He at first declares through Aeneas, his mincing master of ceremonies, that he 'cares not' whether the combat is to be *à l'outrance*. This prompts Achilles to comment on Hector's pride:

> 'Tis done like *Hector*, but securely done,
> A little proudly, and great deale disprising
> The Knight oppos'd . . .
>
> (4.5.73–5)

which in turn provokes Aeneas to a fatuous defence of Hector's courtesy:

> Know this,
> In the extremity of great and little:
> Valour and pride excell themselves in *Hector*;
> The one almost as infinite as all;
> The other blanke as nothing: weigh him well:
> And that which lookes like pride, is curtesie . . .
>
> (77–82)

We are clearly being invited to do our own weighing. And we may notice how, despite his promise to 'obey conditions', Hector denies Ajax's wish to 'fight again'; this is improper in chivalric terms, since refusing to continue with a combat is not the challenger's prerogative. When Hector makes the denial an occasion for ostentatiously heroic declamation, his pompous insistence that 'The obligation of our bloud forbids/ A gorie emulation 'twixt us twaine' might make us wonder why, if he feels like this, he fought at all. As in the Prologue, Latinisms signal pretentiousness—and when Hector's rhetoric culminates in *this* ludicrous spouting it is as though we are watching Henry V collapse into Pistol:

Not *Neoptolymus* so mirable,
On whose bright crest, fame with her lowd'st Oyez[1]
Cries, This is he; could'st promise to himselfe,
A thought of added honor, torne from *Hector*.

(4.5.142–5)

Moreover we should notice that this is also discourteous as a response to Ajax's tribute, since it pointedly denies Ajax any place alongside Neoptolemus (presumably Achilles) and Hector. Achilles' earlier comment applies here too: Hector reveals his own pride in disprizing the knight opposed. (We might remember that the unchivalric behaviour reported in 1.2 followed on Hector's being 'coped' by Ajax.) Yet another discourtesy follows, when Hector takes advantage of Greek hospitality by taunting Menelaus as a cuckold. But all of these seeming inconsistencies dissolve if, after weighing Hector well, we *reverse* Aeneas' verdict. That which looks like courtesy is pride—and so are the disconcerting lapses from courtesy.

The last act brings a dissonant crescendo. In 5.3 we hear the noble hero telling his distraught wife to shut up, be gone, and to stop 'training' him to 'offend' her (a nice one, that); we then hear him loftily declaring that he is 'i' th' veine of Chivalrie'. A crucial disagreement follows, which is clearly— like the disagreement between Achilles and Aeneas over Hector's pride—something we are being invited to weigh well. Troylus objects that Hector's chivalry is excessive, whereupon Hector calls him a 'savage'; what this disillusioned Troylus now calls 'Fooles play' is, Hector insists, 'faire play'. What follows puts this to the test; it is worth

[1] '*O yes*' in the Folio.

stressing that the 'scenes' in question are continuous (there are only fifteen scenes proper in the whole play) and that the different impressions follow in rapid sequence.

We first see Hector meeting Thersites, and sparing him on the grounds that he is not worthy enough to be 'Hector's match': is this 'faire play' or pride? A few moments later Hector is slaughtering Greeks with as much discrimination as could be expected from a combine harvester:

> Now here he fights on *Galathe* his Horse,
> And there lacks worke: anon he's there a foote,
> And there they flye or dye, like scaled sculs
> Before the belching Whale; then is he yonder,
> And there the straying Greekes, ripe for his edge,
> Fall downe before him, like the mowers swath . . .
> (5.5.23–8)

The next play in the Folio includes a comparable description of a death-dealing machine:

> as Weeds before
> A Vessell under sayle, so men obey'd,
> And fell below his Stem: his Sword, Deaths stampe,
> Where it did marke, it took from face to foot:
> He was a thing of Blood, whose every motion
> Was tim'd with dying Cryes . . .
> (*Coriolanus*, 2.2.117–22)

But Coriolanus' prowess is also an awesome triumph of *spirit:* the same speech refers to his ready sense, and to that 'doubled spirit' which requickens 'what in flesh was fatigate'. At the corresponding point in the description of Hector the emphasis falls very differently, not on his *spirit* but on his *appetite:*

> Here, there, and every where, he leaves and takes;
> Dexteritie so obaying appetite,
> That what he will, he does, and does so much,
> That proof is call'd impossibility.
> (5.5.29–32)

This disconcertingly recalls the doubts raised in the Trojan debate; once again, the more damaging genealogy is to hand. Moreover, one of the slaughtered victims is Patroclus. This, and the sight of his mangled Myrmidons ('noseless, hand-lesse, hackt and chipt'), finally rouses the weeping, cursing Achilles to vow vengeance on the 'boy-queller', or boy-killer. Earlier, we may remember, Patroclus was described as 'diminutive': was *he* proud Hector's 'match'?

Achilles certainly is a match for Hector, but when they meet Hector stages another exhibition of lofty chivalry. Sparing Achilles is, in Troylus's terms, the culminating, horrifyingly frivolous example of 'fooles play': it dooms Hector, and Troy with him. If we are still trying to believe in Hector's nobility, chivalry and 'faire play', what follows is still more jarring, for we must explain Hector's extraordinary speech when he spies the unnamed Greek in sumptuous armour:

> Stand, stand, thou Greeke, thou art a goodly marke:
> No? wilt thou not? I like thy armour well,
> Ile frush it, and unlocke the rivets all,
> But Ile be maister of it: wilt thou not beast abide?
> Why then flye on, Ile hunt thee for thy hide.
>
> (5.6.27–31)

Here appetite clearly holds sway: hunting a human 'beast' for its 'hide' is not in the vein of chivalry. The unvizarding of Hector's last victim provides one of this play's most haunting images. After catching and slaughtering his victim Hector unlocks the rivets of the 'goodly armour'—and discloses a 'Most putrified core' (5.8.1). The freshly killed man who had seemed 'so faire without' is already rotting, a putrid, mysterious thing. No realistic explanation is provided, yet Hector shows no marked disturbance—which in an odd way makes the casually unrealistic nastiness of the surprise all the more unsettling. The word *corse* (that is, corpse) might have seemed less startling than *core*, but the corruption in question is not textual, and of course the word *core* belongs with all those other references to ulcers, boils, imposthumes and pus-filled eruptions which link this play to *Hamlet*. Indeed, it is tempting to see this curious episode as a grisly, surreal *Gestalt*, which reflects our continuing doubts about what Hector's own fair exterior conceals, and also vividly actual-ises that process of ruthless unpacking which the whole play so persistently enacts, in pursuing its strict enquiry into motive.

In the new Oxford edition of this play, Kenneth Muir describes Hector as 'an heroic figure, who shines by comparison with Henry V and Fortinbras, near to him in date' (34); yet what makes that comparison so inviting, and potentially far more telling, is the framing of discrepant views of all three characters within their respective plays. Indeed, that 'genealogical' uncertainty which is prompted by the various references to Trojan 'spirits' corresponds with the way in which Hamlet's reference to Fortinbras' 'spirit with divine ambition puft' prompts doubts about Fortinbras' motives and Hamlet's own state of mind.

The parameters of the Hector-problem are mapped out within the play by those disagreements between Achilles and Aeneas about Hector's pride and between Hector and Troylus about 'fooles play' and 'faire play'. So far as Hector's character, motives and behaviour are concerned it does indeed seem much easier to agree with Achilles and Joyce Carol Oates than with Aeneas and Muir or Frank Kermode. Harold Goddard offers a kind of compromise in suggesting that Hector 'is Hamlet's modesty and nobility combined with his inability to live up to his convictions'; but that still assumes that Hector *has* convictions, whereas no man who was seriously committed to reason, morality and a belief in Natural Law could first deliver his 'opinion' and then discard the 'way of truth' with Hector's light, stagy, 'yet nere the lesse'. Nor is Hector clearly committed to honour, chivalry and 'faire play'. Noble, chivalrous heroes know that 'bad successe in a bad cause' brings no honour: they don't chase and butcher strangers for their 'hide'. We might wonder how any attentive critic could resist the conclusion that the Hector-problem is properly resolved by seeing through him—as a hollow man who needs to be admired as Cressida needs to be desired.

I take it that one reason why that resolution of the Hector-problem is resisted is that it makes a larger problem all the more pressing: we see and feel what settling for a wholly reductive genealogy entails, immediately after the unvizarding of Hector's last victim. Hector's sharpest critic returns on cue, with his Myrmidons breathing at his heels; Hector is then butchered, put down with no more chivalry or honour than it would be sensible to show to a rabid dog—*and why not*?

That is an ugly question to put, of course, but it brings our own judgemental dilemma into sharper focus. We have just heard Hector addressing his sword as an instrument of *appetite:* 'Rest Sword, thou hast thy fill of bloud and death.' For Achilles, who is still hungry, Hector *is* a deranged, vicious animal, the brutish 'boy-queller' who butchered his own beloved, 'diminutive' Patroclus. What finally drives the raging, weeping Achilles onto the field is not Ulysses' elaborate machinations, but the ruin of a love relation which might, if we judged it by its devastating consequences, be seen as more substantial and deeply felt than any other in the play. We have seen Hector's appetite for self-display erupting into an orgy of destruction, where the only discrimination shown is that of a guzzler who 'leaves and takes' at a bloody banquet. We have seen how, when Hector brings the 'dull and long-continued truce' to an end, when he disregards his own arguments that Helen is 'not worth what she doth cost the keeping', and when he risks prolonging the war by declining to kill Achilles, Hector makes himself responsible for the deaths of countless Trojans as well as Greeks. Achilles is not playing a game, and has not the slightest interest in establishing whether he or Hector is the 'better man': he wants Hector speedily and efficiently disposed of, like garbage that has begun to stink. The play is effectively over, when somebody at last refuses to treat either war or love as a 'sport'.

This suggests why the contrast between Hector's chivalry and Achilles' murderous calculation cannot be as straightforward as Frank Kermode evidently takes it to be when he comments that 'the noblest of heroes is killed by the vilest of heroes' (186). But if the idea of war as 'sport' is stupid or wicked, what happens to the ideal of honour and 'faire play'? Hector has represented that ideal inadequately, but it survived as an aspiration or as a pretence. It is altogether eclipsed in that 'night' which is described in Achilles' coldly contemptuous address to Hector:

Looke *Hector* how the Sunne begins to set;
How ugly night comes breathing at his heeles,

139

Even with the vaile and darking of the Sunne.
To close the day up, *Hectors* life is done.

(5.8.7–10)

When Troylus and Hector argued about whether 'faire play' is 'fooles play' they were going over ground covered in Chapter 18 of Machiavelli's *Il Principe*. Hector's butcher is the brutally effective practitioner of that Greek *Realpolitik* which the play opposes to the Trojans' doomed, medievally-minded code of honour—the code which the disillusioned Troylus had already repudiated. And in this sense Hector's death has a symbolic resonance which derives much of its paradoxical, jarring force from recent, Renaissance history. When Achilles addresses *his* 'half supt Sword, that frankly would have fed' he is too much the realist to pretend that appetite is anything but appetite. Now, 'The dragon wing of night ore-spreds the earth' like the portent of a new age: this may be evolution, but is it progress?

In characterising our judgemental dilemma we might say that the reductively diagnostic view of Hector is compelling because Hector represents his own professed ideals so inadequately, but that seeing these ideals altogether eclipsed produces a moral shock which is inconsistent with the terminal scepticism or nihilism of a Thersites. And here we should notice how Thersites is representative in two ways which are sharply opposed within the play. On the one hand, his unvaryingly nihilistic view of human motives and behaviour articulates that conclusion which corresponds with the general drift of this play's reductive genealogies. When Una Ellis-Fermor observes that the other characters are also being propelled towards Thersites' conclusion she sees very well how this bears on the issue of the non-objectivity of values:

> he, to whom all the argument is a cuckold and a whore, who sees the common curse of mankind, folly and ignorance, as deserving only the dry serpigo and war and lechery to confound them, has arrived at his conclusion by the very road that they are travelling—Ulysses by his own reasoning, Troilus by the conversion wrought in him by event, and the rest by their betrayal of or at the hands of their codes. The starting-point of his interpretation is the conclusion to which they are proceeding: there is no absolute value inherent in the universe imaged in the loves and wars of Greeks and Trojans. There *is* no 'image of the affected merit'. (127)

But Thersites' 'conclusion'—which is indeed also his 'starting-point', so that we might speak of a terminal starting-point—*pleases* him. Here the Prologue's sardonic venture into the overlapping realms of ethics and aesthetics is a pointed reminder that our responses to the characters may be measured against their responses to their world: 'Like, or finde fault, do as your pleasures are . . .' Ellis-Fermor's pioneering essay shows that she finds Thersites' 'conclusion' forceful and even authoritative within the play's world, but also painful, not pleasing. And this, I suggest, is a very significant part of that larger problem which the play frames.

For Thersites also represents the kind of person to whom such a conclusion would appeal. His rancour is that of a 'ranke', despised bastard who is 'placed', within the play, as a physical and an emotional cripple. As a *cynic*, he is the currish incarnation of that word's etymology: *kunikos*, the Greek word for the cynic, also suggests a dog-like creature, *kuōn kunos*, and this play's Greeks repeatedly refer to him as a 'dogge' or 'horson Curre' or 'Bitch-Wolfes-Sonne'. He lives as a kept animal: we see him changing one despised master (Ajax) for another (Achilles), but his place remains that of a puny performing freak who must entertain powerful and contemptuous patrons with the filth he chews in his 'Masticke Jawes'. Moreover, his levelling reductivism is his only means of exalting himself, which is logically inconsistent but psychologically transparent: its *function* is 'compensatory' in Alfred Adler's sense. In other words, his reductivism is given its own reductive genealogy. Achilles and Patroclus both recognise this in 5.1, when they sneer at Thersites as a 'core of envy' and a 'damnable box of envy', and Thersites himself comes close to admitting as much when he is alone in 2.3 and furiously wishes that 'it were otherwise':

> How now *Thersites*? what lost in the Labyrinth of thy furie? shall the Elephant *Ajax* carry it thus? he beates me, and I raile at him: O worthy satisfaction, would it were otherwise: that I could beate him, whil'st he railed at me: Sfoote, Ile see some issue of my spitefull execrations . . .
>
> (2.3.1 f.)

Like Gulliver, proudly decrying the stench and pride of human Yahoos as he stinks in his stables, Thersites cannot allow his eye to turn inward. He is lost in the labyrinth of his fury because he is always running on the spot, always ending where he began. His scepticism is terminal, never reflexive and radical.

So, even as we recognise Thersites' deceptively authoritative place as the mouthpiece of that view of human motives which the play's 'unpacking' energies seem to promote, the play is unpacking its own unpacker: only a sub-human thing like that would find it pleasing to think like that. That irony is radical, reflexive, and self-consuming—like Ulysses' genealogy of 'Appetite':

> Force should be right, or rather, right and wrong,
> (Betweene whose endlesse jarre, Justice recides)
> Should loose her names, and so should Justice too.
> Then every thing includes it selfe in Power,
> Power into Will, Will into Appetite,
> And Appetite (an universall Wolfe,
> So doubly seconded with Will, and Power)
> Must make perforce an universall prey,
> And last, eate up himselfe.
>
> (1.3.116–24)

Ulysses is imagining a world without Degree, a universe in which Nature is a seething, morally meaningless process, so that terms like 'right and wrong' lose their names and are emptied of meaning. But then we have seen how our own judgemental dilemma, in considering the Hector-problem, involves a similarly self-consuming paradox. So far as Hector's particular character and motives are concerned, it is indeed easier to resolve the seeming inconsistencies by taking a reductive view like that represented within the play by Achilles himself, and seeing Hector's talk of honour, chivalry and fair play as the product of pride, egotism and an appetite for self-display. But this leaves no obvious standpoint from which to express whatever moral shock we feel when Hector is butchered and the dragon-wing of night covers an earth in which the ideal of honour has lost its name and been supplanted by a ruthless *Realpolitik*.

Hamlet struggles, unsuccessfully, with a similar dilemma in the 'How all occasions' soliloquy: as I argued in Chapter 1, his equivocation over Fortinbras' 'spirit with divine ambition puft' expresses both his sceptical fear that honour may be 'a fantasie and tricke of fame' and his unwillingness to surrender the ideal altogether by thinking like a thoroughgoing materialist. And we saw in Chapter 2 how the second tetralogy poses similar dilemmas, in framing its various perspectives on honour: if we have relished Falstaff's genially prosaic and materialist 'catechism' it becomes all the more difficult to justify whatever moral shock we feel in contemplating his treatment of the recruits or Prince John's dishonourable treatment of the rebels, which of course saves many lives. However, in *Troylus and Cressida* this kind of moral 'inquisition' (to borrow Rossiter's term) is extraordinarily sustained, and is rigorously organised so that each judgemental dilemma represents another approach to the underlying issue: if there are no objective values, what follows? The Hector-problem, which I have considered in detail as a kind of test case, is only one example of the way in which we are repeatedly called upon to inspect what might be called genealogical rifts.

So, we might similarly speak of a 'Thersites-problem', after noticing how the play makes him representative in two sharply opposed ways. And once we have registered those subtly orchestrated doubts about the provenance or genealogy of Trojan 'spirits' it is clear that the 'Troylus-problem' complements the 'Hector-problem'. As Arnold Stein observes, 'Troylus will not graduate, like Romeo, from affected romantic to true romantic to tragic lover' (147), and the object of his idealistic but stylistically strained attempts to 'spiritualize the sensual' is characterised 'not by strain and excess but by defect' (149): the 'particular quality of her shallowness is that she is an ephemeral creature of the present with no intensity of attachment to the present' (157). Consequently, Troylus's continual attempts, and continual failures, to feel and sound like a Romeo establish the parameters of the continuing critical disagreements. A critic like Kenneth Muir is disposed—or as the Prologue would say, 'pleased'—to attach weight to the idealistic *aspiration*, whereas its *defeats* are decisive for a critic like Michael Long—who gleefully enumerates the all too numerous 'pudendal slips' in Troylus's language, and the 'unfortunate images of luxury, soilure, staling, digestion and trade which give the scurril lie to his adolescent fantasies' (109).

Shakespeare customarily shows how any character's views are also the expression of what he or she *is;* the Prologue's challenge reminds us that our responses show where and what *we* are. In saying that I am not supposing, hubristicly, that the doom of this play's critics can be reversed for me and that we can somehow rise above the critical affray; I am wanting to emphasise what a Renaissance critic might have called the play's design or *disegno*, and the paradoxical ways in which it mirrors various possible responses onstage. When Act 5 powerfully concentrates our doubts about Hector before showing to what 'ugly night' they may lead, the dizzying perspectivism of its second scene pointedly assembles different ways of understanding Troylus's character and motives: with Thersites' 'Nothing but Letcherie? All incontinent Varlets' still ringing uneasily in our ears, we watch Thersites watching the appalled Troylus and the pragmatic Ulysses watching Diomed and Cressida. There is a kind of stocktaking, in which Troylus's would-be tragic intensities have to be weighed against Ulysses' pragmatic coolness ('What hath she done *Prince*, that can soyle our mothers?') and Thersites' cawing commentary ('Will he swagger himselfe out on's owne eyes?'). The result is a peculiarly jarring dissonance: even as we respond to the anguish of Troylus's insistence that this is not *his* Cressida, we may reflect not merely that this *is* Cressida but also that Troylus has never shown much interest in what the real Cressida thinks and feels.

In seeing how the play orchestrates our doubts about both Troylus and Hector, we might distinguish between two kinds of dissonance, which I want now to consider in relation to the Greeks. In the first place we see how characters are exposed to a kind of linguistic satire by their own stylistic dissonances: Hector's 'Not *Neoptolymus* so mirable' and Troylus's references to 'heaving spleenes' and 'lustyhood deject' are cases in point. We also see how they are exposed by, or to, structural discords. These may occur within a scene, as in 5.2 or in 3.2, when the lovers' attempts at a love duet are sabotaged by Pandarus's reductively prosaic and carefully counterpointed view of their situation and feelings. Or the play provides long-range contrasts, so that one scene tells against another: a very striking instance of this occurs in the way that the stylistic dissonances and structural discords within the Trojan debate complement those within the Greek war council, to which we may now turn.

Rank and degree

Linguistic satire always presupposes a peculiarly intense, diagnostic concern with language, and demands from us a corresponding vigilance. We must first detect the matter for diagnosis, picking up the signal in a stylistic dissonance or unexpected image, in an illogicality, verbal slip or seeming inconsistency; only then can we uncover or unpack the real motive, the unacknowledged explanation, the underlying consistency. '*Language* most shewes a man,' observes Ben Jonson, with a hint of menace: 'speake, that I may see thee'. Our language is so revealing because its revelations are so often involuntary. It shows where we are, which is frequently not where we had wanted to be, and linguistic satire measures that intervening distance, reminding us that we mean what we say, whatever we meant to mean.

Yet, with the single, great exception of Ben Jonson, Elizabethan critics persisted in regarding language as a kind of dress or costume, applied from without to a thought which already had a prior, independent existence. The basis for a fundamental challenge to this naive assumption and the prescriptive educational methods it encouraged had been provided in Erasmus's *Ciceronianus* (1527) and elaborated by Erasmus's great Spanish disciple, Juan Luis Vives, whose *De Disciplinis* and *De Causis Corruptarum Artium* provided Ben Jonson with the stimulus for some of the most remarkable comments on language in *Timber*. With all the passion, inwardness and authority of a great poet whose classicising never made him waver—like Milton, or even Pope—in his commitment to the vernacular, Jonson there insists on the revelatory nature of language:

Neither can his mind be thought to be in tune, whose words doe jarre; nor his reason in frame, whose sentence is preposterous . . . (VIII, 628)

Language most shewes a man: speake that I may see thee. It springs

145

out of the most retired, and inmost parts of us, and is the Image of the Parent of it, the mind. No glasse renders a mans forme, or likenesse, so true as his speech . . . (625)

There cannot be one colour of the mind; an other of the wit. If the mind be staid, grave, and compos'd, the wit is so; that vitiated, the other is blowne, and deflowr'd . . . Wheresoever, manners, and fashions are corrupted, Language is. It imitates the publicke riot. The excesse of Feasts, and apparell, are the notes of a sick State; and the wantonnesse of language, of a sick mind . . . (592–3)

The first of these extracts looks back to Quintilian and the familiar classical concept of *oratio imago animi*, but the second goes further (while drawing on Vives, as the Oxford edition shows). Because language has its own revelatory, dynamic existence—*springing* out of the most retired and *inmost* parts of us—it is ultimately beyond the control of our conscious, detective minds. Moreover, language is not merely vehicular: it carries our perceptions but also shapes them, 'in-forming' them with the determining assumptions and orientations of our particular society and cultural moment. Hence the revolutionary charge in that third extract, which anticipates the critical preoccupations of Wordsworth's preface to the *Lyrical Ballads*, and those of George Orwell and Ezra Pound, by reminding us that language—the 'Instrument of Society'—can reveal the 'sick State' as well as the 'sick mind'.

Indeed, we see this in Jonson's tragedies of state, where the 'sick State' or ailing culture becomes the tragic protagonist. In *Sejanus* the closely observed degeneration in manners, fashions and language accounts for Arruntius's otherwise puzzling claim that Rome itself is responsible for the all-infecting evil:

> 'Tis we are base,
> Poore, and degenerate from th'exalted streine
> Of our great fathers . . .
>
> (1.87–9)

The choruses in *Catiline* point the same moral: the tragic protagonist is Rome itself, the ailing soul of its body politic. The degeneration of the Republic as a moral and cultural ideal is traced in the carefully charted stylistic excesses of the main characters—including Cicero, for the vein of his virtue is no less swollen than that of Catiline's vice. As Cicero launches into his first oration the laconic Caesar murmurs, 'Up glorie!' (3.28); the play ends with Cicero ostentatiously declining—but also *reckoning up*, which is something a Brutus or Cato would never have thought to do—all those 'praises, triumphs, honours and rewards' which he might properly be 'paid'. In its ironic treatment of its flatulent, equivocal hero, *Catiline* reminds us that Jonson's stylistic attitudes, as represented in *Timber*, were very unlike those of the 'Ciceronians' in that controversy which had prompted Erasmus to enter his dissenting, quietly revolutionary minority view.

Here, we may notice, 'linguistic satire' is a helpful term because it distinguishes a mode of working rather than a genre: it helps to suggest what sort of tragedy *Catiline* is, and allows us to isolate the vigilantly diagnostic concern with language which appears in such generically dissimilar works as *Catiline* and *Gulliver's Travels*, Karl Kraus's *The Last Days of Mankind* or Conrad's *Under Western Eyes*, Celia McFadden's *The Serial* or Frederick Crews' *The Pooh Perplex*. Jonson's comedies are also—and many would want to add, more obviously—concerned to 'fix' linguistic idiosyncracies with zestful, deadly accuracy, so that they provide an index to moral, intellectual and emotional disorders. The distinguishing style becomes a means of apprehending, and appraising, an attitude towards experience; a stylistic trait or 'fashion' may mark an ethic or its absence, so that stylistic and moral questions become inseparable. In making linguistic satire the vehicle of a moral satire that is more intense and disturbing than Jonson's because it is less obviously normative, the author of *A Modest Proposal* and *Gulliver's Travels* is also Jonson's greatest heir.

But then it is clear, I take it, that a critical autopsy of the speech which launches the Greek war council suggests conclusions very unlike those the speaker wants to promote. In Agamemnon's case, as in that of the modest proposer or Gulliver, we need to disentangle the argument from its surrounding layers of verbal gristle and fatty pretension:

Princes:
What greefe hath set the Jaundies on your cheekes?
The ample proposition that hope makes
In all designes, begun on earth below
Fayles in the promist largenesse: checkes and disasters
Grow in the veines of actions highest rear'd.
As knots by the conflux of meeting sap,
Infect the sound Pine, and diverts his Graine
Tortive and erant from his course of growth.
Nor Princes, is it matter new to us,
That we come short of our suppose so farre,
That after sever yeares siege, yet Troy walles stand,
Sith every action that hath gone before,
Whereof we have Record, Triall did draw
Bias and thwart, not answering the ayme:
And that unbodied figure of the thought
That gave't surmised shape. Why then (you Princes)
Do you with cheekes abash'd, behold our workes,
And thinke them shame, which are (indeed) nought else
But the protractive trials of great Jove,
To finde persistive constancie in men?
The finenesse of which Mettall is not found
In Fortunes love: for then, the Bold and Coward,
The Wise and Foole, the Artist and un-read,
The hard and soft, seeme all affin'd, and kin.
But in the Winde and Tempest of her frowne,
Distinction with a lowd and powrefull fan,
Puffing at all, winnowes the light away;
And what hath masse, or matter by it selfe,
Lies rich in Vertue, and unmingled.

(1.3.1–30)

Agamemnon's first premise, that *all* earthly designs fail in the promised largeness, cannot be seriously entertained, and is of course blown sky-high by one of the play's most devastating long-range ironies. For the play's most decisive action is the butchering of Hector: Achilles' design is conceived, carefully explained, and then executed some twenty lines later. So much for the Greek commanders' pretension to be the nerves and brain of the great enterprise. All that the superfluous Agamemnon can do, when he has heard the news, is send someone off to 'pray Achilles see us at our tent' and announce—mustering as much dignity as he can manage—that 'Great Troy is ours, and our sharpe wars are ended' (5.9.6–9).

It is in any case obvious that some projects, including some soundly conceived military strategies, meet with even more success than anybody dared to hope. Agamemnon's metaphysics of failure confuses the disillusion which follows an unexpected failure with the disenchantment which sometimes follows success. He then shifts his ground, to argue that failure provides more opportunities for 'Distinction' to appear than 'Fortunes love'. This concedes that there are successes: Agamemnon is maintaining that failure is both invariable *and* a variable test from Jove. The rhetorical question with which Agamemnon began now issues in a remarkable piece of barefaced cheek: he suggests that although a *first* failure ('matter new') might cause a natural (but misplaced) depression, those who have known only failure for seven years should have learned to take it in their stride. This glibly divorces the conduct of the war from its ostensible object: in arguing that failure should be welcomed as a test of distinction (as though one went to war as a spiritual exercise), Agamemnon is conveniently forgetting that a failure to win the war must be depressing if the Greeks have any good reason for fighting it.

Any attempt to draw out the practical implications of the last part of Agamemnon's speech yields results which are ludicrous and even obscene—as appears if we imagine Earl Haig deploying a similar argument. Agamemnon urges the other commanders to regard the extensive Greek losses as a kind of purging or *winnowing* process which establishes the calibre of survivors—or, we might sourly say, establishes the Establishment who don't fight anyway: all that is wanting in this portrait of an Establishment horror is a reminder of the Official Secrets Act. The 'winnowing' plainly does not establish 'Distinction' (Thersites survives, Hector dies) and the very suggestion that it does is monstrously unfair to all those Greeks who have perished under his incompetent leadership.

But then Agamemnon is not thinking about the war dead, and cannot afford to think about anything precise or practical. His argument becomes ever more estranged from reality because its unacknowledged purpose or function is to protect himself and distract others from a realistically adverse judgement of his leadership. Seven years of failure does not command respect. Like a masseur of genius who can see which spot is really hurting, Ulysses brilliantly *inverts* the problem which Agamemnon cannot acknowledge, even to himself: Ulysses argues that the *real* cause of the protracted failures is a decline in respect for the leadership, and the Great Chain of Being is wheeled on to prop up the chain of command. Once Agamemnon and Nestor, his senile poodle, have been offered this far more satisfying way of keeping reality at bay, they are only too happy to abandon all their ill-assorted arguments about pines and boats, failure and fortune, winnowing and Jove. This is yet another reason for not taking those arguments too seriously. Moreover, one of the scene's richest jokes is spoilt if we do not see that Ulysses' account of Patroclus' disrespectful mimicries has the authority of retrospective stage directions:

> Sometime great *Agamemnon*,
> They toplesse deputation he puts on;
> And like a strutting Player, whose conceit
> Lies in his Ham-string, and doth think it rich
> To heare the wooddden Dialogue and sound
> 'Twixt his stretcht footing, and the Scaffolage,
> Such to be pittied, and ore-rested seeming
> He acts thy Greatnesse in: and when he speakes
> 'Tis like a Chime a mending, with tearmes unsquar'd,
> Which from the tongue of roaring *Typhon* dropt,
> Would seeme Hyperboles. At this fusty stuffe,
> The large *Achilles* (on his prest-bed lolling)
> From his deepe Chest, laughes out a lowd applause,
> Cries excellent, 'tis *Agamemnon* just.
>
> (1.3.151–64)

We have already heard the strutting, over-wrested fustian— just as, if the actor playing Nestor knows his business, we will already have seen those 'faint defects of Age' which Patroclus turns into a 'Scene of myrth':

> to cough, and spit,
> And with a palsie fumbling on his Gorget,
> Shake in and out the Rivet . . .
>
> (173–5)

Nestor can do nothing but listen to His Master's Voice and then 'apply' his words; and that joke is given a lovely twist at the end of the scene when Nestor has to admit that he cannot see, with his 'old eyes', where Ulysses' argument is leading.

Agamemnon's speech is also peppered by deflating juxtapositions, echoes and internal contrasts. So, for example, the objectionable implications of the winnowing metaphor are all the more conspicuous because in the previous scene we heard Pandarus's contemptuous reference to the common soldiers as 'chaffe and bran, chaffe and bran'. And immediately before Agamemnon begins to pontificate on ample propositions which fail in the promised largeness we hear Cressida maintaining that in *sexual* affairs 'Men prize the thing ungain'd more then it is'. Later, we might recall both Cressida's and Agamemnon's words when we hear Troylus worrying, like some anxious gourmet, that he may lose 'distinction' in his lovemaking. He fears that he will be overwhelmed by sensation, and incapable of responding adequately to a 'joy too fine,/ Too subtle, potent, and too sharpe in sweetnesse' (3.2.21–2). The contrast with Cressida is sharp but hardly sweet: her fear was that sexual consummation would be underwhelming and disenchanting. That contrast is taken up in 3.2 when Troylus voices a similar fear that 'the will is infinite and the execution confin'd', and Cressida responds only to the pudendal slip, brightly remarking that 'They say all Lovers swear more performance then they are able'. Another such slip occurs a moment later when, after imagining what a 'winnowed puritie in love' would be like, Troylus exclaims, 'How were I then up-lifted!' That reference to winnowing, like the fear that he will lose 'distinction' in his joys, recalls Agamemnon's hunger for a 'Distinction' that can lie 'unmingled'. Such internal ricochets represent exuberantly eruptive variations on the central issue of whether there is an image of affected merit. They also point a contrast, for although both Greeks and Trojans are obsessed with 'Distinction' the obsession manifests itself in different realms of human experience. That point might be made by observing that Adler would feel at home in the Greek camp, Freud in Troy: the Greeks show a more conspicuously Adlerian preoccupation with power, and their position in a social hierarchy, while the ceremonious courtiers of Troy talk of 'love' and 'honour' and are more concerned to achieve 'distinction' in eroticism, aestheticism and self-display.

The dramatic undermining of Ulysses' speech on degree shows why it is helpful to distinguish between the more immediately diagnostic exposures of linguistic satire and those exposures that depend on pointed juxtapositions or long-range structural ironies. In its own terms—and especially if it is extrapolated from the dramatic context or given a privileged, supra-dramatic significance as an expression of current socio-political orthodoxies—Ulysses' speech on degree is very much more impressive than Agamemnon's speeches, just as Hector's parallel speech on Natural Law in the pointedly complementary Trojan debate is more impressive than Troylus's equivocal expostulations about love and honour. Agamemnon and Troylus are exposed as they speak, whereas what is more troubling in the speeches by Hector and Ulysses is the inconsistency or uncertainty of the relationship between the seemingly impressive speech and its speaker.

We may of course observe that the diagnosis Ulysses offers is no less obviously *untrue* than that offered by Agamemnon at the beginning of the scene. As Michael Long remarks in *The Unnatural Scene*, 'It would be a very trivial and reductive reading of the events of *Troilus and Cressida* which concluded, with Ulysses, that what the Greeks lacked was leadership and a hierarchy' (108). But here Long himself is directing attention to the contextual exposure; the *content* of Ulysses' speech, like that of Hector's, is as orthodox as a critic like E. M. W. Tillyard supposes—but the effect of that orthodoxy is far from reassuring, when we see how little support it receives from the *play*.

The sequence of Ulysses' three long speeches suggests the likelihood of an ulterior motive: the manipulative syco-phancy of the request to speak leads, via the speech on degree, to the attempt to disparage (or de-value) Achilles. Just as Hector is keen to demonstrate his intellectual superi-ority in the argument with his youthful brethren, Ulysses is determined to confirm and consolidate his own influence and power at the expense of Achilles: the brain has more 'dignity' than the battering ram. At the moment when Ulysses' massage has taken its effect, Aeneas enters; and although the scene now appears to break apart, as if by accident, into two halves, the effect is anything but accidental.

'How'—Aeneas asks, with blithely insulting courtliness—may he know Agamemnon's imperial looks from eyes of other mortals? 'How?'—echoes the appalled Agamemnon. 'Ay': Aeneas' imperturbably unruffled reply is allowed to sink in, before he continues his suave provocation in another flight of blankly courtly blank verse:

> Ay:
> I aske that I might waken reverence,
> And on the cheeks be ready with a blush
> Modest as morning, when she coldly eyes
> The youthful Phoebus:
> Which is that God in office guiding men?
> Which is the high and mighty *Agamemnon?*
> (1.3.226–32)

Steevens was the first editor to see, in 1793, that the metrical break marks a dramatically held pause—and of course Aeneas' insult is even more timely and provoking than he knows, since we have just heard Ulysses arguing that 'Degree being vizarded,/Th'unworthiest shewes as fairely in the Maske'. Aeneas cannot recognise *un*vizarded distinction, let alone godliness, when it stares him in the face. As we enjoy the comedy of watching the all too mortal, ungodly and undistinguished Agamemnon struggling to recollect his wounded self-esteem, the ironies reflect on Ulysses' sycophantic argument: what Kenneth Palmer nicely terms the 'comedy of misrecognition' deftly implies that Agamemnon's qualities are indeed 'attributed' in the suspect and negative sense of that ambivalent word. So much for the idea that degree can be read off.

But here, once again, we see how this play's brilliantly organised long-range ironies, its seemingly accidental collisions and structural discords, all bear on Troylus's crucial question: 'What's aught, but as 'tis valew'd?' For example, the preceding scene included another little 'comedy of misrecognition' when Pandarus confused Deiphobus with Troylus, and 'mistook' the 'Prince of Chivalrie' for a 'sneaking fellow'. Immediately after the Greek war council we have another scene which passes its own ironic comment on the alleged superiority of brains to battering rams when we hear Thersites insisting, like Ulysses' parody-shadow, on the superiority of his 'braine' to Ajax's brawn. None the less, brute strength determines who is beaten in this case—just as it will at the end of the play, when Ulysses' absurdly elaborate machinations have all come to nothing and the fate of Troy is sealed, in a few bloody and horrifying seconds, by Achilles and his Myrmidons.

In one familiar tradition—seen in Sophocles' *Philoctetes*, for example—Ulysses is the personification of conscienceless craft. Not only does the sequence of Ulysses' speeches in the Greek war council suggest opportunistic self-advancement; our sense of his cleverness depends on our supposing that he is too shrewd to believe his own eloquently manipulative restatement of those orthodox pieties about rank and degree which the play itself incessantly undermines. Because that undermining is also achieved through intricately organised, long-range structural ironies, it very well suggests how the play's mode of 'dramatic thinking' is sceptically interrogative and reflexive, and how that scepticism is radical, not terminal. Indeed, when we ask which of the play's *characters* comes closest to expressing the viewpoint of a truly radical scepticism the answer is—Ulysses. For, as I argued in Chapter 1, the scepticism in Ulysses' speech to Achilles on Time in 3.3 is no less radical and reflexive than that in Montaigne's discussions of miracles or witchcraft. Ulysses will not *deny* that the attributes of value may be inherent—may exist, as the more confident but confused Hector asserts, in the prized as well as in the imagination of the prizer; but, like Montaigne and unlike Hector, Ulysses does not affirm that the human mind is capable of determining this question. The *images* of affected merit are themselves subject to the limits and illusions of imagination and the operations of time:

> man, how dearely ever parted,
> How much in having, or without, or in,
> Cannot make boast to have that which he hath;
> Nor feeles not what he owes, but by reflection:
> As when his vertues shining upon others,
> Heate them, and they retort that heate againe
> To the first giver.

(3.3.96–102)

When Achilles tries (like Hector) to deflect the implications
of this, the point is patiently, and condescendingly, spelt out:

> I doe not straine at the position,
> It is familiar; but at the Authors drift,
> Who in his circumstance, expresly proves
> That no man is the Lord of any thing,
> (Though in and of him there is much consisting,)
> Till he communicate his parts to others:
> Nor doth he of himselfe know them for ought,
> Till he behold them formed in th'applause,
> Where they are extended . . .
>
> (112–20)

The speech on Time follows, explaining why 'Vertue' can
never seek 'Remuneration for the thing it was' (or may have
been):

> for beautie, wit,
> High birth, vigor of bone, desert in service,
> Love, friendship, charity, are subjects all
> To envious and calumniating time:
> One touch of nature makes the whole world kin:
> That all with one consent praise new borne gaudes,
> Though they are made and moulded of things past,
> And give to dust, that is a little gilt,
> More laud then gilt oredusted.
> The present eyes praises the present object . . .
>
> (3.3.171–80)

Ulysses does not specify which 'Author' he has been reading,
but of course the argument he develops in this scene with
Achilles is entirely incompatible with the speech on degree.
So far as ideas of Natural Law are concerned, it is as though
we have moved, all at once, from the ideas enunciated in
Hooker's *Laws of Ecclesiastical Polity* to the scepticism of
Montaigne's essay on custom or Donne's *Biathanatos*. And
of course this is a particularly striking long-range irony:
Ulysses patently cannot believe what he says in *both* speeches, nor can we be sure that he believes what he says in
either of the speeches—since in each case he has a pressing
ulterior motive for seeming to espouse what are mutually
exclusive positions.

Indeed, if we notice it, there is a particularly nice though unobtrusive indication of conscienceless craft, when Ulysses reveals to Achilles that he already knows about Achilles' affair with Polyxena. Achilles is very rattled by this evidence of the efficiency of Ulysses' intelligence network:

Achilles:	Of this my privacie,
	I have strong reasons.
Ulysses:	But 'gainst your privacie
	The reasons are more potent and heroycall:
	'Tis knowne *Achilles*, that you are in love
	With one of *Priams* daughters.
Achilles:	Ha? Knowne?
Ulysses:	Is that a wonder?
	The providence that's in a watchfull State,
	Knowes almost every graine of Plutoes gold;
	Findes bottome in th'uncomprehensive deepes;
	Keepes place with thought; and almost like the gods,
	Doe thoughts unvaile in their dumbe cradles . . .

(3.3.190–200)

We might also be startled, if we reflect that Ulysses took pains to suppress any mention of *this* reason for Achilles' inaction, in the war council: there, Ulysses' primary concern was to discredit Achilles (not least through references to his lolling with his catamite upon a 'lazie Bed') and to advance his own position. That too suggests that the eloquent speech on degree was a calculated rhetorical performance. But then Ulysses' other great set speech—in which a character comes closest to the play's radical scepticism, while professing to represent a 'strange' argument he has just been reading—is no less a cunningly calculated performance: here Achilles is manipulated, very successfully, where before it had been Agamemnon and Nestor. That dizzying irony is a measure of the strain and exhilaration this extraordinary play produces, as it frames and quizzes every character's every utterance.

Unbodied figures in dumb cradles

Those literary critics and historians who discussed Elizabethan humours psychology between the two World Wars tended to assume that its assumptive basis was simplistic and mechanistic. This encouraged accounts of *Troylus and Cressida* as a particularly black comedy of humours in which we see what base appetites and drives 'really' direct the various characters' behaviour. The play aroused more interest than ever before, and it seems likely that the famous production by Sir Tyrone Guthrie appealed to the climate of disillusioned feeling that produced contemporary revampings of classical themes and subjects—for example, in the plays of Giraudoux or in Sartre's *Les Mouches*.

Since the last war, some scientists have been less inclined to scoff at humours psychology—precisely on the grounds that it does *not* attempt to explain human behaviour solely in terms of appetites or Adlerian drives. Melvin Konner, Professor of Biological Anthropology at Harvard, observes in *The Tangled Wing* that much recent research suggests that humours theory has 'a piece of truth that had been missing from analyses of human behavior for some decades', since 'the "humour" metaphor of the Elizabethans is intrinsically closer to the truth as we understand it than in the "drive" metaphor of the early twentieth century':

> Contrary to drive theory, the nervous system is not a hydraulic system. No fluid in it builds up under pressure, forcing or urging us to do this or that action, so that it can relent after 'letting of steam'. Of course, no fluid corresponding to the Elizabethan humour exists either; yet that concept is closer to current ones. Behavioral scientists, especially outside of psychology, but also within it, are turning to concepts like 'state', 'arousal', and 'excitation', which can refer either to a general condition or the organism or a specific tendency to activation of a specific behavioral system (such as sex). Rather than building up pressure until release occurs, these activation tendencies rise and fall according to various causes, often without deprivation or release. The terms used to describe them are nonmetaphoric and epistemologically very conservative, merely describing what can be seen and measured in behavior. But they have the great advantage of having plausible correlates in the neural and endocrine systems, for which 'state', 'arousal', and 'excitation', are highly meaningful terms. (103)

That advantage is absent in 'drive' theory and its associated metaphors and analogies, which do not correspond with what is now known of the body's neural and hormonal systems. Moreover, Elizabethan humours theory had offered to account for 'stable temperament', while supposing that the temperaments were largely innate. Although many obstacles confront acceptance of even a weak modern version of that belief, Konner observes that there is also much recent research showing that there is 'in each of us a residue of characteristics of heart and mind that we brought with us when we entered the womb, a mere few days from conception' (105). And Konner adds, in concluding his own review of such research:

> The denial of this, as liberal as it usually sounds, is really a denial of individuality, in the most fundamental sense, and is every bit as dangerous as the most rigid forms of genetic determinism. Extreme environmentalism had its magnificent heyday when the excesses of genetic determinism were threatening, for decades, not only human dignity, but human survival. It served a noble purpose and was for many years an objectively respectable position. But the sands of scientific time are shifting beneath that position, and those who tend it had best look to a foothold. (105)

When seen in *these* terms, humour theory posits an idea and ideal of balance, or health: instead of providing a rationale for agreeing with Thersites' reductively materialistic account of human drives, it offers a means of diagnosing Thersites.

T. A. McAlindon's essay on *Troylus*, to which I am indebted, very well shows how the exposure of the characters' linguistic excesses may be related to humours psychology. My own concern, in raising these issues while steering my own discussion to a conclusion, is to try to isolate what, in this play's radical scepticism, looks back to *Hamlet* and forwards to *Macbeth*—at those very moments when our minds swivel between different ways of regarding characters and issues, as the play's strict enquiry into human motive suddenly and bafflingly engages our sense of the human *need* to endow life with value and significance.

In discussing *Henry IV* in Chapter Two, I remarked on the way in which that play invokes humours theory not to resolve pressing dramatic questions, or ultimate questions about what men live by, but to make such questions all the more pressing by framing, and bringing into sharp focus, an area of doubt. True, Glendower, Hotspur and Falstaff are all seen, at various moments, as embodiments of humorous imbalance; but then the contrast with Hal cannot function in any reassuring, securely normative way, because there is so much that is disquieting in his contrasted 'balance' and coolly calculating self-control. The disquiet this provokes might well recall *Sonnet* 94, with its ambiguous judgement of those who are the lords and owners of their faces; or the uneasiness which is concentrated, in *Richard II*, by the King's declaration that the most deserving are those that know the strongest and surest way to get (3.3.200–1).

When Ulysses speaks so hauntingly of unveiling thoughts in their dumb cradles, he is of course congratulating himself on his intellectual penetration and the efficiency of his intelligence network (and here an Elizabethan might have thought of Sir Robert Cecil, as we may think of J. Edgar Hoover); the hint of menace in the unveiling image relates it to the play's other images of unpacking and negative exposure. But Ulysses' complacency and manipulative, self-advancing cynicism are also being exposed and unpacked: it is his hubristic humour to think of himself as god-like. Moreover, the image evokes a contrary sense of uncertainty and vulnerability, of the ultimate mysteriousness and *un*fathomability of thought and motive. Amongst other things, the idea of a *dumb* thought engages our sense of what is still a fundamental philosophical dilemma: we are used to being told that we can only think through language and concepts, but language is a communal or collaborative creation, and it is hard to see how new concepts emerge unless in response to new needs. So, for example, there is no classical word for 'chastity' which has the radically inward force of the Christian concept; here, it seems hard not to suppose that the concept *answered to* a need which was in some sense pre-conceptual. At a more trivial or familiar level, we know that it is to feel, when revising something we have written, that this or that is not what we *meant* to *mean:* English allows that play on the senses of *mean*, but it pulls against the important truth that we mean what we say.

Troylus and Cressida not only undermines those notions of Natural Law to which Ulysses and Hector appeal, for reasons of their own, and the corresponding idea that human values are in some sense objective, part of the world's fabric or furniture. It summons another view of the nature of Nature, in which Natural Law becomes a far more menacing affair. Indeed, this point might be made in Schopenhauerian terms, if we substitute Schopenhauer's concept of the 'Will' for the play's repeated references to 'blood' or 'appetite'. Will is primary; intellect or 'reason' is secondary and adventitious; the structure of each animal, including human animals, is adapted to its predatorial and self-assertive needs, and the primary function of intellect is to serve those needs. On such a pessimistic view, each life is an individual manifestation of that Will in Nature which whips a meaningless creation into being—and here we may notice how often the play's language suggests that thought itself is an irrational, convulsive process of being. Cressida's thoughts are 'unbridled children', too 'headstrong' for their mother's head; Pandarus's thought 'seethes'; Ulysses announces a 'young conception' in his brain, and so on. The *prius* is the 'blood', Will, or that 'wanton spirit' which looks out of 'every joint and motive' of Cressida's body; it carries the Greeks through their dances, games and war games, and fuels the 'feverous pulse' and 'firebrand' passions of the Trojans' 'quick sense' and 'heaving spleens'; it generates the 'hot deeds' of 'love', and 'blaze of wrath' and 'heat of action', and the 'flowing' of 'arts and exercise'. How could reason set itself effectively against this teeming, seething world of appetite and will? Hector's intellect serves his will because, in the terms of this Nature, that is the intellect's *job*. Thersites and Ulysses both rely on the brain because, although the crow and the fox cannot fight the ox, they can outwit it. And ideals like 'love', 'honour' and 'chivalry' are, as Thersites insists, mere disguises or excuses for the satisfaction of base appetites and drives.

But there, in various ways, the play repeatedly turns on its own seemingly reductive, terminal energies. We might be reminded here not of Schopenhauer but of Nietzsche. Section XIV of *The Genealogy of Morals* is helpful here, since it provides what is perhaps an unintended, but altogether Nietzschean, irony at that moment when 'Mr. Foolhardy' is forced to peep through a chink in the 'murky shop' where 'ideals are manufactured'. He is appalled, disgusted by the 'stink of lies', and unable to 'stand' the 'smell'—but there, in that revolted wrinkling of the nose and heave of the stomach, is the problem.

We see it in Thersites' case, when we see how he has *two* representative roles, which are opposed to each other. To be the play's most scurrilous unpacker of human motives is his pride and pleasure, but because the play also unpacks that pride, that pleasure, it suggests that such reductivism could satisfy only those who are physically or emotionally warped—are, in human terms, functionally incomplete. What appalls Nietzsche's Foolhardy delights Thersites, and in registering that stalemating irony—which corresponds with two possible, but opposed, applications of humours theory— our own moral noses wrinkle: the strict enquiry into human motives shifts, to engage our sense of that human need for value and significance which Thersites *needs* to deny. And such ironies build on, or fold into, each other: so, for example, as we watch characters exposing their own enlarded pride while laughing at the pride of others (most obviously in 2.3), we are also being richly amused by a poetic drama in which, if the filthily prosaic Thersites were right, the poetry is no more than 'ore-wrested seeming'—a means of deceiving onself, as well as others.

The same problem reappears, as we have seen, when Hector is butchered—and the medievally-toned world of Troy is supplanted by the decentred, late Renaissance world of *Realpolitik*. The Greeks, like Bolingbroke in *Richard II* or, say Octavius Caesar in *Antony and Cleopatra*, are more 'modern'; time and history are on their side. But if this provokes mixed feelings we find that the play is interrogating our own response and sense of predicament. No play better brings out what is potentially disturbing in Blake's great maxim, 'As a man is, so he sees'; and *Troylus and Cressida* does this by reminding us, as tirelessly as Nietzsche himself, that we—as well as each of the characters—interpret the world as we interpret a text.

For a typically witty and intricate example of the way in which the seemingly reductive energies of terminal scepticism suddenly become reflexive and radical, we might recall that scene at the beginning of Act 3, in which a lowly house servant excels Pandarus in the vapid language of a courtly, privileged elite, as the two disagree about the 'attributes' of Helen and Cressida. This in itself is a sly, compound irony, which gives another twist to 'What's aught, but as 'tis valew'd?' while taking another swipe at Degree. It also provides a perfect preparation for our brief but devastating glimpse of Helen, the pearl who has launched a thousand ships. That 'Nell' is so breathtakingly vacuous *seems* to extend the reductive, Thersites-like satire: the Trojan cause becomes as absurd as the empty-headed placket who is its prize or pretext, while the Greeks who are ostensibly there to reclaim this theme of honour and renown did not even discuss her in their council of war. But then this bears in a more unexpected way on the problem of valuing. Not only are Helen and Cressida regularly compared, like beauty queens: the Trojan determination not to relinquish Helen requires that they do surrender Cressida—without regard for what this makes of their, or her, or Troylus's 'honour'. Moreover, Troylus himself acquiesces to the mercantile calculation that Cressida is 'worth' less than the prattling Nell, and less than Antenor, who never utters one word. And if we think that Helen is worthless, that there is far more to, or *in*, Cressida, the question, 'What's aught, but as 'tis valew'd?' becomes all the more pressingly problematic.

On a reductive, Thersites-like view, Troylus's failures as a Petrarchan lover shows nothing less than the failure of Petrarchan, and indeed all other imaginatively constructive, attempts to endow lust with value or meaning. On another view, Troylus's pudendal slips and self-betraying references to soiled merchandise suggest that his failure is personal, a matter of not living *up to* an ideal. Here, what is nowadays called intertextuality is important: our sense that Troylus's language is *self*-betraying is shaped (or 'in-formed') by our sense that he does not sound like a Petrarch or a Romeo, just as the Hector who spouts about Neoptolemus so mirable does not sound like a 'true' hero. But here, once again, is that swivelling between opposed perspectives. The play nowhere shows what a *true* hero or lover is like; where its exuberantly mordant, unpacking energies seem to correspond with those of terminal scepticism, it implies that there is no such thing. But the play also makes us register the life-denying, humanly impoverishing consequences of such a view. This gives rise to a paradoxicality which is not at all Schopenhaurean, but wholly Nietzschean: we might recall, for example, those pages of *Human, All-Too-Human* in which Nietzsche argues that we have great art in order not to perish of the truth, and that we cannot produce or be adequate to great art if we lose our concern for truth. And the play's paradoxicality corresponds with what I suggested, in Chapter One, would be the radically sceptical Shakespearean formulation of J. L. Mackie's observation that there are no objective values: there are, or may be, no objective values, but the need to endow life with value and significance is an objective fact about human nature.

In *Hamlet* the shift into a decentred, 'modern'—that is, late Renaissance—world is felt in various minor ways: for example, in the contrast between the dead King's prowess in single combat and Claudius' diplomacy. But it is felt, above all, in Hamlet's anguished consciousness: for example, in the 'How all occasions' soliloquy where we see Hamlet struggling with the opposed views of values like 'honour' which are generated by opposed views of the nature of Nature. As I argued earlier, Hamlet's predicament is that of the man who will not altogether surrender his notions of value in a terminally sceptical fashion but is tormentedly aware that values cannot be 'read off'. J. L. Calderwood has argued in '*Macbeth*: Counter-*Hamlet*' that *Macbeth* is in many respects 'like a photographic negative of the earlier play, not merely different from it, as the other tragedies are, but in a sustained way the inverse of it' (103). Such a contrast finds further support when we reflect that Macbeth feels, more keenly than any other character in the play, the *need* to commit himself to values while being unable to give imaginative credence to that need: acknowledging it, and trying to live from it, seems—amongst other things—unmanly, and he destroys himself in striving to deny these inner moral and imaginative needs. In this respect both plays may be seen as complementary imaginative explorations of Troylus's question about valuing. In *Measure for Measure*, to which we now turn, the radical scepticism appears, not in a concern with the non-objectivity of values, but rather in the exploration—through Angelo and Isabella, above all—of the incompatibility of different absolute values. But here, once again, the nature of the human *need* to endow life with value and significance becomes the subject of a sceptical exploration that is radical, not terminal.

FIVE

On Tempering Mercy with Justice:
Measure for Measure

'Judge not, *that* ye be not judged. For with what judgment ye judge,
ye shall be judged.'—What a conception of justice, or a 'just' judge!
Nietzsche, *The Anti-Christ*

Vain pity

After agreeing that *Measure for Measure* is a play in which
Justice itself is put on trial, many critics, including our two
greatest Christian critics, find the final verdict faulty. For Dr
Johnson, there is 'perhaps not one of Shakespeare's plays
more darkened than this by the peculiarities of its Author',
and Angelo's pardon is especially provoking: 'every reader
feels some indignation when he finds him spared', since his
'crimes were such, as must sufficiently justify punishment,
whether its end be to secure the innocent from wrong, or to
deter guilt by example' (103, 105). Coleridge is even more
vehement: '*Measure for Measure* is the single exception to
the delightfulness of Shakespeare's plays. It is a hateful work,
although Shakespearean throughout. Our feelings of justice
are grossly wounded in Angelo's escape. Isabella herself
contrives to be unamiable, and Claudio is detestable'
(1888:48). These critics are far more shocked by the mercy
shown to Angelo than by the pardoning of Barnardine, a
man who has killed more than once and shows no sign of
remorse. They concur, too, in assuming that the Duke's final
verdicts correspond—vexingly—with those of the play and
its 'Author': if the verdicts trouble us, the play must be
faulty.

True, its final scene is not like that of Beethoven's *Fidelio*, in which apocalyptic trumpets announce a sublime vision of justice on earth, or that of Molière's *Tartuffe*, in which the *deus ex machina* arrives to represent the *roi soleil*, sanity and *la juste Nature*. Shakespeare's Duke evidently thinks that his own final dispensation of justice is no less elevating: but then, if his elaborately engineered stagy resolutions actually fail to satisfy us, why should his failure be regarded as Shakespeare's?

In fact, Johnson is too confident about what 'every reader feels'. Some readers, like Wilson Knight, profess satisfaction with the play's final clutch of pardons and punishments. Here, we might rather ask whether such approval has practical and theoretical consequences which reach beyond the play: this is a way of asking whether the play is as serious as the problems it treats. Do we merely feel relief at the particular outcome, because (*pace* Johnson and Coleridge) we have no wish to see Angelo, Claudio, Barnardine or Lucio executed —or are we impressed by some more challengingly principled process of legal and ethical judgement?

Yet another question must be asked if we think that the contrast between the Duke and Angelo as judges and governors is a contrast between unprincipled benevolence and unbenevolent principle. Might the play's own final verdict or verdicts be problematic by design—both more ironically unsettling, and more challenging in its implications for our own attempts to *think* about law and morality, than those piecemeal judgements which the Duke so confidently offers as examples of an ideal and exemplary justice? If we want analogies, would we do better to think of *Antigone* or of Melville's *Billy Budd, Sailor*?

Such questions are not usually asked, since critics have tended to follow Johnson and Coleridge in assuming—with differing degrees of satisfaction or consternation—that the Duke's verdicts do correspond with Shakespeare's. This assumption seems all the more arbitrary and strange when we begin to consider where—and why—Shakespeare has departed from his sources. In Cinthio Giraldi's and George Whetstone's versions of the story—as in *Fidelio* and *Tartuffe*—other men's messes are unravelled and resolved by an immaculately detached figure of authority, who is brought in at the end like a *deus ex machina*. But Shakespeare *implicates* his Duke from the first act: more precisely, from that moment in the third scene when we hear the Duke explaining to the Friar that the Viennese mess is the result of his own lax government during the past fourteen years:

> We have strict Statutes, and most biting Laws
> (The needfull bits and curbes to headstrong weedes,)
> Which for this fourteene yeares, we have let slip . . .
> (1.3.19–21)

The Duke himself believes, rightly or wrongly, that the statutes he 'let slip' are now more than ever 'needfull' in a city which requires surgery rather than medicine. When the Friar observes, discreetly but pointedly, that the Duke could have unloosed this tied-up justice whenever he saw fit, the Duke explains why he has not done so:

> Sith 'twas my fault, to give the people scope,
> 'Twould be my tirrany to strike and gall them,
> For what I bid them doe: For, we bid this be done
> When evill deedes have their permissive passe,
> And not the punishment: therefore indeede (my father)
> I have on *Angelo* impos'd the office,
> Who may in th'ambush of my name, strike home,
> And yet, my nature never in the fight
> To do in slander . . .
> (35–43)

Here the Duke is doubly implicated. The 'fight' is, on his account, necessary because he has governed laxly for fourteen years and given crime its 'permissive passe'; but he seems less concerned with the innocent victims of crimes he has permitted than with 'slander' and his own 'name', and he anticipates (with some relish) that the man he has appointed to do the dirty job he cannot face will draw on himself the charge of 'tirrany'. Angelo is being given rope to hang himself by his future judge; yet our greatest Christian critics would sooner see him hang than go scot-free.

Far from being an embodiment of Divine Mercy, the Duke here appears to embody Misrule: in less allegorical terms, he is a negligent governor who now believes that he must confront, but still wants to evade, a problem which he has helped to create. If we are not to defuse or short-circuit this play's power to challenge and disturb, it is important that we do not minimise or disregard the 'Vienna-problem'. The point that immediately matters is not whether *we* believe that Vienna requires surgery, but that the Duke himself believes this and feels obliged to act accordingly. After indulging an inclination to be merciful in the short term, for fourteen years, the Duke is convinced that this was a 'fault', and not merciful at all in the long term. The Friar hints that the task of correction should not be 'impos'd' on a deputy, but does not question the need for urgent measures; nor is this need questioned by Escalus, Isabella, the benign and impartial Provost, the Justice or Angelo. When Escalus and Isabella plead on Claudio's behalf, they do not argue that the strict statutes are bad law and not 'needfull': they want the law to be *bent*, not changed. By departing from his sources and implicating the Duke, Shakespeare is also uncovering a particular kind of judicial and governmental problem, in which what is deemed 'needfull' for the common weal may entail a measure of ethical injustice to the individual: the law which condemns Claudio is (in modern terms) a strict liability law admitting neither mitigation nor excuse, and the 'Claudio-problem' arises from the Duke's attempt to deal with the 'Vienna-problem'.

In short, the play's exposition sets up a problem very like that which Sir Thomas Elyot discussed in *The Boke named the Governour*, before distinguishing between true mercy and 'vain pity'. What is to be done, asks Elyot, when the failure to enforce the law has produced a situation in which 'many proclamations . . . have been divulgate and not obeyed' and 'many commissions directed and not executed'? In characteristically admonitory fashion Elyot adds: 'Mark well here, that disobedient subjects and negligent governors do frustrate good laws.' He might here be referring to Shakespeare's Duke, and his next remarks show what this grave and orthodox writer would think of Escalus's wish to spare Claudio on the grounds that he is a 'gentleman' who had 'a most noble father' (2.1.9–10), or of Isabella's irresponsible plea that Angelo could 'Condemne the fault, and not the actor of it' (2.2.37). Elyot complains that those who have 'authority to them committed concerning the effectual execution of laws' and who recognise in theory that any 'offendor' should be 'punished according to the laws' all too often fail in their duty—when they discover that the accused is a 'seemly personage', an 'acquaintance, or a gentleman born (I omit now to speak of any other corruption)'. Moreover Elyot continues, the truly upright and zealous commissioner who strives to check the 'continual increase' of disorder will be defamed and said to lack charity or mercy:

> if any one commissioner, moved with zeal to his country, according to his duty to execute sharply and frequently the law of good ordinance, wherein is any sharp punishment, some of his companions thereby rebelleth, infaming him to be a man without charity, calling him secretly a pickthank, or ambitious of glory, and by such manner of obloquy they seek to bring him into the hatred of the people.

It is at this point that Elyot distinguishes sharply between true mercy and 'vain pity'—'wherein is contained neither justice nor yet commendable charity, but rather ensueth negligence, contempt, disobedience, and finally all mischief and incurable misery . . .' Escalus himself allows the force of this fundamental distinction, when he concedes that Angelo's severity is 'needfull':

> Mercy is not it selfe, that oft lookes so,
> Pardon is still the nurse of second woe.
> (2.1.269–70)

And Angelo makes the point even more strongly, in replying to Isabella's plea that he should be mercifull and 'shew some pittie':

> I shew it most of all when I show Justice;
> For then I pittie those I doe not know,
> Which a dismis'd offence, would after gaule . . .
> (2.2.100–2)

In Elyot's terms, the Duke and Escalus are both 'negligent' in their misplaced and short-sighted benevolence; it is Angelo who upholds what Elyot regards as a fundamental principle, when he reminds first Escalus and then Isabella of the harmful consequences of 'vain pity' and insists that this is *not* true mercy.

The final scene provides a particularly forceful—and, I take it, deliberately problematic—reminder of the dangers of 'vain pity', when the Duke pardons Barnardine. Nothing could be more at odds with Elyot's conception of what good government and the protection of the common weal requires than releasing a man who has killed more than once, becomes uncontrollably violent when drunk, and shows no trace of remorse. But, as we have seen, our greatest Christian critics find Barnardine's pardon far less offensive than Angelo's; in our own century, those critics who see the Duke as an embodiment of Divine Justice have tended to disregard, rather than defend, the Duke's judgement on Barnardine. Darryl Gless does address the issue directly, in *Measure for Measure, the Law, and the Convent*, and allows that we may indeed worry that 'the Duke's grace towards Barnardine is entirely undeserved' and that 'there is no clear provision for the charitable justice that protects society' (228). None the less, Gless discounts these worries in favour of an argument which rests on a necessarily speculative concern with the *inner* states of the Judge and the accused:

> Duke Vincentio's exhortation that Barnardine take his mercy 'to provide/ For better times to come' imitates and paraphrases the august principle that 'the goodness of God', expressed in his forbearance and long suffering, 'leadeth thee to repentance' (Rom. 2:4). Barnardine's silent acquiescence in the Duke's sentence—a significant silence because it contrasts strongly with his earlier obstreperous desire to hear 'not a word' (4.3.52–62)—suggests that he may be willing, like his yet-unborn kinsman Caliban, to 'be wise hereafter,/ And seek for grace' (*Tempest*, 5.1.294–5). If this likelihood should prove wrong, then at least the Duke will have erred in the right direction. He has correctly weighed Barnardine's essential fault and applied the only remedy likely—so far as human judgement can ascertain —to succeed. (229)

Significantly enough, Barnardine's pardon is interposed between Angelo's second confession and the Duke's sentence on Angelo. For Gless, this convinces us that 'Angelo's more explicit, willing submission to the will of God's substitute, and thereby to God himself, makes the Duke's mercy to him still more clearly just': Angelo 'has acknowledged his depravity, and has felt the bitterness of true repentance'(229).

One difficulty here is that Angelo's agony of shame and self-disgust makes him unwilling to accept mercy. He insists that 'immediate sentence' and 'sequent death' is 'all the grace I beg' (5.1.380–1); Lucio's insistence that he would sooner die than marry a punk provides a grimly dissonant parody. Nor are Angelo's last words those of a man persuaded that he would sooner live and marry:

> I am so sorrie, that such sorrow I procure,
> And so deepe sticks it in my penitent heart,
> That I crave death more willingly then mercy,
> 'Tis my deserving, and I doe entreat it.
>
> (472–5)

And the contrast with Angelo's self-lacerating penitence makes Barnardine's silence all the more disconcerting. That Barnardine acquiesces to his pardon need not surprise us; but the Duke's pious hope that mercy will of itself produce repentance and reformation meets with no response other than silence. Gless's reference to Caliban is hardly helpful, since Barnardine does not say that he will 'seek for grace'. The crucial point is that his inner state is unknown to us and unknown to his judge. There is no evidence that it has changed since Act 4. Yet in that Act the Duke gave the order to have Barnardine dragged to the block—even though he thought it 'damnable' to transport a man in that condition. If the Duke's subsequent decision to pardon Barnardine is not to seem unprincipled, capricious and stagy, we need to know what principles apply in Act 5 which did not apply in Act 4, when the Duke wanted a substitute head.

Moreover, another contrast emphasises the rift between the principles of retributive earthly justice and those of the Sermon on the Mount. The Sermon is indeed more concerned with the inner state of an agent than with the effects and consequences of an action: it internalises external acts, and those Mosaic ordinances which governed external acts. As Jesus warns (Matthew 5: 21–8), the God who sees to the bottom of the heart may regard lustful intent *as* adultery, and anger *as* murder: in that case we are all, to a terrifying degree, sinners, although we are plainly not all criminals. The warning that we shall be judged as we have judged others is above all a warning against spiritual presumption and self-righteousness. But such considerations accentuate the problematic juxtaposition of Angelo's and Barnardine's pardons.

To pardon a convicted murderer is *not* merciful, when considered from the point of view of prospective future victims. It matters very much in legal terms, but not in the radically internal terms of the Sermon, that those crimes which Angelo was prepared to commit did not actually take place, while Barnardine is a convicted murderer who may kill again when he drinks again. To claim, like Gless, that in that case the Duke will at least have 'erred in the right direction' is to disregard not only society's right to be protected but also the implications of the obvious fact that we could never speak of *God* erring in the right direction. For although the Duke takes pride in his 'ancient skill' of reading brows (4.2.148), he has no divine omniscience: to imitate Divine Mercy might seem spiritually presumptuous and hubristic; indeed, it prompts the thought that the Duke is now returning to his old form, regardless of the consequences for Vienna.

Since Shakespeare has invented Barnardine, it is worth adding that everything we learn about Barnardine's case in Act 4 casts doubts on the Duke's judicial competence and motives. Although the Provost has to remind the Duke who Barnardine is, we learn that the Duke tried that case himself—and that, after listening to those friends of Barnardine who 'wrought Repreeves for him', the Duke eventually declared that matters could not be brought to 'an undoubtful proofe' (4.2.128–30) and forgot all about the case. In sharp contrast, it transpires that Angelo has been working through the backlog of ducal messes and has established, quickly and firmly, that Barnardine's guilt is 'Most manifest, and not denied by himself' (4.2.131): here, perhaps, is an example of what the Duke has in mind when he sneers that his deputy is 'precise'.

The Provost, who more than once provides a touchstone of sanity and basic fellow-feeling, compares Claudio's case with Barnardine's and declares:

> Th'one has my pitie; not a jot the other,
> Being a Murtherer, though he were my brother.
>
> (4.2.56–7)

This provides a nice example of the way in which, in this

play, ironies tend to interlock. Not long before, we heard Isabella withholding all pity from *her* brother:

> Die, perish: Might but my bending downe
> Repreeve thee from thy fate, it should proceede.
> Ile pray a thousand praiers for thy death . . .
> Mercy to thee would prove it slefe a Bawd,
> 'Tis best that thou diest quickly.
>
> (3.1.145–52)

When she thinks her own salvation threatened, Isabella wholly forgets her earlier concern that Claudio is 'not prepar'd for death' (2.2.84). But this yields a further pungent contrast with the Duke's ruthless determination to find a substitute head, even if this involves executing *another* 'creature unpre-par'd, unmeet for death' (4.3.63). The other creature is of course Barnardine, but this unleashes a particularly ferocious and devastating irony. The Duke has taken it upon himself to 'prepare' Claudio for death with a wholly unChristian lecture on the need to 'Be absolute for death' (3.1.5–41), in which he tells Claudio that life is a thing which 'none but fooles would keepe' and compates youth and age to 'an after-dinners sleepe'. Now the Duke finds himself confronting a subhuman wretch who really *is* 'insensible of mortality' and really *does* apprehend 'death no more dreadfully, but as a drunken sleepe, carelesse, recklesse, and fearlesse of what's past, present, or to come' (4.2.132–8). The irony cannot puncture the Duke's self-esteem, of course, but even though he declares that 'to transport him in the minde he is/Were damnable' (4.3.64–5), he is wholly determined to get his substitute head—and orders that the newly condemned Barnardine be executed at once:

> Unfit to live, or die: oh gravell heart.
> After him (Fellowes) bring him to the blocke.
>
> (4.3.60–1)

Within seconds of that order the good Provost brings news that will save Barnardine from a damnable end and the Duke from a 'damnable' act:

> Heere in the prison, Father,
> There died this morning of a cruell Feavor,

One *Ragozine*, a most notorious Pirate,
A man of Claudio's yeares: his beard, and head
Just of his colour. What if we do omit
This Reprobate, til he were wel enclin'd,
And satisfie the Deputie with the visage
Of *Ragozine*, more like to *Claudio?*

(4.3.65–72)

'Oh, 'tis an accident that heaven provides', exclaims the delighted Duke—reminding us that the 'accident' is an all too conspicuous contrivance of the dramatist. But in the play's sources only one substitute head is required: Ragozine's would do, and in the end does do. So why has Shakespeare gone out of his way to invent a seemingly redundant, implausible complication which requires a last-minute substitute for the substitute, when he could simply have followed Whetstone and tried to make his *novella*-like contrivance more plausible?

One answer is, as I have already suggested, that this extends the various interlocking ironies about being 'prepar'd for death'. It also shows the lengths to which the Duke will go, when Barnardine presents an obstacle to his attempt to contrive a factitious solution to the 'Claudio-problem'. But here there is another intricate irony, for in the space of a few scenes we see how Angelo, Isabella and the Duke all have extra-legal reasons for wanting to see legal death sentences carried out. As Angelo confirms in the next scene (4.4.26–30), concern for his personal safety had made him resolve to have Claudio executed, despite his promise to Isabella that what the law requires will not be done. Isabella, in her hysterical concern for her chastity, promises to pray for her brother's death, travestying those religious principles she is determined not to transgress. And the Duke is so determined to save Claudio and triumph over the exposed Angelo that he gives that 'damnable' order to 'transport' a 'creature unpre-par'd, unmeet for death'. Whereupon Shakespeare at last produces Ragozine—and what might be thought the most sardonic reflexive irony in the Works.

Being the man he is, the Duke does not reflect on his narrow escape—and entertains no worries about the rightness of pardoning a man in Act 5 whom he was fully prepared to execute in Act 4: if the pardon is proper, the execution would have been a legal (but 'damnable') murder. In the final act the agonised Angelo has indeed discovered the most profound, radically internal import of the Sermon on the Mount: he has realised what he has it in him to become. But the incorrigibly complacent Duke makes no such discovery; indeed, unlike Angelo, and unlike the disguised dukes in Marston's *The Malcontent* and *The Fawn* and Middleton's *Phoenix*, he learns nothing. Instead he plays God, pardoning Barnardine along with Angelo and Claudio, and only punishing the man who offended him personally. The sentencing of Lucio is, as we shall see later, as densely and damagingly ironic as the pardoning of Barnardine. The more important point to notice here is that, just as the 'Claudio-problem' was released by the Duke's attempt to deal with the 'Vienna-problem', the 'Vienna-problem' is aggravated by the contrived resolution of the 'Claudio-problem' and by releasing a murderer into the streets of a city which is already, if the Duke himself is to be believed, boiling and bubbling with corruption (5.1.316). (This point is made very succinctly by A. D. Nuttall when he observes of the Duke's final 'orgy of clemency' that 'we can approve his behaviour at the end of the play only at the cost of condemning his behaviour at the outset' (239).) By inventing Barnardine and giving him a history which tells against the Duke at every point, Shakespeare is not only continuing his mordant exposure of the play's self-appointed *deus ex machina* and surrogate dramatist; he is also finding another means of accentuating that problematic distinction between true mercy and 'vain pity'.

I am of course arguing that the play's interlocking ironies, which are often produced by deliberate departures from the sources, show that the final scene, the Duke's verdicts, and the Duke himself are all problematic *by design*. But here we need to isolate what I take to be the most fundamental objection to those numerous Christian readings which have proliferated in our unChristian century, and which have been so influential that by 1963 Ernest Schanzer described them as forming 'the now dominant view of the play, the new orthodoxy' (73). Schanzer attributed this chiefly to the influence of R. W. Chambers' British Academy Lecture of 1937, while remarking that Christian interpretations can be traced back to Ulrici. Indeed, they go back further—

although, as we have seen, our greatest Christian critics were disposed to put Mercy, rather than Justice, on trial, and were most disgusted by the pardoning of the penitent Angelo for crimes which, unlike Barnardine's, were not actually committed. In his epoch-making Vienna (!) lectures, A. W. Schlegel had claimed that in *Measure for Measure* 'the true significance of the whole is the triumph of mercy over strict justice: no man being so free from error as to be entitled to deal it out to his equals'; and so far as I can tell, Schlegel was the first to associate the play's *morality*, as well as its title, with Matthew 7:

> Judge not, that ye be not judged. For with what judgment ye judge, ye shall be judged: and with what measure ye mete, it shall be measured to you again.
> And why beholdest thou the mote that is in thy brother's eye, but considerest not the beam that is in thine own eye?
> Or how wilt thou say to thy brother, Let me pull out the mote out of thine eye: and behold, a beam is in thine own eye?
> Thou hypocrite, first cast out the beam out of thine own eye. . . .

It might seem odd that Johnson and Coleridge failed to recognise in this the curiously simple moral which Shakespeare's curiously complex play promotes. Of the more recent critics who made this discovery, the most influential was probably not Chambers but Wilson Knight who argued in *The Wheel of Fire* (which was published in 1930, seven years before Chambers' lecture) that 'the simplest way to focus correctly the quality and unity of *Measure for Measure* is to read it on the analogy of Jesus' parables', and that 'the Duke's ethical attitude is exactly correspondent with Jesus"(82–3). Presumably, on this view, we might imagine *Jesus* castigating Julietta for her 'sin' and then assuring Mariana that sleeping with Angelo will be 'no sin' (2.3.19–34;4.1.71); or explaining the meaning and value of life to the condemned Claudio in the wholly irreligius 'Be absolute for death' speech and then giving his unsavoury 'Fellowes' the order to execute Barnardine; or sneering at Angelo's abstinence (1.3.50–3) and proposing to Isabella in that final scene where, according to Wilson Knight, 'all difficulties are here resolved' (89). To be fair, Wilson Knight does also allow that we are not exactly 'told what will become of Vienna'; but he posits a symbolic resolution, through the Duke's marriage to Isabella, of the unsymbolical problems posed by rape, illegitimacy, syphilis and murder (95). Doubtless, if we can manage the other exercises in 'exact correspondence' we will not strain at that, or ask what would become of any commonwealth in which the Gospel ethic of mercy continually triumphed over justice while the authorities picked at their motes. We may rejoice, with Wilson Knight, at the prospect of 'the marriage of understanding with purity; of tolerance with moral fervour': the 'ultimate splendour of Jesus' teaching' is revealed and dispensed by a Duke 'who is incapable of executing justice on vice since he finds forgiveness implicit in his wide and sympathetic understanding'; 'Love asks no questions, sees no evil, transfiguring the just and unjust alike' (95–6). But although this sounds rather wonderful, and although we might not care to contemplate this prospective (but uncertain) marriage, or Angelo's marriage to Mariana, in anything but 'symbolic' terms, we should notice that Justice is here not so much tempered as abolished by Mercy. What has happened to Sir Thomas Elyot's distinction?

Equating the Duke with Christ is shocking in religious terms, and no more defensible in critical terms than equating the Duke with Shakespeare. But the fundamental objection to Wilson Knight's Christian reading, and to every other Christian interpretation of this play which I know, is that they are too little concerned with those problems of secular government and justice which exercise Sir Thomas Elyot: Angelo's arguments correspond with Elyot's, and are not to be routed, like a vampire, by a brandished cross.

Shakespeare makes this clear within the play through another, particularly momentous departure from the earlier versions of the story: by making the condemned man's sister a novice, he ensures that Angelo's Elyotic principles are opposed not merely to Escalus's compassionate inclinations but to Isabella's invocation of the Gospel ethic. Like Gless and the other 'Christian' critics and Jesus, Isabella is far less concerned with the effects and consequences of an action than with the inner state of the agent. Because she is primarily concerned with the soul's salvation, and ultimately concerned with *her* soul's salvation, she is innocently and naively indifferent to the social consequences of any attempt to make the

Gospel ethic the basis of secular justice. If the black-hearted—whom Isabella would regard as sinners, and Angelo as criminals—are given their 'permissive passe', they will use it. But Isabella cannot see, and does not care to reflect, that the consequence of extending 'vain pity' or indiscriminate mercy must be that numberless innocents who might other-wise be protected by the law will suffer. When Angelo tells her that he shows most pity by showing justice, and pitying those whom he does not know, Isabella disputes his right to judge. And because her appeal to the principles of the Sermon on the Mount calls into question the basis of all earthly retributive justice, there is a dreadful irony—or justice, or 'measure'—in what follows: she finds *herself* in the situation of an innocent victim, deprived of legal protection and redress. The irony bites deeper through the contrast with Mariana, another innocent victim: although Mariana is more worldly, she has retired to her moated grange and private devotions. But the enskied and sainted Isabella is neither willing to retire to her convent nor content to refer earthly injustice to her heavenly Maker: she makes her way to the city gate, to cry for 'Justice, Justice, Justice, Justice'(5.1.25).

The argument which Angelo offers Isabella when she asks him to show some pity is an argument to which he is morally, as well as legally, committed. But because Isabella's beauty, passionate purity and simplistic idealism arouse in Angelo emotions which he has never before known (2.2.186–7) and can now only pervert, there is a complementary justice—once more, of that cruel and ironic kind that is unfairly called 'poetic'—in what follows, which exposes the inadequacy of Angelo's no less idealistic, passionately ascetic and simplistic commitment to the law's systematic classifications. As a *judge*, Angelo is not convinced by Isabella's arguments he is right—morally and legally right, according to his quite different premises—to refuse to bend the law, and to reject the suggestion that he has no right to condemn another man: a judge is not entitled *not* to judge. But as a *man*, Angelo is indeed moved, in a quite different and unexpected sense, by Isabella as she argues: he begins to learn what he has it in him to feel and become, which establishes the real relevance of the radically internal Gospel ethic to his own case even as he argues, quite correctly, that it has no bearing on his legal judgment of Claudio's case.

The play's title thus provides a richly ironic comment on what these two novices do to each other. They provide the perfectly complementary centres of poles around which the play's dialectical exploration of justice is organised. Both are inexperienced, youthfully zealous moral absolutists; both are highly principled, and uncompromising in their commitment to their respective religious and secular ethical systems —unlike the capriciously pragmatic, fudging Duke. Moreover, although we are accustomed to respect those principles to which each appeals—the needs of the soul on the one hand, of the common weal on the other—the principles are here in conflict, are indeed irreconcilable: as I remarked in Chapter 1, this play's scepticism differs from that of *Troylus and Cressida* in that the earlier play explores the *non-objectivity* of values while the later play explores the incompatibility of different *absolute* values. In restating Elyot's distinction between true mercy and 'vain pity', the upright judge insists that he is morally, as well as legally, obliged to protect the common weal. That distinction becomes more, not less, problematic when the robed nun invokes the Gospel ethic and the Christian conception of a comprehensive Christian *caritas*.

In other ways, which call forth an irony which is as compassionate as it is acerbic, the two novices resemble each other beneath their robes. As has often been remarked, both show a fear of sex that becomes denaturing; in a more general sense, corresponding with Nietzsche's remark that the will to a system is a form of cowardice, both are frightened of life. Not unlike those French critics who replace Catholicism with Marxism while shamelessly professing their admiration for Nietzsche, Angelo and Isabella both *need* to view life through the spectacles provided by their respective ideologies; both are consequently disposed to recognise only one aspect of any complex and demanding issue. They both suffer appallingly, when each presents the other with the kind of problem which he or she is least equipped to confront. Each, we might say, throws the other into the world.

The main objection to the 'Christian' readings is, then, that produced within the play itself. When he *admires* the

Duke for being 'incapable of executing justice on vice',
Wilson Knight is in excellent company: like Isabella, and
indeed like Jesus in the Sermon on the Mount, he is choosing
not to address those governmental and judicial problems
which Sir Thomas Elyot discusses. It is not enough, and is
not even true, to say, like Berowne in *Love's Labour's Lost*,
that 'Charity it selfe fulfills the Law' (4.3.360). In the first
act the Duke believes that he must confront a state of emergency like that envisaged by Elyot. Although, in the final act,
the Duke has abandoned his attempt to deal with the
problem, his own words forcefully remind us of the consequences of a failure to execute laws which he himself has
declared to be 'needfull':

> I have seene corruption boyle and bubble,
> Till it ore-run the Stew: Lawes, for all faults,
> But faults so countenanc'd, that the strong Statutes
> Stand like the forfeites in a Barbers shop,
> As much in mocke, as marke.
>
> (5.1.316–20)

That, of course, is the problem which Elyot addressed, and
his discussion helps us to see why this problem becomes so
much more pressing in the play's second act.

Like Elyot, the play's exposition presents a situation in
which what is deemed 'needfull' for the common good may
entail harshness to the individual. As Elyot recognises, a
'zealous' governor who revives and enforces a 'needfull' law
will be criticised. Moreover, the law's first victim will inevitably feel that he is being made the object of exemplary
severity when a 'permissive passe' is suddenly withdrawn.
So, Claudio complains that the 'new Governor' has put a
'drowsie and neglected Act/Freshly on me: 'tis surely for a
name' (1.2.158–64). No plea of mitigation or excuse is
admitted: in modern legal terms Claudio's offence is treated
as a matter of strict liability, and this further accentuates the
conflict between the presumed needs of the common weal
and the individual's expectation of legal and ethical justice.
Escalus's legally atrocious argument for bending the law to
spare a well-born gentleman is quite properly demolished by
Angelo, but Escalus continues to be troubled, unlike Angelo,
by the conflict between legal and ethical justice. Here the

Folio editors' act divisions obscure the play's structure, since the exposition proper ends with this crucial exchange between the Justice and Escalus:

> *Escalus*: It grieves me for the death of *Claudio*
> But there's no remedie:
> *Justice*: Lord Angelo is severe.
> *Escalus*:   It is but needfull.
> Mercy is not it selfe, that oft lookes so,
> Pardon is still the nurse of second woe:
> But yet, poore *Claudio;* there is no remedie.
>
>   (2.1.266–71)

After being reluctantly convinced of the force and relevance of Elyot's distinction, Escalus restates it, while also reiterating the absence of any 'remedie'. This prepares us for the great confrontation between Angelo and Isabella in which the scope of the problem is both extended and internalised: the conflict between legal and ethical justice is further complicated by Isabella's invocation of the principles of divine justice and of the radically internal Gospel ethic. Here too there is, far more disturbingly, 'no remedie'—unless, like Wilson Knight, we regard one term of the problem as its resolution and stop thinking about the legal and moral obligations of the governor and judge.

But why—it might be asked—did Shakespeare not make the initial problem clear at the outset, by *beginning* with the play's third scene? To answer that question, we need to see why timing is of crucial importance in this play.

Timing

The first two scenes present a startling contrast which establishes the thrustingly interrogative, dialectical character of the play's dramatic rhythm. The first scene is largely taken up with the Duke's markedly abstract discourse on government, which is curiously at odds with his tributes to Angelo and Escalus for being in no need of such instruction. The discourse has a flatulent dignity and resonance, but is markedly more concerned with theory than practice, or as Bacon might say, with manner not matter. Rude matter erupts in the second scene: we are abruptly removed from the Duke's headily abstract realms of discourse to real streets, where conversation is riddled with trench jokes about syphilis and where respectable burghers have an interest in preserving the brothels. This initial impression of the Duke's Vienna might well recall the second part of *Henry IV*, where the low-life scenes show a commonwealth running to seed in the absence of effective government; but whether this should be telling against the Duke as governor is for the moment left perplexingly unclear. This in itself suggests how, in this play, Shakespeare keeps us asking questions. If he had begun with the third scene, placing it before the second scene, it would have been immediately clear that the Duke now believes that Vienna requires surgery, and that the attempt to treat the 'Vienna-problem' releases the 'Claudio-problem'.

As it is, the Duke rushes off at the end of the first scene, leaving 'Matters of needfull value' unspecified as well as 'unquestion'd'. We have no idea what he is talking about, and are made to share in Angelo's and Escalus's uncertainty over the nature and purpose of their written 'Commissions':

> *Escalus*: A powre I have, but of what strength and nature,
> I am not yet instructed.
> *Angelo*: 'Tis so with me . . .
>
> (89–91)

And when the Duke tells Angelo that

> There is a kinde of Character in thy life,
> That to th'observer, doth thy history
> Fully unfold . . .
>
> (32–4)

we are all the more conscious of being observers for whom nothing, as yet, has unfolded. Later, and only later, we may see why these words are ironic; but critics who call attention to that proleptic irony—because it tells against Angelo— customarily fail to notice another proleptic irony which tells against the Duke: 'Heaven doth with us, as we with Torches doe' is astonishingly brazen, once we are in a position to reflect that this governor has done too little for fourteen years.

The first part of the second scene prompts more questions, and supplies one deliberately misleading answer to an earlier question. Lucio and his chums gossip about 'war' and an apparently urgent need (which actually never troubles the Duke) to come 'to composition with the King of Hungary'. Anybody reading or watching the play for the first time might reasonably suppose that this is why the Duke rushed off—and would then be surprised when the Duke reappears in the next scene, disguised as a friar and explaining that he has 'strewd' this rumour in 'the common eare' (1.3.14–16) because he wants Angelo to think that pressing political affairs have taken him to Poland. It matters, dramatically, that we too were misled, while we were straining to make sense of what is going on. It matters in another way, too: hearing this idle street gossip about current affairs helps to establish the reality of the dramatic world in which we are trying to find our way; Whetstone's *Promos and Cassandra* is less confusingly life-like, less convincingly confusing.

But this experience of perplexity, and of a consequent need to keep revising earlier impressions, turns out to be of the utmost significance to the play of ideas. It brings out, and brings home, the precarious and provisional nature of judgement. So, in the second scene, we share in the general alarm at Claudio's harsh treatment, and in the suspicion that the new governor is a tyrant. Only then do we learn, in the next scene, that the Duke himself wants the strict statutes to be enforced and has 'impos'd' this task on Angelo. To hear the Duke coolly (or even gleefully) anticipating that Angelo will be regarded as a tyrant is far more disturbing when we have already entertained that very suspicion. Similarly, when we watch the stunned Claudio reeling under the shock of finding himself condemned by a law which has not been enforced for many years, it matters very much that we respond to his agony and confusion *before* we hear the Duke arguing that the urgent need to protect the common good must outweigh compassionate consideration for those individuals who will suddenly be sacrificed to this common good. This *kind* of argument may be good, or indeed compelling, and is regularly used to justify strict liability laws; but Shakespeare makes the abstract and theoretical argument hard and concrete by ensuring that the cost of the attempted cure for the 'Vienna-problem' registers, very painfully, *before* we hear the justifying argument. If the third scene preceded the second it would indeed be clearer that the 'Claudio-problem' follows from the attempt to deal with the 'Vienna-problem'; but the effect would be quite different, and the given sequence of scenes is more jolting.

In other words, Shakespeare has an excellent reason for withholding crucial information; here and elsewhere—for example, when he withholds the information about Angelo's promise to marry Mariana, and Lucio's promise to marry Kate—the result is a shock that is emotional as well as intellectual. But precisely because it is intellectually and emotionally demanding, this dramatic procedure is risky—as appears, in this case, when we notice how often critics go on believing that Angelo has *chosen* to revive the statute which condemns Claudio. To make that assumption in the second scene is natural enough, particularly after hearing the Duke tell Angelo in the first scene that

>   your scope is as mine owne,
> So to inforce, or qualifie the Lawes,
> As to your soule seemes good.
>   (1.1.65–7)

But these lines are delivered like an afterthought, after the first 'Fare you well' (59); they involve us in another confusion which, as we discover in the third scene, the Duke wants to establish. For although it is not immediately clear what the *written* 'Commissions' contain, or why the Duke will not reveal their contents in front of the assembled 'Lords' mentioned in the stage direction, it *is* clear that the Duke expects his 'Commissions' to be executed. He tells Escalus not to 'warpe', and peremptorily dismisses Angelo's real or assumed diffidence: 'No more evasion' (1.1.15,51). And in the third scene the Duke explains that although he is determined that the 'needfull' laws be revived and enforced, he has 'impos'd' that office on Angelo precisely because he does not want to invite 'slander' on his 'Name'. The slipperiness of the Duke's notions of 'slander' and 'tiranny' is a consequence of his self-esteem: he speaks, with no obvious disturbance, of 'my fault', but will countenance no criticism.

Because the play's revelations are so carefully timed, we must attend very closely to the given sequence of scenes: if we read back into one scene what we learn only in a later scene, we misrepresent those intellectual and emotional dilemmas which the play sets out to produce and explore. After our first brief glimpse of Angelo in the first scene we do not see him again until 2.1, and after seeing Claudio in the second scene we do not see him again until 3.1. But the intervening scenes modify our attitudes to both men in subtle and important ways. In particular, a subtly elaborate contrasting of different attitudes towards love and sexuality runs through the whole exposition, and has the important function of providing an explicit or implicit commentary on Claudio's situation and Angelo's view of it.

The third scene provides a striking instance, since there is no other obvious reason why it should open so abruptly with the Duke's indignant correction of the Friar—apparently for supposing that his disguise is part of some lover's stratagem. But the correction (which looks forward to Othello's no less disquieting speech to the Senate on Cupid and skillets) shows a curiously dismissive attitude towards sexual love: 'Beleeve not that the dribling dart of Love/Can pierce a compleate bosome . . .' (1.3.2–3). This is one of many points at which we might dissent from Leavis's emphatic contention that the Duke's 'attitude, nothing could be plainer, is meant to be ours'(163). In dismissing love's dribbling dart, the Duke contrasts his own 'grave, and wrinkled' purpose (or end) with the 'aimes, and ends' of 'burning youth'. This is all the more disquieting, if we have just found Claudio's quiet assertion that he *loves* Julietta coming like a small but welcome gust of fresh air, amid the brothel humour of the second scene and in the face of Lucio's reductive references to 'Lechery' and games of sexual tick-tack. For Lucio there is only 'the sport': there is no distinction between appetite and desire, or lust and love. 'Call it so', says the exasperated Claudio, when he cannot prevail upon Lucio to see that anything other than 'Lechery' is at issue.

When the Duke says that his own end is grave and wrinkled, not youthful, burning and dribbling, the Lucio-like lewdness of the play on words leads to a sharper irony: the inconsistency in the Duke's remarks on Angelo shows that he is disposed to have this particular cake and eat it too. For after admiring his own complete bosom and ineffable superiority to burning youths, and commending Angelo once again as 'A man of stricture and firm abstinence' (12), the Duke reveals a barely concealed animus—criticising the one young man who does not burn or dribble with desire for scarce confessing 'That his blood flowes: or that his appetite/Is more to bread then stone . . .' (1.3.51–3). This anticipates Lucio's more wittily malicious Theophrastan 'character' of Angelo in the next scene:

> A man, whose blood
> Is very snow-broth: one, who never feeles
> The wanton stings, and motions of the sence;
> But doth rebate, and blunt his natural edge
> With profits of the minde: Studie, and fast . . .
>   (1.4.57–61)

Since we are still awaiting a fuller, more extended view of Angelo we cannot know what truth there is in this. But it is clear that Lucio is not qualified to pronounce on the dangers involved in 'profits of the minde'; it is less clear why the Duke should be disparaging sexual love on the one hand and Angelo's firm abstinence on the other. Having anticipated that Angelo will be reviled as a tyrant if he executes his 'Commissions', the Duke concludes the third scene by anticipating (in a satisfied couplet) that 'if power change purpose'— that is, if Angelo does not execute his 'Commissions'—he will be exposed as a 'Seemer'. Here indeed we may guess what is later confirmed: that the 'precise' deputy disapproves of the Duke's letting the law 'slip' for fourteen years, and has dared, as the Duke later puts it, to 'weede my vice' (3.2.252). If this suggests one reason why the Duke has 'impos'd' the unpleasant 'office' on Angelo, despite Escalus's seniority and experience (1.1.47), another, more reputable reason becomes clear in 2.1, when we see how Escalus is disposed to bend (or 'warpe') the law for a well-born gentleman.

The interplay of contrasting attitudes to sex and asceticism now throws out a wonderfully rich contrast with the elderly Duke's *navrant* condescension—in the form of a youthful, blushing girl, who is about to give herself, with passionate abandon, to a life of celibacy. I take it that the main irony is thoroughly engaging, not hostile: there is a delightful, gauche girlishness in Isabella's preposterous exchange with the nun (in a sisterhood famed for its exceptional strictness), and in the typical way in which she can forget both her concern for her brother and her flustered irritation with Lucio for long enough to give the latter a mini-lecture:

> *Isabella*: Some one with childe by him? my cosen *Juliet*?
> *Lucio*: Is she your cosen?
> *Isabella*: Adoptedly, as schoole-maids change their names
> By vaine, though apt affection.
>
> (1.4.45–8)

Pare un libro stampato, as Mozart's Leporello would say!—she talks like a book. But although there is indeed something stiff and primly self-regarding in Isabella's rebuke to Lucio—'You doe blaspheme the good, in mocking me'—that stiffness also suggests girlish nerves, like the blushes or 'cheeke-roses' which Lucio admires. And the self-regard proceeds from a self-respect which Lucio conspicuously lacks, so that he cannot respect others either.

Even as we smile at the beautifully ironic aspects of this confrontation between a polished rake and an inexperienced girl—between a man who will not answer questions and a girl to whom one would not lightly put any—the contrasts between the 'strict' and the loose have a bearing on our attitudes to Angelo, Claudio and the law itself. Lucio has only the profligate's blankly uncomprehending scorn for any kind of high-mindedness and finds Isabella's Dorothea-like hunger for 'strict restraint' as ludicrous and incredible as Angelo's asceticism, study and fast; in appraising Isabella, we are prompted to think about issues which are no less relevant to our shifting, uncertain impressions of Angelo. And Claudio, although he is morally undistinguished and obviously no ascetic, is also no profligate: the contrast with his sister and his judge on the one hand and with Lucio on the other helps to establish his rude but healthy normality. So, while we respond to the other characters, we are thinking about human potentialities and the apparent conflict between Nature and the Law: our attitudes to Claudio and his offence, to Angelo and his judgement, are being modified.

As the fourth scene progresses, Isabella becomes less self-consciously nunnish: her passionate longing for 'Strict restraint' has a poignant, as well as a comic, aspect. Shakespeare's heroines not infrequently recall the spirited, intelligent girls in Erasmus' colloquies, and Isabella's youthful ardour recalls Erasmus's keenly ironic presentation of the enthusiastic novice Catherine, in *The Girl with no Interest in Marriage* (1523) and its sequel *Repentance* (1523). Like Isabella, Catherine does not very well know herself or that world she is determined to renounce, and she too would 'rather die than give up my resolution of virginity' (106). Isabella shows a frightened recoil from that 'naturall edge' which Lucio declares has been blunted in Angelo, and which has brought her unascetic brother close to the axe's sharper edge. Lucio *may* be speaking out of character in the beautiful lines which see Claudio's crime in natural terms:

> Your brother, and his love have embrac'd;
> As those that feed, grow full: as blossoming Time
> That from the seednes, the bare fallow brings
> To teeming foyson: even so her plenteous wombe
> Expresseth his full Tilth, and husbandry.
>
> (1.4.40–4)

But we are not obliged to suppose that Lucio has become suddenly and uncharacteristically dewy-eyed, since these lines are all the more powerfully disconcerting if they are delivered sardonically. The insinuating rake enjoys the blushing nun's discomfort—and adds to it by reminding her (and us) that what the law has condemned, and what she herself wants to deny by becoming a nun, is the imperious process of Nature. In Lucio's view, Claudio is to die for doing what comes naturally, while Angelo and Isabella are both denatured. This too helps to prepare us for the central confrontations between Angelo and Isabella, and Isabella and Claudio. These later scenes show, through ironies which are far less genial than those of the fourth scene, how idealism and imaginative aspiration do not always ennoble human nature, and may cruelly distort it.

But here we need to consider why Shakespeare waits so long to reveal crucial information about the *other* cases he has invented, which bear very challengingly on the Claudio-

Juliet case and the judgemental dilemmas this play explores. After her confrontation with Claudio, Isabella never speaks to her brother again, and the absence of any 'remedie' is all the more keenly felt. But then, at the very moment when the Duke begins to commandeer the stage and try to engineer a happy and necessarily contrived resolution, Shakespeare begins to uncover further complications and paradoxes. We learn in 3.1 of Angelo's contract with Mariana, and in 3.2 of Lucio's contract with Kate; critics usually have little or nothing to say of the latter, but, by departing from his sources once again, Shakespeare has assembled *three* cases involving promises to marry. Two also involve dowries, and two involve pregnancies. On a more inward view, of just that kind with which the law is not concerned, one case—the Claudio–Juliet case—involves this play's only act of mutual, reciprocal love; in the Angelo–Mariana case only one partner is loving; in the case of Lucio and Kate there was no love, merely a cash transaction and a spilling of seed. When critics complain that *Measure for Measure* is 'broken-backed' they merely betray their lack of interest in those problems which the play explores, and an inability to see what these cases have to do with each other.

To begin with Angelo's case: he was not *legally* obliged to keep his contract with Mariana, since she could not deliver her part of the contract—the dowry—and since there had been no consummation. In this case, and also in judging that of Claudio—who fell foul of the law when he postponed his marriage to secure a dowry—Angelo refuses to recognise that legal justice (to which he is, as we have seen, morally committed) is not identical with ethical justice, and that a moral obligation may exist where there is no legal obligation. Angelo is indeed legally innocent, unlike Claudio. But in moral terms his action was far worse: at a time when the death of the brother and the loss of 'the portion and sinew of her fortune' had made Mariana more than ever vulnerable, Angelo abandoned the woman who loved him, 'left her in her teares, and dried not one of them with his comfort' (3.1.207 f.).

On hearing this story, Isabella's reaction is characteristically simplistic: she reflects, 'What a merit were it in death to take this poore maid from the world'. It is no less characteristic of the Duke to confuse the moral and legal issues: he accuses Angelo of swallowing his vows as though those vows established a legally binding commitment, while at the same time trying to engineer a situation which will be legally binding—that is, by tricking Angelo into sleeping with Mariana. (In fact, if Shakespeare's Vienna were subject to the same laws as Shakespeare's England, it would still be open to Angelo to plead *error personae* after sleeping with Mariana; but Vienna is *not* London, the play tells us what we *need* to know, and the incredibly protracted critical discussions of troth-plighting repeatedly ignore both these points.) Unlike the Duke, Shakespeare is underlining the *distinction* between a legal and a moral obligation.

The parallels and contrasts with Lucio's case are no less pointed. In legal terms Lucio has committed exactly the same offence as Claudio: he has fathered a child without marrying its mother. But although he 'promis'd her marriage' (3.2.189) he had no intention of marrying the woman he describes as a 'punke' and a 'whore'. When he was brought before the Duke 'for getting a Wench with childe', he swore that the child was not his (4.3.165–9); we learn that his fear was that he would otherwise be forced to marry Kate, not put to death—for of course the Duke had 'let slip' that strict statute which Angelo enforces when he sentences Claudio to death 'for getting Madam *Julietta* with childe' (1.2.69). We also learn that although Lucio's child will be 'a yeere and a quarter old come *Philip* and *Jacob*' (3.2.189–90) he has never maintained it and—a particularly dark, Dostoevskian touch—resents the fact that Mistress Overdone has 'kept it'; when he vents this resentment by viciously betraying her to the law Lucio leaves his infant entirely destitute. In the first half of the play Shakespeare has used Lucio to resolve one structural problem which defeated Whetstone: in *Promos and Cassandra* the 'low-life' scenes are never integrated with the main plot. Now, by revealing that Lucio himself has committed Claudio's legal offence (and critics who suggest that Angelo has done this are hopelessly confused), Shakespeare can further accentuate the gulf between legal and ethical justice.

For it is clear that any law which *equates* Lucio's offence with Claudio's is atrociously insensitive in moral terms. True,

Shakespeare has carefully established that the groaning Julietta is about to deliver: months have passed, the child's
legitimacy evidently matters less to the parents than the
dowry they still hope to secure, and in the second scene
Claudio is still vague about when they will marry and
abandon the hope of a dowry. Here Angelo's case is indeed
relevant: his determination to have a dowry made him
abandon Mariana. Moreover, there is a 'mutuall', reciprocal
love between Claudio and Julietta which distinguishes their
case from both of the others. In sharp contrast, Lucio's case
admits no doubt on any of the points where Claudio's is
troubling: he does not love Kate, has no intention of
marrying her, and has already abandoned both mother and
child. If the Duke is still convinced that the need to protect
the public good makes the strict statute which condemns
Claudio more than ever 'needfull', there could be no more
appropriate victim of an exemplary severity than Lucio. But
here the Duke is doubly exposed.

In the first place, his thinking is too capricious and
unprincipled to allow him to see how the three cases bear on
each other. Once they are assembled, the parallels and
contrasts between them provide a basis for the kind of
comparative exercise given to students of law and moral philosophy in Shakespeare's time as in ours. One Renaissance
work which Shakespeare certainly knew, and which exhibits
a zestful delight in contriving prickly test cases, is Alexander
Silvayn's *The Orator* (1596). Declamation 95 presents a
dispute between a Christian and 'a jew who would for his
debt have a pound of the flesh of a Christian'; Silvayn's
translator, 'Lazarus Piot', was Anthony Munday, whose
Zelauto (1580) also provided material for *The Merchant of
Venice*. Declamations 54, 61 and 68 all presuppose a law
which allows a ravished maid to choose between having the
ravisher put to death or marrying him; the law gives rise to
different dilemmas which are carefully and formally disputed.
So, Declamation 61 presents, and invites the reader to
appraise, the respective arguments of 'two maidens ravished
by one man, for the which the one required his death, and
the other desired him for her husband'. Shakespeare carefully
invents three cases which accentuate his play's judgemental
dilemmas but withholds this crucial information until the

play's second half, when the self-appointed surrogate dramatist is attempting to manufacture a factitious 'resolution' to
a problem which has exercised civilised, principled men in
all ages: how are conflicting interests and principles best
served? But in matters of this sort the seemingly benevolent
but unprincipled Duke is entirely out of his depth; like the
highly principled but unbenevolent Angelo, the surrogate
dramatist cannot recognise the problem which the real dramatist has made more than ever pressing.

The second exposure is both mordantly funny and devastating in its implications about the Duke's seeming benevolence. The Duke is indeed determined to punish Lucio—for
offending him personally. This is ironic in itself, in that
Lucio's slanders are far less damaging than the Duke's exhibition of indignant, obsessive self-regard; but the irony is
developed. Just as the Duke forgets his own argument that
the strict statute which condemns Claudio to death is 'needfull', he fails to notice that Lucio has committed Claudio's
offence. Lucio is indeed sentenced to death, but for slandering a prince not for getting a maid with child. The Duke
then adds—remembering that a woman has been 'wrong'd',
while continuing to forget the 'Vienna-problem'—that before
being whipped and hanged Lucio must marry the woman he
'begot with child'. This sentence is then commuted, in an
ostentatious demonstration of mercy: the Duke will 'forgive'
the 'slanders' and 'Remit thy other forfeits', and it will be
sufficient for Lucio to marry the woman he has 'wrong'd'.
But then, when the irrepressible Lucio continues to spoil the
performance and upstage the Duke, by wittily protesting that
marriage to a 'punke' is 'pressing to death,/Whipping and
hanging', the Duke's reply comes back quick as a flash:
'Slandering a Prince deserves it'. Here the Duke irascibly
invokes that very offence which he had ostentatiously
forgiven, and shows how he is still disposed to think it
more heinous than the crimes for which Angelo, Claudio and
Barnardine were, no less ostentatiously, pardoned. The point
is not that the Duke's various sentences are wrong because
alternative sentences are obviously right, but that the Duke
cannot see why it is so very difficult to know what sentences
would be right or wrong, according to the incompatible
demands of legal, ethical and divine justice.

In short, Shakespeare's various departures from his sources, his invention of contrasts and parallels which the Duke fails to notice, let alone appraise, and his carefully timed revelations are all calculated to accentuate this imcompatibility, and to cause a consternation which is emotional as well as intellectual. Indeed, in the central confrontations between Angelo and Isabella, and Isabella and Claudio, we see how hard it is to separate this play's emotional and intellectual challenges: diagnostic astringency and imaginative empathy combine to provide what Pater called—felicitously, but, alas, for rather different reasons—'an epitome of Shakespeare's moral judgments' (183).

Kind pity

Although Isabella speaks of the need to show some pity, prompting Angelo to insist that he shows most pity by showing justice, neither of these highly principled moral absolutists can reach to that basic, unassuming fellow-feeling—or 'Kinde pitty' in Donne's sense—shown by the decent Provost, or by Mistress Overdone when she looks after Lucio's bastard infant. Just as this play's only act of 'mutuall'. reciprocal love is roundly condemned by Angelo, Isabella and the Duke, its one conspicuously disinterested act of human kindness occurs in the lower depths and makes little or no impression on the Duke or those 'Christian' critics who admire him.

And when Lucio, who arranges Mistress Overdone's arrest, brutally refuses the hapless Pompey's plea for help he is, for once, imitating his betters. In gloatingly observing that 'If imprisonment be the due of a baud, why 'tis his right' and in telling Pompey to 'say I sent thee thither' (3.2.59–62), he unwittingly parodies Angelo's legalistic judgement on Claudio; worse still, when he goes on to affirm that he will 'pray [*Pompey*] to encrease your bondage if you take it not patiently', he is unwittingly echoing Isabella's hysterical promise to her brother, in the previous scene, that she will 'pray' for his death, since his 'sin' is a 'trade' , and 'Mercy to thee would prove it selfe a Bawde'.

As for Pompey, we see in 4.2 how he has learned his

lesson: giving up his trade as an 'unlawfull bawd', in which he had been an accomplice to the illegal act of engendering illegitimate life, he declares himself 'content to be a lawfull hangman', and 'glad to receive some instruction' in the legal trade of legal killing (4.2.15–18). The natural mystery of procreation (licit or illicit) is replaced by the 'Mysterie' of dispensing death. With something of the pride the Duke himself takes in 'instructing' and 'fitting' condemned men for death, Abhorson discourses on his 'Mysterie' and fears that it will be discredited by having a pimp for partner. In a mordantly inquisitional interlude, the Provost and the Clown inspect some of these dark ironies and paradoxes: the Provost insists that the unlawful bawd and the lawful hangman 'waigh equallie: a feather will turne the Scale', while the Clown finds 'your Hangman is a more penitent Trade then your Bawd: he doth oftner aske forgivenesse'. In 3.2 Lucio took up the Duke's moralistic censure of Pompey, like an embarrassing ally; in 4.3 the Duke addresses Abhorson and Pompey as his 'Fellowes', in giving the order to have Barnardine dragged to the block. His 'instruction' has not helped Barnardine, while poor Claudio, who could say with some dignity at the beginning of 3.1 'I 'have hope to live, and am prepar'd to die', is reduced to a state of terror and despair by his 'Christian' visitors.

Once again, the ironies interlock in an extraordinary manner. Even Abhorson's name is a blackly ironic pun, of which Joyce might have been proud: I find it hard to think of any play in which Shakespeare takes more pains with his plotting and with such telling details. To say this is heretical, of course, but such details are regularly neglected by those critics who criticise Shakespeare's negligence.

It is indeed often remarked that when Claudio reappears in the final scene Isabella has not one word to say to him; but has anybody remarked that Isabella shows no trace of concern, or 'kinde pitty', for the helpless 'groaning' Julietta— her childhood friend, adopted 'cousin', and prospective sister-in-law? Immediately before the first confrontation between Angelo and Isabella, the worried Provost tells Angelo that Julietta is going into labour, and Angelo gives instructions for the 'Fornicatresse' to be taken 'with speed' to 'some fitter place' where her 'meanes' should be 'needfull' (that word again) but 'not lavish' (2.2.17–24). This is quite understandably said to illustrate his cold inhumanity, like his earlier hope that Escalus will find occasion to have Pompey and the others whipped (2.1.131). The important argument which Angelo is about to restate—that he shows most pity by showing justice, and pitying those he does not know—is indeed powerfully principled; but we also see how little Angelo feels with and for those suffering fellow creatures with whom he is immediately concerned. Yet if Angelo's concern for Julietta is so minimal as to seem inhuman, what are we to make of Isabella's total lack of concern—and why should Shakespeare have taken pains to establish that Isabella and Julietta have been so close, if he did not want us to ask that question?

Shakespeare's presentation of Angelo and Isabella provokes extreme and divergent responses. Moreover, different aspects of their characters may be—indeed, inevitably will be—emphasised in any particular performance; and whatever the emphases of that performance, members of the audience will respond differently. Unending critical controversies, and the absence of any received reading, testify to the play's power to provoke 'undisciplined squads of emotion' and suggest that it is especially foolish, in this case, to attempt to be prescriptive about what our response to the characters 'should' be. But here the concept of 'framing' seems to me especially helpful. It directs attention to the way in which judgemental dilemmas unfold: so, as we have seen, the exposition emphasises the problematic distinction between *true mercy* and *'vain pity'* while timing its revelations so that we register the problem feelingly; and that dilemma is intensified, not resolved, by Isabella's subsequent invocation of the principles of *divine mercy* (a third term) and by our perception that the highly principled moral absolutists who debate these matters are themselves not much swayed by *'kinde pitty'* or compassionate inclination. Indeed, we might here notice how the first confrontation between Angelo and Isabella shows, all the more pressingly, the need to distinguish between moral *obligation* and compassionate *inclination*. After indulging his compassionate inclinations for fourteen years, the Duke is convinced that this was not truly merciful in the long term; Angelo insists—quite correctly, on his own or Sir Thomas Elyot's terms—that his obligation to protect the common weal is moral as well as legal, and he is shocked when first Escalus and then Isabella ask him to bend the law—but then, like Isabella, and unlike the Duke or Escalus, he is hardly troubled by any *inclination* to be compassionate, and this produces a divided response.

Similarly, the contrasts with Escalus in 2.1 point in two opposed directions. In the first place, Angelo refuses to allow that there is anything morally painful or problematic about the sentence on Claudio. His reply to the older, more experienced judge shows the doctrinaire exaltation of the studious theoretician ("Tis very pregnant . . .'); his conclusion ('Sir, he must die') is delivered with a Johnsonian inexorability which suggests the debating chamber, and shows no tremor of that moral disturbance which might accompany any decision to invoke the law's most extreme penalty. Elbow then enters (the law as ass), and brings a pimp who proceeds to caricature simplistic legalism: when asked whether his trade is lawful Pompey replies, 'If the law would allow it, sir'. When the impatient Angelo stalks out and leaves us to watch the scene he found too boring, we see how Escalus is both humane and practically concerned with the law's admininstrative problems. From his patient enquiries, and his eventual request that Elbow supply the names of some 'six or seven, the most sufficient of your parish', we may conclude that Escalus is actually going to do something about the way in which master constables are appointed.

However, the critical eagerness to arraign Angelo is all too often combined with a willingness to sentimentalise Escalus. We have heard him attempting to 'warpe' from his 'Commissions', despite the Duke's instructions, by advancing an extremely shaky argument: Angelo *could* bend the law, if he wished; he, Escalus, is *inclined* to do so, since the 'gentleman,/ Whom I would save, had a most noble father'; the law *should not* be enforced by any judge who might have committed the same offence, 'Had time coheard with Place, or place with wishing' (2.1.4–16). Angelo very properly demolishes this argument. The legal justice of a sentence depends on the law, and is no more affected by the inner state or potentially criminal character of a judge than the efficacy of the sacraments is affected by the moral character of the administering priest. Unlike Escalus, Angelo is morally committed to his task of enforcing the law, and to the fundamental principle that nothing should 'come in partiall'; and in the play's final scene he still wants to be judged as he has judged—whereas Escalus is ready and eager to rack an elderly foreign friar, and promises, with graphic relish, to 'towse' him 'joint by joint' (5.1.309–10). This savagery seems inconsistent with the benign figure some critics describe, but is wholly consistent with Escalus's concern with birth, rank and position: as a man who greatly enjoys exercising authority and shows more regard for persons than principles, Escalus is quite prepared to bend the law for a well-born gentleman, but will not tolerate any criticism—true or not—of those in authority. Here he resembles the Duke, and it is his misfortune that the critic of authority whom he would rack turns out to *be* the disguised Duke.

In other words, the 'framing' of 2.1 not only advances our understanding of an intellectual dilemma; it is also emotionally demanding, because it prompts sharply divergent responses to Angelo as man and judge. And to see how this prepares for the very complex irony that follows, we might turn to *Billy Budd, Sailor* and notice how Captain Vere recalls the first confrontation between Angelo and Isabella at the very moment when he is asking the drumhead court to make his own careful distinction between moral obligation and inclination:

> But the exceptional in the matter moves the hearts within you. Even so too is mine moved. But let not warm hearts betray heads that should be cool. Ashore in a criminal case, will an upright judge allow himself off the bench to be waylaid by some tender kinswoman of the accused seeking to touch him with her tearful plea? Well, the heart here, sometimes the feminine in man, is as that piteous woman, and hard though it be, she must be ruled out.

Shakespeare's exposition finished with Escalus bemoaning the lack of any 'remedie'; the development opens with a scene in which, as Melville reminds us, a beautiful woman is attempting to seduce an upright judge from the path of duty. The troubling irony was anticipated when Claudio hoped that his sister would 'make friends' with the 'strict deputie': for he spoke first of his 'great hope' that the 'prone and speechless dialect' of Isabella's 'youth' would 'move' Angelo—before going on to add ('beside . . .') that his sister could argue well. And the irony is underlined by Lucio as he urges Isabella on: 'Oh, to him, to him wench . . . Hee's comming, I perceive't' (2.2.124–5).

The contrast between Angelo and Melville's Vere is particularly instructive, and less simple than might at first be supposed. In Shakespeare's play the 'Claudio-problem' is precipitated by an attempt to deal with what the Duke regards, rightly or wrongly, as a civic emergency requiring strict measures and exemplary severities. In *Billy Budd* there is a national emergency, since England is at war with France; Billy has struck an officer, which is in itself a capital offence under the Articles of War, quite apart from the blow's lethal effect on Claggart. Moreover, the recent mutinies at Spithead and Nore make Vere consider the effect of the trial on the 'sea-commonalty': any admission of extenuating circum-stances might give mutiny its permissive pass, whereas Billy's execution would (like Claudio's) provide an 'admonitory spectacle'. In judging the case Vere has no doubt that the plea of extenuation would be accepted by 'a court less arbi-trary', and that at 'the Last Assizes it shall acquit'; he even allows that, in terms of 'natural justice', to apply the strict martial law will mean that 'innocence and guilt . . . in effect changed places'. Unlike Angelo, Vere insists that he feels very keenly those 'scruples' which are 'vitalized by compassion'; but he also insists, like Angelo, that his obli-gation to enforce the law is moral as well as legal. As Peter Winch observes in *Ethics and Action*, Vere is not merely faced with a conflict between morality and military law, but with an *internal* moral conflict between genuinely moral 'oughts', since the military code is 'something to which he himself is morally committed' (156). Billy is hanged, and Vere dies not long after this, murmuring Billy's name; but we are told (in italics) that *'these were not the accents of remorse'*.

It is indeed tempting to say that Vere, unlike Angelo, *recognises* the conflict between legal and ethical justice and *suffers* as a result, and that this is why Melville's strict judge engages sympathy while Shakespeare's strict judge repels us. But both works undermine and complicate that contrast. In

Vere's case, it is important to notice how, from first to last, Vere never regards moral and compassionate scruples as other than irrelevant to the 'decision', although he claims to feel their 'full force': 'For the compassion, how can I otherwise than share it? But, mindful of paramount obligations I strive against scruples that may tend to enervate decision.' Just as the dying Vere feels no 'remorse', his initial sense of the appropriate judgement declared itself immediately, and was followed—not preceded—by a painful inner conflict.

Moreover, the historical setting for Melville's 'inside narrative' makes it possible to take external and retrospective bearings, but these increase the pervasive atmosphere of moral perplexity. The Preface reminds us that the 'Revolutionary Spirit' emboldened men to 'rise against real abuses' and 'the Old World's hereditary wrongs'. The naval mutinies were prompted by 'real abuses' like impressment (Billy's fate) which were in time denounced and reformed, but here Melville pointedly refers to a legal judgment of Lord Mansfield's which helped to *maintain* such 'sanctioned irregularities'. In contrast, and rather like Angelo when he explains to Escalus what is 'pregnant' but irrelevant to the processes of legal judgment, Vere first notes and then *discounts* the fact that many of the men pressed into his Majesty's navy would have preferred to fight for the Rights of Man, as promulgated by the revolutionary 'enemy'. It is darkly hinted that Claggart's presence on Vere's ship follows from the way in which the law favoured criminals of high birth, offering them naval commissions as an alternative to prison sentences. In short, even as the tale snipes at 'martial utilitarians' and the 'Benthamites of war', it suggests the need for something like the Utilitarian distinction between the conventions of 'positive morality' (the morality accepted by a given group) and principles of 'critical morality', which may be invoked in criticising established social institutions and 'sanctioned irregularities'. The interests of a people do not necessarily coincide with those of its ruling class, although the ruling class may be relied upon to insist, not least through its laws, that they are identical. In some sentences which Melville later deleted from his Preface, perhaps because they were *too* unequivocal, he wrote that even 'the dry tinder of a Wordsworth took fire'. On this view, Vere condemns Billy to death to defend the 'positive morality' of Lord Mansfield's England and Claggart's class.

In trying to 'make moral sense of' Vere we might indeed employ S. L. Goldberg's distinction (which I discussed in Chapter 1) between 'agents' and 'lives': Melville's 'inside narrative' challenges us to see why Vere cannot but arrive at his decision, being the man he is, while also exposing that decision to the perspectives of 'critical morality' or a still more radical scepticism. Peter Winch's fine discussion of *Billy Budd* appears in an essay called 'The Universalizability of Moral Judgments' in which, significantly enough, Winch opposes a great artist's approach to questions of morality to the philosophical view of ethics as 'a sort of calculus of action, in which actions are considered as events merely contingently attached to particular agents' (153). Winch's challenge—and Melville's—may be focused by a troubling play on prepositions: we may not think it right *of* Vere to sentence Billy to death but it is unquestionably right *for* him, according to his own conception of his legal *and* moral duty.

Here the contrast with Angelo becomes more complex and demanding. My purpose is not to suggest, prescriptively, how we should respond to Angelo, but to isolate the difficulties *to* which we must be responding, if we are responding adequately to the scene's powerfully framed intellectual and emotional challenges. In each case, indulging a natural and easy response—of sympathy for the suffering Vere or dislike of Angelo's inhumanity—circumvents a more complex judgemental dilemma. Vere suffers, but does he suffer enough? The obvious objection to his claim that he feels 'to the full' those 'scruples' which are 'vitalized by compassion' is that if this were true he could not make that decision; the senior officer of marines also *recognises* the internal moral conflict, but is disposed to acquit Billy. Angelo will not even allow that there is a conflict between legal and ethical justice, let alone an internal moral conflict. But *we* see this conflict—or should, if we have been attending to the masterly exposition. This may make us all the more resentful of Angelo as man, but we have also to recognise that sentencing Claudio to death is unquestionably right *for* Angelo, according to his own conception of his legal and moral duty. In arguing that he shows most pity by showing justice and pitying those he does not know, whom a dismissed offence would later gall, he offers Isabella an unquestionably moral argument which forcefully extends the argument to which Escalus has reluctantly conceded. Isabella refuses to concede the moral force of this argument—but does so when *she* becomes one of the innocent victims whom the law should protect, and tells her terrified brother that 'Mercy to thee would prove it selfe a Bawd'.

Isabella's proudly passionate outburst against 'man, proud man' does indeed 'move' Angelo the man: if we allow the watchful Lucio's expertise in these murky areas, this is when Angelo starts 'comming'. A moment later, Angelo observes in a tormentedly punning aside, 'She speakes, and 'tis such sence/ That my Sence breeds with it' (2.2.141–2)—but of course he is not here acknowledging the superior moral force or legal relevance of her argument that he should ask his own heart 'what it doth know/ That's like my brother's fault'. He showed his inflexible rectitude by dismissing that argument when Escalus advanced it. Rather, he is acknowledging with guilt and horror that this pungently ill-assorted trio is succeeding in its attempt to corrupt an upright judge; and when he tells Isabella to 'come againe tomorrow' he is agreeing to bend the law to the extent of postponing the execution.

In the soliloquy that follows, Angelo confirms that he has never before felt those natural emotions which he can now only condemn and pervert—precisely *because* he is so austerely high-minded and habitually sets the requirements of virtue and the law against those of nature. His admission that 'Ever till now / When men were fond, I smild, and wondred how' is grotesquely, wrenchingly tragi-comic. In acknowledging the first access of the natural, human feelings which the Duke and Lucio have mocked him for never feeling, the appalled judge condemns the man: judging his feelings to be criminal, Angelo sentences himself to *be* a criminal. One horribly revealing image allows us to see how Angelo's high-mindedness has perverted his nature and imagination: as editors very properly remind us, the word 'evils' could at this time mean *excrement*, and when Angelo speaks of razing the sanctuary and pitching 'our evils there' he sees the sexual act as an excremental spilling of seed.

Here the distinction between judge and man is crucial to our understanding of the inner dynamics of Angelo's denatured character: the judge condemns the man to be vile, and the man, not surprisingly, never shows any desire to *repeat* his first sexual experience. But this extends the challenge to our own capacity for 'kinde pitty', since the soliloquy reveals a desperately unhappy 'case'; if we remember the radically internal import of the Sermon on the Mount, we shall not be self-righteously censorious in noticing how frequently this play's Christian critics forget it.

Here, though, we need to emphasise that neither Isabella nor the Gospel ethic she invokes is allowed any privileged, supra-dramatic status. The consummately ironic structure depends upon the complementary, interrogative relationship between its two highly principled moral absolutists and their respective religious and legal ethics. Just as Isabella inadvertantly brings about a strikingly comprehensive exposure of Angelo, he brings about an exposure of her lack of 'kinde pitty'; of her inability to 'live up to' the requirements of her ethic; and of the deficiencies within her ethic, in which the profound and radical concern with inner states and personal salvation necessarily takes precedence over any concern for the common weal or the law's moral obligation to protect society.

As soon as Isabella confronts Angelo she false-foots herself—first by conceding that the law which condemns her brother to death is 'just', and also by basing that concession on her declared abhorrence of the 'vice' (2.2.29–41). Not being disposed to distinguish between 'sin' and 'crime', she assumes—like Law Lords in our own times: for example, Lord Denning in his account of the Profumo affair, and Lord Devlin in *The Enforcement of Morals* —that it is the law's business to punish immorality as such. This makes it easy for Angelo to reply that the law cannot 'Condemne the fault, and not the actor of it', and Isabella is ready to retire in defeat. She next resorts to arguments we have already heard from Escalus, and is curtly told to 'be gone'. Her subsequent plea that Claudio is 'not prepar'd for death' is rendered faintly ludicrous by the comparison with killing 'the fowle of season', and this too reveals her underlying indifference to the governor's duty to protect those committed to his charge:

201

Claudio is not being killed to 'serve heaven' (83–7). And when Angelo offers Isabella the moral argument about what the greater good requires—a utilitarian argument which echoes Sir Thomas Elyot and anticipates John Stuart Mill—Isabella (unlike Escalus) fails to see its moral force. This of course unleashes the cruelly exposing irony which follows, when the upright judge betrays his ethic and invites Isabella to betray hers. Although Isabella shows no concern for Juli-etta, let alone for those whom she does not know and whom, as Angelo insists, the law must protect, she will scream for 'justice' when *she* becomes an innocent victim; and her professed concern for her brother's inner state and salvation is entirely forgotten once she thinks her own salvation at risk. 'As much for my poore Brother, as my selfe', she declares to Angelo (2.4.99); by 'as much' she means 'no more', but we have occasion to reflect that 'no more' really means 'far less'. We should notice that this painful irony is not resolved in the final act when she eventually intercedes on Angelo's behalf; she does indeed give up her (unChristian) concern with vengeance at this point, but neither her life nor her salvation are at risk, and she is (like the Duke) exhibiting her own *caritas* to the eyes of men as well as God. Such *caritas* costs less than everything, and does not extend to the brother she ignores.

On the most unsympathetic view, Isabella is not only exposed as a 'self-loving nun' (to borrow a phrase from *Venus and Adonis*, which considers the denaturing effects of high-mindedness); that very principle of Christian love which she invokes is seen as a species of self-love. The repeated refer-ences to rewards and punishments in the Sermon or the Mount do not promote any concept of disinterested good-ness. In *Der Lohngedanke im Neuen Testament* the Prot-estant theologian Gunther Bornkamm remarks that 'the New Testament does not know the idea of the good deed that has its value in itself'; and of course Nietzsche makes this point more virulently in *The Anti-Christ:*

'For if ye love them which love you, *what reward have ye?* Do not even the publicans do the same? And if ye salute your brethren only what do ye *more than others?* do not even the publicans so?' (Matt. 5:46–7)—Principle of 'Christian love': it wants to be *well paid*.

And in his commentary on Matthew, J.C. Fenton contrasts a Jewish rabbinical text ('Be not like servants who serve their lord on condition of receiving a reward'), in order to emphasise that moral disinterestedness is not and cannot be 'a mark of Christianity or of the New Testament' since men are in 'a state of need' and are 'not in a position to speak of disinterestedness and "pure love" ' (25). But this suggests why it will not do to argue that Isabella alienates sympathy by failing to 'live up to' the requirements of her faith. The Sermon on the Mount sets a sharp limit on love: for the Christian, concern with one's own fate in the next world *must* take precedence over concern with one's own, or anybody else's, fate in this world. Shakespeare is accentuating that difficulty which Bunyan confronted with characteristically unflinching, painful honesty by showing how, in the pursuit of personal salvation, 'Christian' plugs his ears to avoid hearing the screams of his abandoned wife and children. Like Bunyan's Christian, Isabella *heeds* Jesus' grave warning that 'a man's foes shall be they of his own household' (Matt. 10:36). And this suggests how Isabella presents an intellectual and emotional challenge which perfectly complements that posed by Angelo: we may not think it right *of* her to refuse to save her brother by surrendering her virginity, but this is unquestionably right *for* her, according to her own conception of her moral and religious duty.

Isabella is not disposed to make any distinction between sin and crime; throughout their first confrontation Angelo's arguments are secular. He refers to 'faults', 'offences', foul wrongs and evil infringements, but only begins to speak of 'sins' in the soliloquy—on seeing *himself* 'that way going to temptation,/Where prayers crosse'. Before the second confrontation we have a chance to consider the Duke's thoughts on 'sin' and 'crime'. Being 'Bound by my charity' to 'minister' to those in prison after learning 'the nature of their crimes', he tells Julietta that her 'most offence full act' was also, because it was loving and 'mutually committed', a 'sin of heavier kinde' than Claudio's; in offering a final blessing he remembers to mention that Claudio 'must die tomorrow', and strolls off to deliver further 'instruction', without waiting to see how Julietta receives this thunderbolt. Julietta sinned by loving; in the next scene we hear Angelo arguing that there might be 'a charitie in sinne', while the uncomprehending Isabella insists that bending a just law would be 'no sinne at all, but charitie' (2.4.62–6). And when Angelo proposes that 'compel'd sins' stand more for number, then accompt' (57–8), he is offering the kind of legal argument used when somebody is compelled to commit a *crime* (*coactus voluit*): in such cases punishment may be appropriate but there is mitigation of the penalty. For some critics Isabella's rejection of this argument shows that she thinks of God as being as legalistic as Angelo, but, once again, such a response fails to recognise the terms of the problem. Isabella is not being raped, she is being invited to *choose* to sin. Moreover, having sentenced himself to be a monster ('I have begun . . .'), Angelo is even insisting, sadistically, that Claudio's death will be prolonged by torture if Isabella does not also simulate sexual pleasure by 'fitting' her 'consent' to his 'sharp appetite' and laying by all 'nicetie' (2.4.159–63). Being the woman she is, and believing what she believes, she cannot but refuse.

However, her manner of refusing further emphasises the two novices' complementary relationship. As Harriett Hawkins shrewdly remarks (1985:69), the sexual masochism of these lines perfectly matches, and might be thought to inflame and inspire, Angelo's sexual sadism:

> were I under the tearmes of death,
> Th'impression of keen whips, I'd weare as Rubies,
> And strip my selfe to death, as to a bed,
> That longing have bin sicke for, ere I'ld yeeld
> My body up to shame.
>
> (2.4.100–4)

Even as they inadvertently expose the incompatibility and human insufficiency of their respective ethics, the two highly principled novices reveal an affinity—in their recoil from sexuality and their own animal natures, and in the dualistic extremity of the images supplied by their denatured imaginations. When Angelo so revealingly equates sexuality with defecation in his image of pitching excrement in temples, we might be reminded of Tertullian's notorious description of woman as 'a temple built upon a sewer'; but Tertullian's patristic *bon mot* might also be said to reveal what Ted

Hughes once called the 'neurotic-making dynamics of Christianity', and in this respect resembles Isabella's fiercely dualistic vision of man as an 'angry ape' ignorant of his 'glassy essence' (1.2.117–23). But the result—in Isabella's case, as in that of Angelo when he discovers that he is no Adonis and sentences himself to be a Tarquin—is a peculiarly intense horror: those very speeches which might prompt a harsh, detachedly diagnostic awareness of Isabella as a 'case' also challenge our own capacity for 'kinde pitty' by registering her own sense of her situation and of an inescapable dilemma which she is particularly ill-equipped to confront.

Angelo's circumspection, and his irritation when he thinks that Isabella is *pretending* to misunderstand him (2.4.73–5), reveal shame and self-disgust; once again there is a pointedly complementary irony when we see Isabella's desperately anxious, awkward circumspection in the first part of her confrontation with Claudio. When she does finally begin to answer his no less desperately anxious questions she appeals to his sense of 'honour', and this unChristian appeal prompts the New Arden editor to censure her 'psychic confusion' *and* the integrity of her professed commitment to Christian values:

> Horror of physical violation has become identified with concern for chastity, and is taken to justify a refusal of Angelo's demands at all costs. Accordingly 'shame' not sin, 'honour' not charity, are seen now as the all-important considerations, and Claudio's duty to Isabella as superseding her duty to him. Her brother is no longer to be thought of as a victim to be rescued but as a potential chivalrous protector; his moral lapse is condoned as due to 'prompture of the blood'—a defence as valid as Angelo's own 'Blood, thou art blood'—and his 'mind of honour' is praised because it alone can redeem his sister's body from 'abhorr'd pollution'. In this transvaluation of values, chastity is yoked not to charity but to 'honour'. Standards have slipped down from a spiritual plane to the level of a brittle social code where nobility is the true virtue and chastity is an aspect of physical self-regard (lxxix)

But although this suggests how Isabella's desperate appeal to 'honour' contributes to the scene's lacerating moral comedy, it fails to suggest why she is driven to employ such arguments.

There is for her a clear categorical imperative: she must not accede to Angelo's proposal. This may also be expressed as a hypothetical imperative: 'If you want X (salvation), you must not do Y (choose to sin).' But Claudio is one of Shakespeare's casual atheists, as his terrified vision of what follows death confirms (3.1.119–33): what he wants, supremely, is his life, and this has for him a value which excludes Isabella's X and requires Y. Isabella's dilemma is precisely that Claudio cannot recognise the force of her imperatives. She must therefore try to question his: so she pleads with the young, all too vigorously healthy Claudio that he would only be prolonging his life by 'six or seven winters' (3.1.77), while desperately invoking other values, like 'honour' and 'nobility', which do not direct her own thinking but might have some purchase on Claudio's. And indeed, for a few moments, they do—until his sense of death is actualised in the unforgettable eruption of a terrified imagination: 'Ay, but to die, and go we know not where . . .' This drives Isabella into a hysterical frenzy, but her 'self-regard' is neither merely 'physical' nor the result of 'psychic confusion': it follows from her commitment to values which she sets above her own life and which can be preserved only at the expense of Claudio's life. Something must be sacrificed: Claudio's life, which is for him of supreme value, can be saved only if Isabella denies the supreme values which for her give life its only meaning and significance. Claudio is reduced to abject begging, while his sister reviles him; but in his case, hers, and indeed Angelo's, the challenge to our own capacity for imaginative empathy and 'kinde pitty' is concentrated at those very moments where the play's acerbically diagnostic ironies might prompt—and for many critics do prompt—a withdrawal of sympathy.

The play frames its moral and judgemental problems in just such a way as to ensure that any response of simple dislike or unqualified sympathy is inadequate *to* the problems. When Johnson and Coleridge angrily invoke the principles of legal justice to insist that Angelo should be punished, they are representing one *term* of a moral and judgemental problem as the *solution* to the problem. 'Christian' interpreters like Wilson Knight or Gless are doing the same thing with another term, when they assume that the judgemental dilemma is resolved—rather than complicated and intensified—by that Gospel ethic which Isabella invokes in

2.2. Pater's promising claim that the play provides 'an epitome of Shakespeare's moral judgements' is rendered suspect by his characterisation of Shakespeare as a Pateresque Oxford don: 'one who sits as a spectator'; 'a humorist also, who follows with a half-amused but always pitiful sympathy, the various ways of human disposition, and sees less distance than ordinary men between what are called respectively great and little things'; an aesthete whose own contented vision of 'true justice is dependent on just those finer appreciations which poetry cultivates in us the power of making' (184). In other words, Pater is satisfied with the notion of a *merely* 'poetical justice', and gives this a privileged status without showing any concern for the problems which exercised Sir Thomas Elyot, or Jesus.

The play's exposition had issued in a deadlock, which was formally emphasised in Escalus' sad conclusion: 'There is no remedie'. When Isabella abandons her brother, the development has established—in more demandingly comprehensive and painfully internal ways—that there is indeed 'no remedie': no way to resolve the incompatible demands of conflicting principles and priorities; and no prospect of a realistic outcome which would not merely rub our noses in a mess and affront those feelings of 'kinde pitty' which the central confrontations of 2.2, 2.4 and 3.1 so challengingly provoke. Everything is as bad as could be.

Here indeed it may seem tendentious to use the term 'development' when the development in question finishes in the *middle* of a scene —to be precise, when the Duke enters at 3.1.152. There is an unmistakably noisy change of gear: the scene suddenly lurches into prose, and we also hear the creaking of contrived plot mechanisms which have hitherto been concealed. In many or most critical accounts this is where the 'broken-backed' play's back breaks. So, for example, Tillyard argues that from this point the tone is lowered, 'antique quaintness excuses the lack of poetic intensity', and Shakespeare cannot control the split between 'realism' and 'folk-lore': 'the realism admits no folk-lore for half of the play, while all the folk-lore occurs in the second half' (1949:140). In other words, Shakespeare is not blessed with the critic's shrewdness, good taste and *savoir-faire:* having shown bad judgement by choosing to graft two very different kinds of story—the Claudio/Julietta story, and the Angelo/Mariana story with its *novella*-like bed-trick—Shakespeare now finds that he cannot control the radical and disquieting 'inconsistency' (140).

But here, since an interpretative choice is involved, I would ask the reader to consider not only what has already been said about Lucio, Barnardine and the play's final scene, but the earlier discussions of Shakespeare's reflexivity and of his habitually interrogative internalisation of novella-like contrivances. The immediately pressing issue is whether we identify the Duke with Shakespeare, and whether we regard the all too conspicuous change of gear—like the later, all too conspicuously contrived débâcle over the need for a substitute for the substitute head—as an unprofessional clumsiness or as a dramatically pointed signal. At the very point when the dramatic situation appears to be most intractable and painful—admitting no solution which can be principled, realistic and aesthetically satisfying—the Duke steps forward as a surrogate dramatist, determined to engineer that kind of factitious 'solution' which we regularly encounter in *novelle*. This jars within the scene, precisely because Shakespeare ensures that it occurs in the middle of the scene. And from this point, as we have already seen, there is a dual development in which the real dramatist (who may have played the Duke) sabotages the surrogate dramatist's contrivances. On the one hand, there is the highly coloured and implausibly contrived movement towards a 'happy' closure, involving Italianate plot contrivances and moated grange lyricism; on the other hand, the 'low-life' scenes become more seamily 'realistic' in the scenes involving Lucio, Barnardine, Pompey and Abhorson, while the ironic parallels between *three* cases involving promises to marry expose the unprincipled, capricious and self-regarding nature of the Duke's legal and moral thinking. The ensuing ironies expose the arrogant naivety concealed within the commonplace Renaissance comparisons (such as we find in Sidney or Ben Jonson) which see the Poet as a Prince or even a god, who creates a universe or commonwealth and dispenses ideal justice; put crudely, it is as if Shakespeare is reminding us that life is not like stories, and that only a moral idiot, or somebody who sees life through the spectacles of books, would expect a work of art to resolve problems which are —as this work of art so disturbingly shows—wholly intractable. The play's title becomes as pointedly ironic as that of *All's Well That Ends Well*, and just as *The Merchant of Venice* seems a far less intelligent and satisfying play if we suppose that Portia's legal trick resolves the problems that play explores, the Duke is unable to resolve, or even recognise, the problems explored in this later 'comedy of appraisal'. Having taken pains to implicate his Duke as Governor and man, Shakespeare exposes the Duke as artist: we appraise the discrepancy between what the Duke wants and what we want, between the expectation of a conventional comic closure and the expectation that a work of art will be morally intelligent, not frivolous, when it addresses a morally demanding subject.

I have never understood why anybody should expect a supreme play of ideas by our greatest dramatist to be easy. If we are attending to this play of ideas, it may indeed be divided into five 'movements', but they do not correspond with the Folio editors' act-divisions. The exposition finishes at the end of 2.1, with Escalus's verdict that the conflict between legal and ethical justice admits 'no remedie'. That judgemental dilemma intensifies in the development, as Elyot's distinction between true mercy and 'vain pitty' is complicated by Isabella's invocation of divine mercy and by the two novices' lack of 'kinde pitty'. A third movement, which splits a scene and indeed the play itself into two parts but should never be seen as the place for an interval, begins at 3.1.152 and finishes with the Duke's complacent octosyllabics at the end of Act 3: here, after outlining his contrived resolution for the Angelo–Mariana problem, the Duke encounters Lucio, Mistress Overdone and the others, and is too preoccupied with the slanders to his 'name' to see how the Lucio–Kate case bears on the others. In the next, complementary movement, the lyricism of the start leads to the still more compromising encounters with Barnardine and Abhorson, and culminates in Angelo's soliloquy in 4.4: unlike the Duke and Isabella, Angelo repudiates his own extra-legal reasons for assenting to a legal execution. The last two scenes of Act 4 and the final act are continuous: we see the Duke proceeding towards the city gate (4.5), awaited by the gate (4.6), and finally delivering his problematic verdicts.

Real and fancied problems

The 'strict' but hitherto 'drowsie, and neglected' statute which condemns Claudio to death is, beyond question, exceedingly severe. In *Promos and Cassandra* the revival of a rusty statute which punishes fornication with death leads to the immediate arrest and sentence of *thirty* men: this is quantitatively worse, but seems less arbitrary than the way in which the revived Viennese statute 'falls' on Claudio. In Cinthio Giraldi's story the Claudio-figure is sentenced for rape, which is a serious crime; but critic after critic has objected that a Viennese ban on extra- or pre-marital sex is not only ludicrously severe in its penalties but is also imposs-ible to enforce. Making the point that it would have seemed ludicrous in Shakespeare's day, the shrewd and learned New Arden editor notes that with the possible, solitary exception of Stubbes even the Puritan extremists of the time never demanded that fornication be punished with loss of life (lxvi). Moreover, while pimps and their numerous clients are threat-ened with milder punishments or left alone, Claudio is to have his head chopped off for a 'mutual' act of love—or as Pompey puts it, for groping in a peculiar river, instead of groping a paid whore. Worse still, Claudio tells Lucio that there had been a 'contract', of a kind recognised in English common law although discountenanced by the Church; and we hear from Lucio that Claudio was 'ever precise in prom-ise-keeping' (1.2.72).

From these difficulties others follow. If the 'contract' is an important consideration, why is it that Isabella never so much as mentions it when she is pleading for her brother's life? In 1.4 her first response to Lucio's news is 'Oh, let him marry her', and in 3.4, when the Duke mentions Angelo's contract with Mariana, Isabella neither objects to the Duke's proposal nor requires further explanation. Moreover, if the revived statute is inherently ludicrous and morally atrocious, why don't any of the play's decent, intelligent and responsible characters demand that it be removed forever from the stat-ute-book? Why doesn't the Duke condemn Lucio for this offence, if he still believes that the biting laws are 'needfull'? His own machinations depend on an act of fornication, which he easily persuades Mariana and Isabella to accept by appealing to the status of a 'contract' which had been ignored in Claudio's case. If we are taking the play seriously, such problems cannot be wholly alleviated by discussions of folk-lore, fairy tales or generic expectation; they produce that widespread dissatisfaction which Richard Wheeler succinctly reformulates in his thoughtful book on the 'problem comedies':

> The range of feeling dramatized in *Measure for Measure* is diminished rather than sustained and controlled as the play moves towards completion. Shakespeare seems not to finish quite so large and powerful a play as the one he starts, but to change the rules—excluding powerful trends of feeling already admitted into the action—so that the play can be finished at all. (5)

At the very moment when the revived statute is first discussed, editors and critics convict Shakespeare of negligence. We hear Mistress Overdone explaining that Claudio was sentenced to death 'for getting Madam Julietta with child' (1.2.69–70); but then, only seventeen lines later, we hear her asking, 'Is there a maid with child by him?' Elaborate arguments have been produced to account for this 'textual anomaly'. So, for example, the New Arden editor posits the inclusion of discarded material from a first draft (xx); Mary Lascelles argues that Pompey's 'yonder man' (about whom Mistress Overdone asks her curious question) is some *other* victim of the statute, even though we never learn anything more of this shadowy second offender (51–2).

The so-called 'textual anomaly' is itself an editorial invention. Mistress Overdone has just seen Claudio 'arrested' and 'carried away'—as she naturally assumes, to prison. Pompey then enters, reporting that 'yonder man' (still offstage) is being 'carried to prison'; no less naturally, Mistress Overdone supposes that this must be somebody else—and asks whether there is also a maid *by him*. She cannot know what will be explained to Claudio himself, when he asks the Provost why he is being dragged through the streets: Angelo has given a 'special charge' that Claudio must be shown 'to th' world' as an example, since the purpose of reviving the statute is to frighten the Viennese into behaving better. The 'man' Pompey has seen is Claudio, and once Claudio enters—

asking the Provost the relevant question—the confusion is cleared up.

But this does not merely resolve an invented 'anomaly'. We are being told, twice, what we immediately need to know about the statute which condemns Claudio. Mistress Overdone does not say—like countless editors and critics—that Claudio is to have his head chopped off for fornication. She says that he has been sentenced 'for getting Madam Julietta with child'. In the fourth scene we are given the same information: upon learning that her brother is in prison Isabella exclaims, 'Woe me; for what?', and is told: 'He hath got his friend with childe' (1.4.29). Later, when the Duke asks to know the 'nature' of Julietta's crime, the Provost explains that Julietta is 'with childe,/ And he that got it, sentenc'd' (2.3.14–15). In short, Claudio's offence does indeed depend on, but does not *consist in*, an act of 'fornication'.

I want to give this heretical idea its head for a few paragraphs, since what emerges throws a very interesting light on what are usually taken to be weaknesses or problems in the play. Why, in adapting the story, did Shakespeare introduce a pregnancy, and show us a Julietta who is about to give birth to an unwanted child?

There is obviously a *loose* sense in which—as is claimed by Lucio, or Loose-io: his logic is as loose as his morals—Claudio has been sentenced to death 'for' fornication. The logical looseness involves a familiar kind of confusion between necessary and sufficient conditions. It is no surprise that Lucio should protest to the Duke that it is 'ruthless' to 'take away the life of a man' *for* 'the rebellion of a Codpeece' (3.2.106), but this is immediately followed by another reminder of the true nature of Claudio's offence:

> Would the Duke that is absent have done this? Ere he would have hanged a man for the getting a hundred Bastards, he would have paide for the Nursing a thousand . . .

In another example of this play's finely calculated timing, we then learn that Lucio has fathered a son he did not want and refused to support. In referring to *hanging*, his protest suggests that he is thinking of what the law may yet do to *him:* as a gentleman Claudio is to be beheaded, but Lucio's slip is instructive in the Freudian way—this is Vienna, after all.

Although the decent, compassionate Provost tells the Duke that Claudio is to be executed for having 'got' a child, we do also hear him ruefully reflecting that 'all Ages smack of this vice, and he/ To die for't' (2.2.5–6), and here 'vice' seems to refer to illicit sex. The (moral) 'vice' is a necessary condition of the (legal) offence, but Claudio is sentenced not for yielding to natural passion but for the unplanned consequence of that passion. It is easy to see why the sternly chaste Isabella is not concerned with such distinctions: her first words to Angelo show that she is content to believe that a law which punishes the 'vice' she 'abhors' (as a sin) is indeed 'just'. Yet she does not make the mistake of those critics who think that Claudio's 'contract' makes all the difference, and therefore cannot understand why Isabella does not mention it to Angelo. The contract is legally irrelevant, first because Claudio is condemned 'for getting Madam Julietta with child' and not for fornication *per se*, and secondly because the law makes this offence a matter of strict responsibility, admitting neither mitigation nor excuse. Isabella can only plead for mercy, and beg Angelo to bend the law.

But here we may notice that the Provost's loose use of the word 'for' suggests how moral and compassionate considerations enter in two ways. They enter first, precisely because the 'strict statute' (like all strict liability sentencing) specifically excludes them: that is the legal force of the word 'strict'. The justifying arguments for such strictness may be good, or even compelling: in this play they turn on the assumed gravity of the 'Vienna-problem'; in *Billy Budd* they turn on the war and the continuing threat of mutiny; in modern English law a shopkeeper who unwittingly sells adulterated milk is sentenced as a criminal because, once again, it is argued that the need to protect society outweighs the ethical requirement that justice be shown to the individual. Unlike Lucio or Pompey, the Provost never disputes that such laws are 'needfull'; we first see him in the act of enforcing this law. And yet, like Escalus and unlike Angelo, he is morally troubled by the conflict between legal and ethical justice. Moreover—and here moral and compassionate considerations enter by another route—he is deeply troubled by the extreme and irrevocable penalty attached to Claudio's case. Given the naturalness of the passions which led to (although they do not constitute) the offence, such extremism is appalling: 'all Ages smack of this vice, and he/ To die for't.'

None the less, although such moral and compassionate considerations provide a basis for objecting to the refusal to allow any pleas of mitigation or excuse, they do not establish any *legal* injustice. As governor, Angelo is not obliged to consider such arguments; as a man, he is not disposed to. The moral and compassionate arguments do not meet that argument which we hear from the Duke in 1.3 and from Angelo in 2.2, that there are pressingly urgent social reasons for enforcing the strict statutes. And here it should be emphasised that the particular statute which triggers the main action is only one part of a menacing judicial package. In the general alarm of the second scene we also learn that brothels are being pulled down, and we hear of other 'proclamations'. In the third scene the Duke admits that he has 'impos'd' on Angelo the task of enforcing *various* 'strict Statutes, and most biting Laws'. In the fifth scene we hear Escalus warning Pompey of the 'pretty orders beginning', in which it is 'but heading and hanging'. In dramatic terms, the specific statute which condemns Claudio focuses our response to, and in this sense stands for, what is evidently a far more comprehensive attempt to enforce morality by law. But if we actually assume that Claudio is sentenced *for* fornication, and in effect consider the specific statute as though it were the whole judicial package, a host of difficulties arise. Critics and editors do make that assumption, and then argue at length about whether these difficulties are minor, considerable, or ruinous. If, on the other hand, we suppose that Shakespeare's exposition tells us what we immediately need to know about this very specific statute, these difficulties appear to have been imported. Let us quickly review them.

There is no 'textual anomaly' in 1.2, and no need to posit textual corruption, revision, or the hand of another dramatist. Nor is there any puzzle about why, when the play starts, this specific law 'falls' only on Claudio, since he is the only man who is known to have broken it. The fact that Isabella never presents Angelo with an argument about the 'contract' ceases to be troubling since, quite apart from the fact that she is disposed, like Angelo, to condemn fornication *per se*, the argument would be legally irrelevant and inadmissible. Much of the discussion of this play's 'contracts' is seen to be distracting: at the end of the play Lucio is forced to marry the woman 'whom he begot with childe' because he fathered a bastard son, not because there was a 'contract'; and in Angelo's case the 'contract' with Mariana underlines the *difference* between legal and moral obligations. When the Duke so easily persuades Mariana and Isabella to assist with his plan, we need not suppose that they are all conniving to break that very law which condemned Claudio, since his legal offence presupposed, but does not consist in, fornication. It remains absurd for the Duke to lecture Julietta on her 'sin' just before he assures Mariana that it is 'no sin' to sleep with a man who neither loves her nor wants to marry her; but that beautifully pointed irony tells against the Duke and is a 'difficulty'—an insuperable difficulty, I think—only for those critics who suppose that we should admire the Duke's unprincipled and compromised benevolence.

Moreover, this suggests why Shakespeare was unwilling to take over the unhelpfully far-fetched statute in *Promos and Cassandra*. A law which makes fornication a capital offence could be justified only by the religious extremist's argument that an absolute sin should be treated as a capital crime; this would make Shakespeare's Vienna as remote as the Ayatollah Khomeini's Iran. But a statute which punishes fathers who have shown no intention of legitimising and maintaining their offspring is very much less arbitrary and unenforceable; it is customarily agreed, now as in Shakespeare's time, that this is an area in which the law is properly and necessarily concerned. Lucio's timely revelations in 3.2 underline this: unmarried mothers and their offspring need maintenance and support, and here we see why Shakespeare's revision of the story introduces *two* illegitimate infants. To make Claudio's (and Lucio's) offence capital is brutally severe, of course, and does not help the mother or child. But sentencing is a logically distinct part of the judicial process, and the justifying argument for such severity turns on the assumption that

Vienna's state makes it 'needfull'—not on an insanely extreme religious argument. And the severity of the sentence is intended to have a deterrent effect: this is why Angelo gives that 'special' order to parade the sentenced Claudio—and we learn that the worried Lucio has changed his diet!

Having given this heretical argument about the statute its head, I shall admit to being unsure at what point, if any, it seems over-ingenious or over-literal. To be sure, it offends against received assumptions; but this, although it is a serious objection, need not be conclusive. Although it may seem immodest to say so, I am more swayed by a 'genetic' consideration: the controversial interpretation of the statute's content was something which presented itself only at a late and relatively uninfluential stage of my thinking about the play, and seemed the startling but logical consequence of two more general conclusions. For this reason, it seemed best to hold back the discussion of the statute until the end of this chapter; I shall conclude by offering these two less provoking conclusions, while referring the most controversial issue to the reader's judgement.

The first is that that very distinction between necessary and sufficient conditions which I may seem to have been driving too hard had already been forced, but in the opposite direction—by all those discussions of the play which assume, as though it were obvious from the second scene on, that Claudio is sentenced to death for fornication *per se*, not 'for getting Madam Julietta with child'. This, I suggest, is partly the result of not attending to the process of the play's unfolding, as it releases information from scene to scene, and partly the consequence of a blurring assimilation: although there is indeed a sense in which the statute which condemns Claudio 'stands for' all those 'strict Statutes' and 'most biting Laws' which the Duke wants Angelo to enforce, the particular statute which triggers the main action is still only one part of the menacing judicial package.

The second is that Julietta's pregnancy matters profoundly in the play's imagery. The play bristles with stark antitheses involving birth and death, and the engendering or taking of life. Even where other words might have served the prosaic sense and situation, we find images of conception, pregnancy and birth. Angelo and Escalus debate a 'very pregnant' point

(2.1.23). The Duke talks of 'fine issues' (1.1.37) and 'bring-ings-forth' (3.2.135); he tells Isabella that Mariana's brother 'miscarried at sea' (3.1.205), and tells Julietta that she *carries* a 'sin of heavier kinde'—which prompts her ambiguous affirmation that she will 'beare the shame most patiently' (2.3.19–28). One of the Duke's more obscure asides, on vice's 'quick celeritie', can only be unravelled if we pick up the underlying idea of propagation (4.2.107–11). Claudio is determined to 'encounter darkness as a bride', before his natural love of life reasserts itself in the terror of death (3.1.183). Angelo considers what his sense 'breeds' (2.1.144) and is horrified by the 'strong and swelling evil of my concep-tion' (2.4.6–7); he fears that his own crime 'unshapes me' and 'makes me unpregnant' (4.4.18), while trying to assure himself that his authority still 'bears credent bulk'. In an extraordinary speech which loses much of its point if we do not see how it refers to Claudio's offence, he also speaks of evils which are 'conceiv'd', 'hatch'd' and 'borne' (2.2.97–8). In another difficult but revealing passage he observes that women, like 'glasses' or mirrors, 'make forms', while men— forms made in God's likeness—'their creation mar/ In profiting by them' (2.4.125–7). In this speech the 'profiting' involves sexual exploitation but also plays on the idea of forging—just as Angelo's name reminds us that he is (by now) heaven's counterfeit image, an angel with horns, a coin that has been tested and found wanting. This is not an exhaustive list of examples, but it sufficiently suggests how the statute which condemns Claudio to death for getting a maid with child connects with the poetic drama's central nervous system.

In yet another speech which shows the *poetic* appropriate-ness of launching the play's main action through a statute which makes the illegitimate engendering of life a crime punished by death, Angelo explains why he cannot pardon Claudio:

> it were as good
> To pardon him, that hath from nature stolne
> A man already made, as to remit
> Their sawcie sweetnes, that do coyne heavens Image
> In stamps that are forbid . . .
>
> (2.3.42–6)

This shows why forging and pregnancy are closely associated in the image clusters. Angelo's coining metaphor compares the forging of counterfeit currency with the creation of new life: the one involves the illegal counterfeiting of the King's image or stamp, while the other involves the illicit production of 'heavens Image'—that is, of man as God's image. And since the metaphor also compares illicit creation with murder, this passage also suggests what prompted Shakespeare to invent Barnardine. The 'sawcie sweetnes' of extra-marital intercourse is incidental to the powerful paradox of punishing illegal procreation with legal murder: the Law is doubly at odds with Nature, in making the consequence of a natural act a crime punished by an unnatural act. That paradox reappears when Isabella insists to the disguised Duke, 'I had rather my brother dies by the law, than my son should be unlawfully born' (3.1.198).

These image clusters remind us that, here as elsewhere, Shakespeare thinks through his images, which carry thought and feeling. In responding to them, we *apprehend* a peculiarly rich, complex and vivid mode of thinking. If we are also trying to *comprehend* their import, we may reflect that these image clusters depend for their force upon that plot-innovation in which Shakespeare himself created Claudio's child, and Lucio's.

SIX

Imaginative Openness and the *Macbeth*-Terror

> The artist is responsible for everything that happens in his work—and not just in the sense that it is done, but in the sense that is *meant*. It is a terrible responsibility; very few men have the gift and the patience to shoulder it. But it is all the more terrible, when it is shouldered, not to appreciate it, to refuse to understand something meant so well.
>
> Stanley Cavell, *Must We Mean What We Say?*

Is *Macbeth* frightening?

A wit once remarked that we are all born originals, and become imitations. 'Eng. Lit.' has much to answer for if, as I suspect, it teaches us how to make trifles even of *Macbeth*'s terrors. After thirty years, I still remember my own fright when, as an eight-year-old boy in Brazil, I first encountered these lines from the bleeding Captain's speech:

> For brave *Macbeth* (well hee deserves that Name)
> Disdayning Fortune, with his brandisht Steele,
> Which smoak'd with bloody execution
> (Like Valours Minion), carv'd out his passage,
> Till he fac'd the Slave:
> Which nev'r shook hands, nor bad farewell to him,
> Till he unseam'd him from the Nave to th'Chops,
> And fix'd his Head upon our Battlements.
>
> (1.2.16–23)

My measureless fright at the idea of a *smoking, unseaming* sword was followed by a measure of incredulity when I came to Duncan's response: 'O valiant Cousin, worthy Gentleman'. *Gentle*man? Was the King of Scotland *listening*?

219

Scotland was then no more than a name, but became an infinitely imaginative territory or country of the mind. Years later, 'doing' English in an English school provided me with the familiar kind of explanation of what the inattentive Duncan really 'represents', and of what Killing the King consequently meant, in England, Scotland or anywhere else:

> The holy King who represents the stable decencies of the traditional sovereignty; his murderer who is forced to rule with blood and iron, proceeding from enormity to enormity; the eventual mustering of the powers of outraged pity and justice; their return and the overthrow of the ungodly rule—this is also the shape of the first chronicle tetralogy.

That representative passage appears in John Danby's *Shakespeare's Doctrine of Nature* (161). True, Danby does go on to add that this reassuring 'formal outline' is complicated by Shakespeare's concern 'not only with the evil man's impact on the world, but also with the manner and process of his entry into evil':

> So we see Macbeth at first almost equally poised (as anyone might be) between the good and the bad . . . We then see how, his reason having been hypnotized by the fortune-telling witches, he leads his will to the foretold event, and catches the nearest way. (161–2)

Yet this still suggests that the terrors of *Macbeth* are contained within a reassuringly firm moral framework.

Although we might, after an abstracting moral effort, see Macbeth in this way, our first dramatic impression is of a man of terrifying power and courage, such as not 'anyone' might have. We hear reports of an *un*poised, unseemly unseamer who is commended for being

> Nothing afeard of what thyself didst make:
> Strange Images of death . . .
>
> (1.3.96–7)

We then hear Macbeth himself revealing that he is indeed 'afeard'—terrified by one particular 'horrid Image', which unfixes his hair, sets his seated heart knocking at his ribs, and makes him find his 'Present Feares' only less 'horrible' than his 'Imaginings' (1.3.134–7). Once we have been admitted to Macbeth's convulsed consciousness, nothing could seem further from the truth than Duncan's imperturbable fancy (which Rosse merely reports) that this man is 'Nothing afeard'.

This adds to our difficulties if we are making another abstracting effort to see Duncan as the 'holy King'. Once again, our first, unmediated impressions are difficult to fit into a formal framework. We see an elderly, anxious noncombatant, waiting on the outskirts of a battlefield, and greedy for the uncertain, infrequent reports of what is happening in that second Golgotha which Macbeth is memorising. We hear Duncan trying to impose some moral order on the ghastly reports; he is in this sense the first of *Macbeth*'s providentialist critics.

So, Duncan transforms the terrifying, terrified unseamer into a 'worthy Gentleman', while regretting that he was not more perceptive about the *first* Thane of Cawdor; and he sees the Captain's reeking 'gashes' as decorations which 'become' him and 'smack of Honour', like his 'words'. As loyal subjects, the Captain and Rosse do indeed search for words which smack of honour. As has often been remarked, the Captain's description of a 'doubtfull' conflict between 'two spent Swimmers' who 'cling together, And choake their Art' makes the two men seem indistinguishable, while his attempt to provide a distinction by calling one 'mercilesse' and the other 'brave' is itself exposed by the interchangeability of these adjectives: it is hard to think the unseamer more merciful than the man he unseams. Just before he faints, the Captain's effort to edit horror is abandoned, and he speaks of an impression which is all the more nightmarish for being logically and syntactically uncertain:

> Except they meant to bathe in reeking Wounds
> Or memorize another *Golgotha*
> I cannot tell . . .

> (1.2.40–2)

Rosse describes yet another 'dismall Conflict' in which the effort to distinguish two men who confront each other with 'selfe-comparisons', 'Point against Point', again accentuates the uncertainty of the distinction. The outcome of these 'doubtfull' conflicts appears to depend on chance and

Macbeth's Might, *not* on Right or providential powers. Nothing dismayed, Duncan edits Rosse's report—'Great happinesse'—and promptly declares Macbeth Thane of Cawdor!

I doubt whether even the most strenuous abstracting effort could discover any sign, in these scenes, of Danby's 'stable decencies of the traditional sovereignty'. The 'common weal' is not present, even as a memory, nor does Macbeth's later retrospective account of Duncan's reign suggest that things were ever very different:

> *Duncane* is in his Grave:
> After Lifes fitfull Fever, he sleepes well,
> Treason has done his worst: nor Steele, nor Poyson,
> Mallice domestique, forraine Levie, nothing,
> Can touch him further.
>
> (3.2.22–6)

In the opening scenes the 'multiplying Villanies' are everywhere in evidence; but Order is not. From every seeming comfort 'Discomfort swells'. Acts of appalling savagery obliterate any steadying, sustaining sense of the values which are ostensibly being defended. Attempts to provide a moral framework seem inadequate to the horrifying realities they edit: the 'words' and moral concepts smack of honour, but melt into the miasma of fog, filth and reeking blood. But then, if this is so, why should so scrupulously attentive a critic as A. P. Rossiter refer to 'the breakdown of ordered nature' which is 'released by Duncan's murder' (221)? How could we speak of a 'breakdown' which is only 'released' in the second act, when the play *starts* with 'another *Golgotha*', in which Nature's multiplying villainies are already swarming?

The strange thing is that we do indeed have an impression of something being 'released' through Duncan's murder— even though this 'Scotland' has afforded no strong impression of 'ordered nature', and 'disorder' would be a tame word for the initial havoc. There is a concurrence of impressions which are—on any more detached, comfortably retrospective view—incompatible. That Thing which is most obviously 'released' is the 'horrid Image' which has hitherto possessed Macbeth's imagination—to the extent that 'Nothing is, but what is not' (1.3.141): this Macbeth releases, or exorcises, by discharging it from his head into the world, like some monstrous birth. Until he has done this he has force but no drive; his asides and soliloquies show him dreaming an uninterrupted, unmanning nightmare while the rest of the play goes on elsewhere. And yet as soon as we ask where this 'horrid Image' comes *from*, we confront another set of concurrent, conflicting impressions.

One answer, the most familiar, is that the witches ensnare Macbeth and impregnate his mind. The guilty fearful 'start' which Banquo observes marks this moment of conception, like Leda's shudder in the loins. On this view the witches are firmly 'placed'—as Satanic instruments of darkness. Good and Evil are opposed, as antithetical conceptual abstractions, which then buttress that analogic 'world picture' in which the little state of man is an inseparable part of an all-encompassing moral and spiritual order. 'Faire is foule, and foule is faire' (1.1.10) thus represents a sinful attempt to reverse the natural, divinely ordained hierarchy of values—while providing (like Satan's 'Evil be thou my Good' in *Paradise Lost*) an indirectly reassuring *confirmation* of that hierarchy's natural and supra-natural reality. We know where we are, and most accounts of *Macbeth* show that assurance. L. C. Knights refers to 'the main theme of the reversal of values', and assures us that *Macbeth*'s 'pattern is far easier to grasp than that of *Lear*' (1959:122).

Yet 'Faire is foule' is ambiguous. Instead of providing an indirect confirmation of the conceptual abstractions it may assert their *unreality*, in relation to the elemental 'Hurley-burley' (that word suggests amoral Chaos rather than immoral Evil), and to the obscene, elemental savagery of battles which are (in a comparably ambiguous way) 'lost and wonne' (1.1.4). For Satanic instruments in a Christian universe, these weird sisters seem curiously capricious and infantile, hardly less concerned with pilots and chestnuts than with Macbeth and Scotland. Such nursery horrors would not be so alarming if they were not associated with the concretely savage but morally indefinite 'Hurley-burley'. What bears in on us in the opening scenes is something terrifyingly inchoate—a violent reality of which Macbeth is already part, but of which Duncan seems to know little or nothing.

In the first, reassuring account Banquo becomes the Good Man who successfully resists temptation. His dramatic function is to establish Macbeth's damnable guilt by contrast—rather as Milton invented Abdiel in order to 'establish' (with the methodological resourcefulness of a Stalinist historian) that if *one* fallen angel can see through Satan's specious logic then God is justified in withholding his otherwise infinite mercy from all the others.

Yet we may also notice how the *Macbeth*-terror affects Banquo. His fear of those 'cursed thoughts that Nature Gives way to in repose' will keep him from his bed (2.1.8–9). After Duncan's murder he stirringly affirms that he stands 'in the great Hand of God' and is ready to fight 'undivulg'd pretence' (2.3.129–30); but he prudently chooses not to divulge what he knows, and soon declares himself 'knit' to this new king by a 'most indissoluble tye' (3.1.17–18). Indeed, if the conventional, providential-moralistic readings of *Macbeth* have not persuaded us to accept the abstract and schematic notion that Banquo represents the Good Man, we might even think that those strong, inward moral promptings which Lady Macbeth so fears in her husband's 'Nature' are altogether beyond the range of the prudential Banquo. The Christian providentialist accounts tend to *flatten out* Banquo's character. And not only Banquo's: I shall return to this point.

I am not wanting to suggest that such accounts *import* the suggestions of an all-encompassing order; nor am I wanting to argue that the play denies that any such order exists. The suggestions appear in the play, where they correspond with human hopes and fears—not with theological and ideological certitudes. In *Macbeth* as in *Lear*, the vividly apprehended reality of these pressing *human* needs and aspirations does not of itself guarantee the existence of a corresponding moral and spiritual order; it may leave man all the more terrifyingly 'unaccommodated'. *Macbeth* terrifies, not by denying the existence of 'order' in some dogmatically sceptical or nihilistic way, but by making its reality so alarmingly uncertain.

This appears, for example, if we consider how Banquo's wry comment that 'There's Husbandry in Heaven' (2.1.4) applies to the way in which the two 'worlds' or 'halves' of Nature figure in the play as a whole. Banquo's joke is a grim one, not unlike Woody Allen's description of God as an 'under-achiever'. And in *Macbeth* the world of 'seeling Night' is everywhere present and frighteningly palpable: it envelops and smothers us, like Hopkins' 'fell of dark, not day'. In contrast, the world of Day is longed for but rarely seen, either before or after Duncan's murder; a typical image like 'Scarfe up the tender Eye of pitifull Day' (3.2.47) makes Day itself seem Duncan-like in its frailty and wincing vulnerability. In conceptual terms, the opposition between a world of Day and a world of Night or between two halves of Nature promises a degree of clarity, like the opposition between Good and Evil. As has often been remarked, the suggestion that these opposed forces are equal is not very sound in the terms of Christian theology, and rather recalls Manichaean or Zoroastrian conflicts between the powers of Light and Darkness. But it seems more important to notice the disparity between the *conceptual* clarity such oppositions seem to promise, and the *experiential* uncertainty the play provokes. It is as if the play set its own moral categories adrift on the wild and violent sea—inviting us to distinguish between the two Thanes of Cawdor, or to see the weird sisters as Satanic instruments and Banquo as the man in the Hand of God, while it undermines these very distinctions.

'So faire and foule a day I have not seene' (1.3.38): Macbeth's first words do nothing to resolve this uncertainty. To be sure, a rational and reassuring explanation is available: the victory is fair, the weather Scottish. But the echo of the weird sisters' equivocal words also prompts an identification, even before Macbeth has seen them or heard their prophecies. Lady Macbeth's first speech reveals that Macbeth's 'Ambition' to be 'great' is nothing new, but that he has *hitherto* made her fear that his 'Nature' is 'too full o'th'Milke of humane kindnesse' (1.5.13–14):

> What thou would'st highly,
> That thou would'st holily: would'st not play false,
> And yet would'st wrongly winne.
>
> (17–19)

But this too increases our uncertainty, by making that question Macbeth asks himself seem all the more pressing:

Why doe I yeeld to that suggestion,
Whose horrid Image doth unfixe my Heire,
And make my seated Heart knock at my Ribbes,
Against the use of Nature?

(1.3.134–7)

Even as he asks this, Macbeth recognises that the 'supernaturall solliciting . . . cannot be good'. Banquo's prudential perspicacity is certainly not beyond the range of the Macbeth who goes on to reflect that if Chance will have him King it may crown him without his stir (142–3). So why is Macbeth yielding now, and observing his yielding with such fascinated horror, as if intent observation might supply an answer to his question?

Most critics of *Macbeth* ask that question, of course; what is strange is that the difficulty or impossibility of answering it is not seen as a major obstacle to all those readings in which, as Wilbur Sanders observes, 'evil is *somehow* subordinated to the good and the natural, and the military victory of Malcolm's forces is seen as the *elimination* of the *Macbeth-evil*'. After quoting the same speech, L. C. Knights observes that 'This is temptation, presented with concrete force'; but his answer to Macbeth's question is, in effect, that Macbeth should have known better. He *did* know better: that is exactly what worries his wife. What his speech presents with 'concrete force' is a moral and psychic confusion which we share, in not knowing to what extent the prophecies account for the strengthened 'temptation' or Macbeth's diminished power to resist it. In *The Dramatist and the Received Idea* (which contains what I take to be the most searching of all critical discussions of *Macbeth*) Wilbur Sanders observes:

The very predictions seem to presuppose the effect they will have on Macbeth—as if a deterministic net has been cast over the whole action. Yet Macbeth proceeds, with every appearance of freedom, to draw the *un*necessary conclusion from the prophecies: that chance will *not* crown him without his stir. (280)

And here we may recall that when Macbeth invokes 'Fate' (3.1.70) and tries to have Fleance killed, he apparently believes that the future is *not* pre-ordained. His attitude to the prophecies is unstable and uncertain, nor is it clear what, if anything, the witches implant in his mind. The 'Ambition'

was already there, and the 'horrid Image' seems very like
one of those 'strange Images of death' which Macbeth is
commended for 'making'—while serving King and Country
on the battlefield. After the battle, the witches set out to
'meet with' the man who is hero of the hour and saviour of
Scotland.

Here we might ponder another suggestion which the play
includes, and which, although it is consonant with the
repeated suggestion that 'Blood will have Blood' (3.4.122)
and with what we know of the psychologically unhinging
effect of prolonged savage combat, also cuts across any simple
moral framework. Macbeth is already steeped in blood: he
has bathed in it, become Bellona's bridegroom, memorised
another Golgotha, and been initiated into those obscene
reeking realities which Duncan edits or disregards. Duncan's
imagery of planting and growing draws on, and as it were
cherishes, those beneficent aspects of a Nature which is not
alien, indifferent or hostile to man. Nor is he exposed to the
engulfing horrors of the 'Hurley-burley'. But Macbeth is.
The descriptions of his brave defence of the realm and its
values also include the hints of unholy initiation, symbolic
marriage, foul rituals and baptism in blood. The King sends
for his worthy gentleman, while the weird sisters set out to
meet Bellona's bridegroom, as a familiar.

Here once again is that duplicity or multiplicity, that
concurrence of contradictory impressions which characterises
the play and makes *us* feel that

> we feare, yet know not what we feare,
> But floate upon a wilde and violent Sea
> Each way, and move.

(4.2.20–2)

The play presents us with a Macbeth who, as in the providentialist readings, shows a progressive dehumanising deterio-
ration; it also shows Macbeth growing in stature, as Nietzsche, appropriately enough, seems to have been the first to
remark (in *Daybreak*, 4.240), and as Lascelles Abercrombie,
Wilson Knight and Wilbur Sanders have more recently
argued. In his final speech Malcolm dismisses the inhuman
'butcher' (5.8.69). Yet in the battles of the first act (which

were too much for Malcolm, who had to be rescued, and then stayed in safety with his father) Macbeth's skill in carving and unseaming brought Honours and Golden Opinions. What should establish the difference between the butchers of the first and last acts is some nicely firm sense of the values which Macbeth first represents and then subverts. But the butcher of the first act cannot give any imaginative credence to those values: they have been displaced by the 'horrid Image' and the 'strange Images of death' which he himself makes. And here, if we feel that Duncan's moral categories seem smaller and more fragile than the terrors they have to order and contain, the play implicates us: we don't feel and rejoice in a holy King's 'Great happinesse', because our responses are preparing us to follow Macbeth into the heart of darkness.

Of course, this is at odds with Knights' view that Malcolm's final speech provides

> a fitting close for a play in which moral law has been made present to us not as convention or command but as the law of life itself, as that which makes for life, and through which alone man can ground himself on, and therefore in some measure know, reality. (141)

And many critics have fastened on the suggestion of providential Nemesis in Malcolm's declaration that Macbeth

> Is ripe for shaking, and the Powers above
> Put on their instruments . . .
>
> (4.3.238–9)

as though this sufficiently confirms the existence, and deep concern, of such Powers. But when Malcolm announced, a moment earlier, that 'our power is ready' (236), he was referring to those earthly, and largely English, powers for which he has prudently waited, as Macbeth ripens. Earlier still, he expressed a more tentative hope:

> Now wee'l together, and the chance of goodnesse
> Be like our warranted Quarrell.
>
> (136–7)

Of course, the reiterated seasonal imagery, and the hopeful

evocations of outraged natural order, have an effect; but their effect is not to establish the supra-human, supra-dramatic reality of the 'Powers above'. In 5.4 both Macduff and old Siward warn Malcolm of the dangers of optimism; as old Siward says, 'certaine issue, stroakes must arbitrate' (20). Of course we feel the symbolic felicitousness of the moving wood, and of the fancy that Nature itself is rising against Macbeth—but it is not. Men are carrying the branches, and the battle's outcome depends on a man-to-man combat between Macbeth and the vengeful Macduff. That is why 'So great a day as this is cheaply bought', as old Siward says— suddenly yielding to optimism, before he is shown his dead son.

A feeling that we have been here before is what we must stifle, if we are to share in L. C. Knights' great happiness. Macduff's longing to confront Macbeth 'Front to Front' (4.3.232) disconcertingly recalls the earlier 'Point against Point' confrontation between the first and second Cawdors. Although Shakespeare has no occasion to mention Donalbain's future role as the murderer of Malcolm's son, we know that the throne must pass, somehow, to Fleance. We hear Malcolm making strategic promises, just like his father, that the next Honours list will 'reckon with your severall loves, And make us even' (5.8.61–2).

Another echo is still more ominous. When Malcolm dismisses Macbeth and Lady Macbeth as 'this dead Butcher, and his Fiend-like Queene', this attempt to reduce human complexities to starkly simple categories should produce both a tremor of protest (Macbeth was more than that) and a tremor of premonitory alarm. Here the obvious parallel is with the first Thane of Cawdor, who was first seen as a 'Gentleman' on whom Duncan could build 'an absolute Trust', and then became 'that most disloyall Traytor', and finally managed to die so that it *seemed* that 'Nothing in his Life became him, Like the leaving it'. In each case the moral categories are imposed on and (in their awkward discontinuity) exposed to the actual unfathomability of the first Thane. One thing 'became' him, another did not, and the word *become* is in this play regularly associated with appearances, which are deceptive. Macbeth was concerned with what *becomes* a man, and wanted to *wear* his latest Honours and 'Golden Opinions' in 'their newest glosse' (1.7.33–4). 'There's no Art, to finde the Mindes construction in the Face', but Malcolm trusts his art and his categorising terms—unlike Macduff who, when he finally confronts Macbeth, calls him a bloodier villain than 'tearmes can give thee out' (5.7.7–8). Like his father, Malcolm must rely on reports, and observes that the 'Fiend-like Queene' committed suicide—'(as 'tis thought)'; but fiends *do not* commit suicide. Malcolm must also rely on the force of Macduff's arm to secure his realm, as his father depended on his unseamer— and does our sense of the poetic inevitability of Macduff's victory over Macbeth altogether exclude a suspicion that the outcome of this later point against point conflict might have been different, if Macbeth were not unmanned by his superstition?

The play ends, as it begins, with a battery of opposed impressions. There is indeed a strong sense of closure, of an inevitable process working itself out; there are also the various unnerving suggestions that the satisfying idea of a re-established natural order may prove to be yet another Seeming comfort, from which Discomfort will swell.

The interpretative leap

I have so far been trying to suggest why *Macbeth* is frightening, while the play most critics describe is not. Here I need to make a disagreeable suggestion, before producing my excuse for thinking that it may be helpful, not merely self-betraying. It often happens that when critics speak of what we may *learn* from a work of art the lesson in question sounds all too familiar, while the critic sounds more like a tired but dutiful museum guide than like a man who has been startled into new knowledge. But if even very good critics like Knights and Leavis discuss *Macbeth* in ways which prompt this disagreeable and hubristic reflection, might that tell us something about the *kind* of imaginative challenge which *Macbeth* presents?

Here, for example, is Knights:

Clearly then we have in this play an answer to Shakespeare's earlier

questionings about time's power, as we have also a resolution of his
earlier preoccupation with the power of illusion and false appearance.
Macbeth *has betrayed himself* to the equivocal and the illusory. So too
time appears to him as meaningless repetition because he has turned his
back on, has indeed attempted violence on, those values that alone give
significance to duration, that in a certain sense make time. (141)

One effect of this passage is to seal off that whole area of
imaginative doubt about the nature of Nature and Value
which I considered in Chapter 1. Knights' confident reference
to 'those values that alone give significance' posits values with
an agreed, external and objective reality: they are 'out there'
to be 'read off', so that it seems a pity that nobody took the
trouble to explain this to Macbeth or Hamlet—not to
mention poor Kleist, Nietzsche or Montaigne. And when
Knights explains where he locates these values, and why
Macbeth fails to do so, we should watch the critic's own
language closely. Apparently, even as Macbeth watches
himself yielding, he fails to see how his own 'words do not
only point inward . . . but, as it were, outward to the play
as a whole' and to those 'major themes' which 'emerge as
themes because they are what the poetry—reinforced by
action and symbolism—again and again insists on' (121).
The gap between 'inward' and 'outward' is negotiated by a
rhetorically conspicuous shift, from the tentative 'as it were'
to the assertive 'again and again insists on'.

In that pregnant sentence from 'Tragedy and the
"Medium" ' which I quoted in Chapter 1, Leavis sounds
very alive to the fundamental 'challenge' he addresses; and
yet he too speaks, like Knights, of things which 'give' life
value:

> It is as if we were challenged at the profoundest level with the question
> "In what does the significance of life reside?", and found ourselves
> contemplating, for answer, a view of life and of the things giving it
> value, that makes the valued appear unquestionably more important to
> the valuer, so that significance lies, clearly and inescapably, in the willing
> adhesion of the individual self to something other than itself.

This provides a valuable way into *Macbeth*, which Leavis
goes on to discuss. But the sentence also equivocates in a
subtle and instructive way, since it is very hard to see what

force 'as if' and 'appear' are to have, in relation to what is then seen as being 'clear' and 'inescapable'.

It is obvious that the value of the valued may seem inescapably clear to the valuer—to Othello, for example, or to Mark Antony when he rejects the absolute values of Rome and proclaims, before kissing Cleopatra, that the 'Noblenesse of life' is 'to do thus'. But Leavis is evidently concerned with a 'significance' which may also be 'clear' to our 'contemplating' selves. This 'significance' is neither a demonstrably self-evident and constantly apprehended truth nor a mere illusion into which we sometimes sink: rather, it is a 'view of life' to which we may rise—when we are in the grip of the greatest works of art, and feel ourselves 'challenged at the profoundest level'.

Perhaps inadvertently, the sentence implies two quite different accounts of value, without confronting the possibility of a collision like that Shakespeare explores in *Troylus and Cressida*. For in asking what the significance of life resides *in*, and then referring to 'things' which 'give' it value, the first part of Leavis's sentence implies that values are inherent in the valued and independent of the valuer. This, as we have seen, was Hector's position when he tried to deflect the force of Troylus's question 'What's aught, but as 'tis valew'd?' by arguing that 'value dwels not in particular will'. And of course Hector wants to have it both ways: a value he values is 'precious of it selfe' as well as precious to the 'prizer', whereas a value he does not countenance only seems precious to those who make 'the service greater than the God'. In this way Hector both protests against and unwittingly illustrates our human readiness to accord our values the status of objective values.

But then the last part of Leavis's sentence locates 'significance' within the act of valuing—not, that is, in the 'things' which give life value, but rather in 'the willing adhesion of the individual self to something other than itself'. For all the felicitousness of the formulation, it seems in danger of disregarding Hector's warning about the dangers of the doting or idolatrous will. To locate significance in the 'willing adhesion', without consideration of whatever it is to which the individual self adheres, is to make the service greater than the god. I am reminded of Kierkegaard's argument that 'An

apostle has no other proof but his own assertation, and at
the most by his willingness to suffer everything for the sake
of the doctrine'; and Leavis's sentence might suddenly seem
very shocking if we were to think of the young Nazis' 'willing
adhesion of the individual self to something other than itself'
in Leni Riefenstahl's *The Triumph of the Will*.

It is less difficult to see how a reading of *Macbeth*, with
which Leavis is immediately concerned, might very well
encourage us to locate 'significance' within the distinctively
human *need* to endow life with significance and value, and
in the corresponding human capacity for ego-transcending,
morally and imaginatively constructive acts of self-commitment which answer to the urgently apprehended need.
Macbeth feels that need but refuses to give it imaginative
credence. Like the Coriolanus who declares

> Ile never
> Be such a Gosling to obey instinct: but stand
> As if a man were Author of himself
> And knew no other kin . . .
>
> (5.3.34–7)

Macbeth denies and suppresses those promptings of his own
nature which make his wife speak of the milk of human
kindness; and the result of the self-mutilation is catastrophic.
Leavis's essay seems to promise an 'existential' account of
Macbeth which could acknowledge, without being defeated
by, that gap between 'inward' and 'outward'. Instead, just
like Knights, he *externalises* Macbeth's inner promptings by
making them correspond with an 'order' which Macbeth
subverts:

> He has confounded 'this little state of man' and the impersonal order
> from which it is inseparable . . . his valedictory nihilism is the vindi-
> cation of the moral and spiritual order he has outraged, and which is
> re-established in the close. (122)

It is one thing to say that Macbeth shows a 'fatal ignorance'
of his own nature (250), but can we also say, and say so
confidently, that he fails to perceive the world—his world—
as it really is? It is one thing to suppose that Macbeth's
actions are inevitably self-destructive because he is the man

he is; but has anybody ever supposed that some reassuringly inevitable process will ensure that the men who butcher Banquo or Macduff's family feel a corresponding mental agony?

Some remarks which Gustav Janouch attributed to Kafka, in his somewhat unreliable memoir, help us to characterise that critical and interpretative leap which Knights and Leavis are making. In discussing an old Czech legend with Janouch, Kafka observed:

> The longing for the divine, the sense of shame at the violation of holiness which always accompanies it, men's innate demand for justice—these are mighty and invincible forces, which grow stronger as men try to oppose them. They exert a moral control. A criminal must therefore suppress these forces in himself before he can commit an objectively criminal act. For that reason, every crime is preceded by a spiritual mutilation. (50)

That Macbeth feels such forces in himself and strives to suppress them, so that his own crime is 'preceded by a spiritual mutilation', is not likely to be disputed. What I think is in dispute is the claim that the play reveals an all-encompassing moral and spiritual order, which exists *outside* Macbeth's tortured consciousness and above or beyond the cataclysmic 'Hurley-burley'. The 'mighty forces' to which Kafka refers are not Divinity and Justice, but the human *longing* for the divine and men's innate *demand* for justice.

Macbeth's great soliloquy in 1.7 testifies to the power of those imaginative needs and moral promptings which 'grow stronger' even as he tries to discount them, or see them as unmanly, womanish fictions. And when, in her own soliloquy, Lady Macbeth says 'Yet doe I feare thy Nature', she does not fear that 'order' which critics invoke: she fears her husband's nature. Macbeth is—as Leavis and almost every critic who writes on the play remarks—'fatally ignorant of his nature'; but this inwardly apprehended truth about Macbeth does not establish the reality of any 'Powres above'; and Macbeth is also the most feeling register, within the play, of that terrifying moral and metaphysical uncertainty which the play also provokes in us.

Knights and Leavis both make what I take to be an unjustified interpretative leap, which closes that intensely troubling gap between the urgently apprehended *inner* need and an *external* order which could contain the Macbeth-terror. We might similarly notice the editor of the New Arden *Macbeth*, Kenneth Muir, briefly alludes to Macbeth's 'Existential "anguish" of choice' (lxi), but devotes much of his critical discussion to an amplification of Danby's 'formal outline'. The play is 'about damnation' (li); Shakespeare presents a 'general antithesis between good and evil' (lii), creates 'a picture of an orderly and well-knit society, in contrast to the disorder consequent upon Macbeth's initial crime', and emphasises the 'naturalness of that order, and the unnaturalness of its violation' (liii). Such a view provides no basis for 'Existential "anguish" ': the moral framework is clear, firm and simple. Macbeth then fails to *see* the 'order' which is evident to the prudential Banquo, the patriotic Macduff, and all those critics who suggest that Macbeth wilfully betrays himself. At the end of Beckett's early story, 'Dante and the Lobster', the lobster disappears into the pot:

It had about thirty seconds to live.
Well, thought Belacqua, it's a quick death, God help us all.
It is not.

After making the interpretative leap to an externalised order, Muir, Knights and even Leavis all report that *Macbeth* is relatively simple. It is not.

I believe that we *want* to make some such leap precisely because the play makes the gap between 'inward' and 'outward' so alarming, and that the leap testifies to the play's imaginative power by trying to deflect it. As I suggested earlier, the critics do not *import* the idea of 'order'; rather, there is a tendency to misrepresent the ways in which we apprehend it within the play. Here we might well think of the way in which Montaigne's essay on custom produces its 'official' conclusion, while at the same time exposing the apparently orthodox submission or genuflection to immensely subversive imaginative energies. What breaks down in Act 2 of *Macbeth* is not the 'ordered Nature' we have never seen, but the basis for human hope and collaborative effort: in this Scotland Duncan is the only possible point of growth, through which higher human aspirations might be realised, and through which life might indeed be endowed with value and significance.

The natural touch: two marriages

Another significant feature of L. C. Knights' account of *Macbeth* could be seen as a paradoxical consequence of his celebrated assault on Bradley's preoccupation with 'character'. In preferring to approach the play as a 'dramatic poem', Knights is surprisingly ready to assume that what is said by one relatively minor charcter has an overriding, supra-dramatic authority, and carries the dramatist's clear *imprimatur* as well as the censor's necessary *non obstat*. Such an assumption is necessary to the interpretative leap; but it also denies the perspectival nature of Shakespeare's poetic drama.

I am of course thinking of Macduff, and of Knights' assumption that Macduff's view of Duncan as the 'Lords anoynted Temple' has a coercive authority which we would not allow, say, to Lady Macbeth's levelling view of Duncan as 'the old man'. Lady Macbeth is speaking in character; but so is Macduff. He is the man whose abstract allegiances to God, King and Country are even stronger than his 'natural' or biological instincts, so that his own abandoned wife bitterly comments that he is *unnatural:* 'He wants the naturall touch' (4.2.9). Macbeth can neither give imaginative credence to Macduff's view of the King as God's quasi-divine represen- tative, nor can he rest with his wife's pointedly unmetaphys- ical view of the King. His instincts are more natural than those of the wife who invites spirits to unsex and denature her; but they are also more 'naturall'—in precisely Lady Macduff's sense—than those of the man who was untimely ripped from his mother's womb and presents himself as Macbeth's timely executioner. Indeed, Lady Macduff is wishing that her husband were more like Macbeth, and that irony will only seem grotesque or gratuitous if we are over- looking Shakespeare's remarkable presentation of the Macbeth's marriage, and the accompanying contrast with the family Macduff.

In certain respects the Macbeths' marriage is normative,

and deeply touching in its essential domesticity. For Macbeth, even an appalling cry of agony can be accompanied by an unthinking acknowledgement of that corner of his mind which is not infected:

O, full of Scorpions is my Minde, deare Wife . . .

'My dearest Love', 'dearest Chuck': the very casualness of such tenderness suggests how much these lovers can afford to take for granted in each other, and testifies to continual reciprocities of feeling—as does the tenderness of Lady Macbeth's breathtakingly simple language in the sleep-walking scene:

Wash your hands, put on your Night-Gowne, looke not
so pale . . .
Come, come, come, come, give me your hand: What's done,
cannot be undone. To bed, to bed, to bed.

(5.1.60 f.)

Such intimacy is magnificently domestic, far removed from the heavens and hells of Grand Passion. In Lady Macbeth's case it is also clear that her collapse is in part the result of the increasing enstrangement we saw her feeling in 3.2 ('why doe you keep alone?'); we might be reminded of Portia in *Julius Caesar*, who could not endure the breakdown of a trust and intimacy she had learned to take for granted.

But the intense bond contains its own solvent, in that preoccupation with manliness which the sleepwalking scene also recalls ('Fye, my Lord, fie, a Souldier, and affear'd?') and which proved so decisive in 1.7. The capacity for affection which Macbeth shows in his relations with his wife is also present in the generosity of his tributes to the gracious Duncan and the royal Banquo; but this potential lifeline to a larger community is severed within the marriage itself, which is at best a refuge or sanctuary, when it is not a campaign headquarters. The Macbeths' marriage neither establishes nor looks for any further connection with a community. Having no metaphysical dimension, repre-senting no morally constructive aspiration, it is never more than—if sometimes not less than—'mating' at its most human and engaging. Macbeth lives vigorously in that 'Chaos' which

Othello feared, and refuses to give credence to that need for value and significance which directed Othello's whole life. For all its attractive, normative aspects, this marriage remains socially, morally and of course literally sterile, providing no vantage from which Macbeth might assess his relations with others or with those parts of his own nature which Duncan would 'plant' and cultivate and which his wife fears. The marriage is in this sense *merely* natural.

As is well known, Shakespeare adjusted his sources to compress the length of Macbeth's reign and to highlight the practical and symbolic issue of childlessness. This was essential to the subtle and elaborate contrast with the Macduffs— I should say contrasts, since Shakespeare contrasts the two men, the two women, and the couples' respective relations with each other and the larger world. For Macbeth, a 'deare Wife' takes precedence over all other allegiances, including those which dictate Macduff's behaviour. Lady Macduff— who is identified in the Folio as 'Macduffes Wife' and then becomes 'Wife'—provides another charged contrast: not only does she complain of her husband's unnaturalness, she is herself altogether *too* natural—so that our distress on her behalf might be expressed through the words she addresses to her poor, doomed son: 'Poore pratler, how thou talk'st' (4.2.63). Two men risk their lives in trying to persuade her to take her children away: 'I pray you schoole your selfe', pleads the desperate Rosse—but she will do nothing but talk, making her son the bewildered receptacle of her paralysing terror, self-pity and resentment:

> . . . He loves us not,
> He wants the naturall touch . . .
> (8–9)
> . . . Sirra, your Father's dead,
> And what will you do now? How will you live?
> (30–1)

This, in its helpless naturalness, is beyond her control or our censure; but we still notice how—like many another much wronged, abandoned single parent—she gives no thought to the likely effect such remarks will have on the boy.

And there is a wrenching psychological truthfulness in the way the poor lad picks up one word which has nagged at his mind since he heard his mother say, 'Our feares do make us Traitors'. She refers of course to Macduff, not to herself, and after Rosse's departure the boy would understand this:

Son: Was my Father a Traitor, Mother?
Wife: I, that he was.
Son: What is a Traitor?
Wife: Why one that sweares and lyes.
Son: And be all Traitors, that do so.
Wife: Every one that do's so, is a Traitor,
And must be hang'd.
(44–50)

Another brave messenger comes and goes, Wife rattles on, and the horror arrives—whereupon the boy promptly and bravely dismisses his mother's catechism as he dismisses the Murderer's charge:

Murd: He's a Traitor.
Son: Thou ly'st thou shagge-ear'd Villaine.
(81–2)

Indeed his father is not a Traitor, in the normal sense: he is a Patriot, and will become his country's saviour in the fifth act by killing the man who was its saviour in the first. But in the catechism on loyalty and betrayal Lady Macduff provides the *natural* perspective: wrens own no allegiance to Holy Kings.

In the next scene this irony is given a particularly ferocious twist, when the incredulous Macduff discovers that his readiness to set King and Country before wife and family is what actually arouses Malcolm's suspicion:

Macduff: I have lost my Hopes.
Malcolm: Perchance even there where I did finde my doubts.
Why in that rawnesse left you Wife, and Childe?
Those precious Motives, those strong knots of Love,
Without leave-taking . . .
(4.3.24–8)

That echo may remind us that in his own hour of crisis Malcolm thought it best to 'shift away' without being 'daintie of leave-taking' (2.3.143–4). Here Malcolm displays another kind of prudence as he stalks, quizzes and tests Macduff: in seeing the need to be wary of Macbeth's 'trains', and in putting to work his knowledge that there *is* an 'Art, to finde the Mindes construction', Malcolm is less gracious than his father, and more astute. Where his father had committed himself to constructive acts of love and trust, the wary, frightened son loves and trusts nobody. As he tests Macduff we appraise both men, and the testing is far more elaborate than that in Holinshed. But to see this we need to recognise why Shakespeare has placed this 'English' scene between the scene in Fife and the scene in which Lady Macbeth is observed.

In a way, the naturalistic vivacity of 4.2 almost distracts us: Lady Macduff and her son appear but once, and are both unforgettable. The wife's terrified prattle and the boy's nervous pertness are caught with an astonishing sharpness of ear, and the keen relishing of human behaviour provides an indirect characterisation of domestic life in this corner of Fife. Evidently this household affords much intimacy, but the child is at the same time treated as a small, inept adult, whose presence does not inhibit the conversation of his elders; we see him trying to be manly, and striving, more poignantly, to stand in for an absent husband. Although the frantic mother cannot stir for his sake or her own, his last thought is for her safety: 'Run away, I pray you.' For all its local naturalism and psychological penetration, the scene also shows a powerful organising intelligence at work—carrying forward those troubling contrasts between a wife who would denature herself and a 'Wife' who is disabled by her own naturalness; between the 'Traitor' who disregards the 'Knots of Love' and 'precious Motives', and the hero whose regard for his 'dearest Love' helps to make him a traitor; between natural and unnatural manliness, between natural and more than natural bonds; between a marriage which is destroyed when the husband goes to 'pray' to 'the Holy King' (3.6.30), and a marriage which is an eyrie for predatory human eagles.

The 'English' scene picks up and extends these contrasts, adjusting the details of the test in Holinshed in subtle, discreetly pointed ways. Malcolm is not only less 'holy' than his father: he tests Macduff's genuineness by establishing his readiness to do what all official Tudor and Stuart propaganda expressly prohibited—to judge, and condemn, a rightful king. We have already heard Banquo fearing that Macbeth has played 'most fowly' for the throne, and then—just a moment later—assuring Macbeth that he is 'For ever knit' to him by 'a most indissoluble tye' (3.1.3;17–18). Now we hear Macduff prevaricating: 'The time you may so hoodwinke' (72), he falters, adding a moment later, 'All these are portable' (89)—until the magnificent, heretical explosion finally comes: 'Fit to govern? No not to live' (102–3). There indeed is the 'Noble passion' which proclaims his 'integrity' (114–1), as Malcolm concludes: it is one of the most moving—and deeply subversive—moments in Shakespearean drama.

But Macduff's goodness and naturalness—his *natural* integrity, which would shame and alarm a more perceptive Malcolm—are established twice over, and each time in a painfully paradoxical way which affords an illuminating contrast with Macbeth. First, the very man who spoke of the King as 'the Lords anoynted Temple' repudiates his own code of absolute allegiance when confronted, as it seems, with an incorrigibly vicious man. The contrast with Macbeth is more subtle than the contrast with Banquo: for Macbeth could not make his own sense of obligation, to a king whose natural holiness he recognised, the basis for 'the willing adhesion of the individual self to something other than itself'. Secondly, Macduff's response to Rosse's terrible news is indeed searingly natural, and includes another repudiation in the form of a desperately bitter self-reproach: 'Sinful *Macduff*, They were all strooke for thee' (224–5). Other echoes are heard, as Malcolm insists on *manliness*:

Malcolm: Dispute it like a man.
Macduff: I shall do so:
  But I must also feele it as a man;
  I cannot but remember such things were
  That were most precious to me . . .
                        (219–23)

We might remember not only the dispute on what becomes a man in 1.7, but also the response of two terrified sons to their father's death:

Donalbain: Our Teares are not yet brew'd.

241

Malcolm: Nor our strong Sorrow
         Upon the foot of Motion.
                (2.3.123–4)

Like the Duncan who spoke freely and touchingly of his own tears, Macduff avers that he could indeed 'play the woman with mine eyes', although he will not—and the callow Malcolm comments approvingly, 'This tune goes manly' (230,235). But the most telling contrast is yet to come. In the next scene we see and hear Lady Macbeth, estranged and deranged—and when Macbeth hears the news of *her* death his response is cauterised, utterly unyielding:

> She should have dy'de heereafter;
> There would have beene a time for such a word . . .
>   (5.5.17–18)

Although he is now prompted to pass his final verdict on life itself, Macbeth can no longer be pierced by the memory of those things that were most precious to him. Instead of pulling his hat over his brows or mourning, he pronounces life a tale told by an idiot, signifying nothing: the profoundly searching comparison between two marriages is complete.

And this is the manly, denatured tune Macbeth's marriage helped him to master. Even before learning of his wife's death, and before he believes that the battle cannot be won, Macbeth sees that he can never 'looke to have' those things which 'should accompany Old-Age': 'Honor, Love, Obedience, Troops of Friends' (5.3.24–6). But then the Macbeths—perched in their marital eyrie—had never looked to have these things, since they convinced themselves that the requisite acts of loving, morally constructive self-commitment were unmanly. They deny the human need for shared, communal values, before destroying the community in which that need might be acknowledged, expressed and fulfilled: to use Duncan's metaphor, they will not be planted. The 'tragedie of Macbeth' is that he also responds to that moral and imaginative challenge which Duncan presents—a challenge to recognise his need and capacity for such a commitment (or 'willing adhesion'). The incidental but pointedly complementary tragedy of Macduff is that his initially unquestioning commitment to a natural and supernatural order must be paid for—both by the loss of his 'pretty Chickens, and their Damme', and in that moment when he is driven to pronounce that a rightful king is unfit to govern and unfit to live. The 'Noble Passion' which is the 'Child' of Macduff's natural 'integrity' shows how far the play has travelled, since Macduff spoke of 'the Lords anoynted Temple'. The instinctive, pious patriotism which the earlier Macduff represents is explored in its natural and unnatural aspects. It is seen as unnatural by Lady Macduff, and in relation to the Nature that is red in tooth and claw, the natural world of eagles and wrens, martlets, kites, chicks and eggs. It is natural, as an expression of higher *human* aspirations, and of the human needs which the early Macduff acknowledges without question but which Macbeth cannot credit.

As Hugh MacDiarmid once remarked, 'A force evolves a form'. Macduff's 'Noble Passion' contrasts with Banquo's ignoble submission, and in an important sense Macduff takes over from Banquo: he and his family provide a complex but illuminating perspective on Macbeth and his marriage. His dramatic *function*, in relation to the forces which evolve this play's form, is not wholly unlike that of the Shakespearean 'sub-plot', which this play is usually said to lack; in the fourth act we might even speak of a double plot. This may seem a rather abstract or schematic reflection, but it is not likely to occur to us at all unless we are attending to Macduff as a character who speaks in character, and whose character shows a momentous development.

Mindfalls

In taking an unorthodox view of the Macduffs' significance I find my nerve steadied by the reflection that conventional accounts of *Macbeth* not only describe a play which is less frightening than Shakespeare's: they also make *Macbeth* seem unShakespearean in two rather striking respects. In the first place they suggest that the chameleon poet does not here display that prodigal, zestful imaginative energy which endows even minor characters in, say, *Hamlet*, with a rich dramatic existence. I have already mentioned the tendency to see Banquo as an exemplary Good Man: to do this, we must disregard the suggestions that he is vulnerable, equivocal, and in some ways less morally sensitive than Macbeth. Similarly, if we give Macduff's untested pious patriotism an oracular or vatic significance in Act 2, we shall be less likely to attend to the testing developments in the next two acts. In both these cases there is, I take it, a clear relation between the tendency to stabilise or 'flatten out' character and the tendency to deflect the *Macbeth*-terror by externalising 'order'.

The conventional, providential accounts of *Macbeth* also tend to suggest that when Shakespeare raided the *Chronicle* for *this* play he suppressed—and had to suppress—those alert political and psychological interests which he brought to his reading of Holinshed on every other occasion. Here Duncan is a crucial figure, and my own view is that the 'holy King' of the providentialist readings is a less inspiring, movingly courageous figure than Shakespeare's vulnerably human monarch. To some extent this is already conceded by those critics who suggest that Macbeth's crimes escalate, or compare Duncan's human qualities with those of Malcolm, to the latter's disadvantage. For of course, in the terms of that 'moral and spiritual order' which Knights, Leavis and Muir all invoke, no crime *can* be worse than killing the King; and Malcolm's human qualities cannot affect his status as rightful heir. But here it is most instructive to see how Shakespeare retains and reworks some of the details of Holinshed's account of the historical Duncan.

The Duncan of the *Chronicle* is repeatedly presented as a feeble and ineffectual ruler whose very virtues were disabling. He was seen by one warrior rebel as 'a fainthearted milksop, more meet to gouerne a sort of idle moonks in some cloister, then to have the rule of such valiant and hardie men of warre as the Scots were'. He was, Holinshed reports, 'so soft and gentle of nature' that the people wished him 'more like his cousin Makbeth', who, 'if he had not been somewhat cruell of nature, might have been thought more worthie the gouernement of a realme'. Makbeth himself scorns the King's 'softness', and has a far more pressing and specific motive for discontent: he became 'sore troubled' on seeing how the weak but cunning Duncan did 'what in him lay to defraud him of all maner of title and claim' to the throne. For as Kenneth Muir explains in the New Arden edition, which conveniently assembles the relevant passages from Holinshed, Makbeth had a 'genuine grievance against Duncan, who by proclaiming his son Prince of Cumberland went against the laws of succession, and took away from Macbeth the prospect of the throne' (xliii). Muir hastens to add that Shakespeare 'suppresses these facts' and disregards the various suggestions in Holinshed that Duncan was a 'feeble ruler'; on the contrary, by 'making the victim old and holy and by passing over his weaknesses, Shakespeare deliberately blackened the guilt of Macbeth'. But this, I would argue, is far too cut and dry, and has the effect, once again, of flattening out Shakespeare's characterisation.

It is indeed true that Macbeth tells the witches that to be king 'Stands not within the prospect of beleefe' (1.3.74); moreover, despite Lady Macbeth's problematic reference to having given suck, the play contains no explicit reference to the fact that the historical Makbeth could claim the throne on behalf of his wife and her son by her first husband. Since Shakespeare makes no attempt to explain the very complicated laws of tanistry and succession (which even Holinshed understood imperfectly), Malcolm's investiture may be seen, and has been seen, as a mere formality—somewhat hastily managed, but with no taint of irregularity, let alone illegality. Unlike his historical counterpart, Macbeth does not express any 'grievance' or suspicion that Duncan would 'defraud' him. In the great soliloquy in 1.7, he reviews the possible motives for killing Duncan and rejects them all, without mentioning any such grievance; and whereas the historical Makbeth was contemptuous of Duncan's 'softness', Macbeth is impressed and touched by the way in which Duncan has been so 'meeke' and 'cleere in his great Office' (1.7.17–18).

Yet this, we might reflect, tells us much about Shakespeare's Macbeth, as well as Duncan. Macbeth's tortured, reluctant registering of the king's 'Vertues' tells in Duncan's favour more than any interested or disinterested testimony; but it also reveals his own capacity—which has no counterpart in Holinshed's Macbeth—for intense loyalty, affection and imaginative inwardness. It reveals his own 'Nature', and that 'Milke of humane kindnesse' which makes Lady Macbeth fear that her husband will always be determined to proceed 'holily', without playing false or catching the nearest way. Yet here we touch a difficulty, since her opening soliloquy makes little sense unless Macbeth has *some* unspecified claim to the throne—some 'prospect', however near or remote, which he has discussed with his wife before he ever meets the witches. Moreover, we need to understand why Malcolm's investiture so stuns Macbeth. For if Malcolm's claim to the throne were hereditary, Macbeth would certainly have anticipated that obstacle 'in my way'; as it was, the Scottish laws of succession were not based on primogeniture and Macbeth's response is that of a man confronting a quite unexpected development:

> The Prince of Cumberland: that is a step,
> On which I must fall downe, or else o'releape,
> For in my way it lies . . .
>
> (1.4.48–50)

And once Malcolm has taken flight, it is simply taken for granted that the throne will pass to Macbeth: as Rosse says, ''Tis most likely' (2.4.29). Within the extended Scottish royal family, the man whose courage has made him Scotland's martial saviour is also the king's 'worthyest Cousin' (1.4.14) and 'peerelesse Kinsman'. If Shakespeare really was determined to 'suppress' the historical 'facts' as reported by Holinshed, he seems to have nodded over significant details.

Alternatively, *we* should be more vigilant, particularly in registering the political and psychological tensions in the fourth scene, when Malcolm is proclaimed Prince of Cumberland. There is no suggestion that Duncan does not have the best interests of Scotland at heart, as well as those of his family; but what he is doing is unexpected, difficult and potentially dangerous, since its success depends upon his preserving the loyalty of the lords and nobles, particularly Macbeth. The abrupt and awkward transitions in his speeches are frequently attributed to textual corruption, but might rather be regarded as dramatic signals which show how Shakespeare has retained and developed—not eliminated— Holinshed's sketch of a king who is saintly, feeble and necessarily cunning.

Before taking his calculated risk, Duncan sends first Rosse, and then Angus, to summon Macbeth with the offer of magnificent rewards. Rosse duly reports to Macbeth that the king 'bad me, from him, call thee Thane of Cawdor', and that this is only 'an earnest of a greater Honor' (1.3.104–5). Editors are conspicuously unhelpful about what this 'greater Honor' might be, and of course we never find out because it never materialises. The excited Macbeth's response is hardly surprising:

Glamys, the *Thane* of Cawdor:
The greatest is behinde . . .
            (1.3.116–17)

But here, although 'behinde' may be understood in different ways, it seems curious that so many editorial annotations explain that Macbeth is recalling the witches' prophecy, but without allowing for any connection between Macbeth's 'greatest' and the immediately preceding promise of some 'greater Honor'.

Duncan has no 'greater Honor' to confer on the peerless kinsman who has done more than any man to preserve the realm and throne. He offers Macbeth gracious words instead:

. . . Thou art so farre before,
That swiftest Wing of Recompence is slow,
To overtake thee. Would thou hadst less deserv'd,
That the proportion both of thanks, and payment,
Might have been mine: onely I have left to say,
More is thy due, then more then all can pay.
            (1.4.16–21)

If we assume what seems obvious—that Macbeth had a strong interest in knowing what the 'greater Honor' might be—we must also assume that its failure to materialise is a bitter disappointment. But of course Macbeth now has more than this to endure. Having been told how he is 'so farre before' all others, he hears the king go on to tell Banquo that he has 'no lesse deserv'd'; having been assured that more is *his* due than 'more than all' could pay, he next hears the king suddenly and unexpectedly bestowing 'all' not on Scotland's saviour but on the son who had to be rescued from captivity.

Yet Macbeth's public response to his king's gracious words is wholly consistent with that capacity for loyalty and devotion which makes his wife fear his 'Nature':

> The service, and the loyaltie I owe,
> In doing it, payes it selfe. Your Highnesse part,
> Is to receive our Duties: and our Duties
> Are to your Throne, and State, Children, and Servants;
> Which doe but what they should, by doing every thing
> Safe toward your Love and Honor.
>
> (1.4.22–7)

By dismissing talk of payment, Macbeth's reply also directs attention to one of the main dramatic points in this scene's characterisation of the King: Duncan knows very well—unlike, say, Shakespeare's Henry IV—that loyalty cannot always be commanded, and that it is sometimes an economy to buy it by offering thanks *and* payment. The emphasis on payment is conspicuous both in the message Duncan sends through Rosse and Angus and in his own speech to Macbeth. Once he has settled his estate on his son, Duncan rushes on in an anxiously calculating, propitiatory manner, to promise that Malcolm's

> Honor must
> Not unaccompanied, invest him onely,
> But signes of Noblenesse, like Starres, shall shine
> On all deservers.
>
> (39–42)

That promise shrewdly glosses over the fact that being a star is not like being the sun, and that Malcolm's particular 'Honor' does 'invest him onely'. Later, Duncan's intimacy with Lady Macbeth similarly combines graciousness with yet another bid for continuing affection and loyalty:

> Give me your hand:
> Conduct me to mine Host we love him highly,
> And shall continue, our Graces towards him.
> By your leave Hostesse.
>
> (1.6.28–30)

Here we may notice the nice shift from the flatteringly intimate 'me' and 'mine' to the promisingly regal 'we' and 'our'.

This is worth emphasising, I think, because it can be critically unhelpful to theologise a word like 'Graces', or to get dewy-eyed over the natural imagery in lines like 'I have begun to plant thee, and will labour/To make thee full of growing'. When translated into the material terms of Tudor court life, such promises would mean a new title, a profitable ward or a fat monopoly. When Duncan invites his lords to 'binde us further to you', when Banquo anticipates a 'Harvest' and when Lady Macbeth speaks of an 'Audit', there is no abrupt lurching from the spiritual to the material; rather, Duncan offers his lords and all 'deservers' the vision of a community which might satisfy higher aspirations *and* guarantee material well-being and safety. If we insist on sentimentalising Duncan as a *holy* king we are likely to miss the various suggestions that he is a *good* king in practically realistic and worldly ways. And in noticing his shrewd concern with 'payment' and 'Recompence' we should not be less realistic than the play or Duncan himself—who plainly cannot afford to take anything, including loyalty, for granted in his savage realm. The fourth scene opens with the question, 'Is execution done on *Cawdor*?', and with Duncan's sorrowing reflection,

> There's no Art,
> To finde the Mindes Construction in the Face:
> He was a Gentleman, on whom I built
> An absolute Trust.
>
> (1.4.11–14)

And this suggests what makes Shakespeare's vulnerable, movingly human king so much more complex and interesting than Muir's holy king. Knowing the risks and dangers, Duncan will not abandon the constructive effort to 'build' and 'trust' and purge the realm with gentle, humane statutes. He is both calculating and warmly emotional, frightened and couragous. He is Scotland's point of growth because he alone offers the hope of a community which might satisfy man's material and moral-imaginative needs. And his 'Vertues' are most sensitively registered by his murderer.

All of which suggests, disconcertingly, that Macbeth's

unquestioning assumption that Duncan is good, meek, gentle and *not* attempting to defraud him of his own claim to the throne, is a measure not only of Duncan's capacity to inspire tenderness, loyalty and hope, but also of Macbeth's moral generosity—that same generously imaginative responsiveness which makes him describe Banquo in terms of unqualified approbation. And this points towards Shakespeare's most obvious and fruitful departure from his sources. Makbeth, in the Chronicle, is the foremost example of those sturdy Scottish warriors who think Duncan's 'softness' more suited to a monastery; Shakespeare's Macbeth is still the terrifying warrior—but a warrior with an intensely moral imagination which makes his own wife fear his 'human kindness', his determination to proceed 'holily'. This is the crucial innovation—that Macbeth's instinctive response to Duncan is so keenly, reverentially responsive to the King's inspiring human qualities and to what Keats called the 'holiness of the heart's affections'. The other crucial complication, and the rich suggestiveness of the contrasts with the Macduffs, follow from this. For whatever reason—and we have seen how hard it is to determine the reason: reasons abound in the *Macbeth*-world, as in our own—the Macbeth of Act 1 can no longer give imaginative credence to the deepest inner promptings of his own nature. Even in the great soliloquy of 1.7 he is still commending Duncan's meekness; but now he can no longer credit his own corresponding inclination to behave 'holily'. He does not despise the King for being unmanly, but does not know how to believe that his own impulse to loyalty is not unmanly.

Belief, as Nietzsche sardonically noted, is a form of not *wanting* to know: that unengaging but amenable maxim might be appropriated by the terminal, as by the radical, sceptic. Like Wilbur Sanders and, more recently, Stephen Booth, I have been concerned to stress the terrifying uncertainty this play induces, and the consequently short-circuiting effect of those Christian-providentialist accounts which assume that man's intensely apprehended needs here find some cosmic confirmation and are, as it were, ontologically right. But my concern is also to stress the *radically* sceptical, interrogative nature of the play's summoning energies, as it explores the gap between what Theseus calls apprehension and comprehension. There is no rainbow bridge from the intensely apprehended need to objective and external sanctions—but in denying his own 'Nature' and morally constructive need for self-commitment Macbeth destroys himself.

I have tried to show how the 'interpretative leap' which seeks to close that gap is characteristically betrayed by the critic's own linguistic manoeuvring, and by the tendency to attach an unaccountably privileged, supra-dramatic significance to particular characters and speeches. Indeed, such accounts of Shakespearean tragedy characteristically expect us to swallow one particularly large ostrich. Shakespeare's villains are to be recognised, it seems, by their modernity, their tendency to view the world through the spectacles of an emergent scientific materialism rather than those of Christian humanism: because Iago or Edmund do not believe in God or the Great Chain of Being or the Divine Right of Kings, we, who probably also have difficulty in believing in such things, know them as evil opponents of that order for which Shakespeare is supposedly fighting a wistfully desperate rearguard action. Worse: when Hamlet or Macbeth find it difficult or impossible to sustain their faith in sustaining illusions, we are to think their souls imperilled—instead of feeling a shock of recognition at the modernity of protagonists who are fully alive to the imaginative terrors of an unaccommodated universe. But then inverting Tillyard is no corrective, as a book like Jonathan Dollimore's *Radical Tragedy* may remind us. In ideological terms Dollimore's book is as far removed from Tillyard as could be, yet its interpretative method is in one important respect similar: the statements of particular characters are still given a privileged, supra-dramatic status and are even, on occasion, assumed to correspond with the dramatist's beliefs. This, to my mind, is more worrying than the more obvious awkwardness that those characters whom Dollimore in effect commends—for advancing materialist, anti-essentialist views which 'anticipate' or are 'identical with' views held by Marx, Foucault or Althusser—are almost invariably 'villains'. And in this respect *Radical Tragedy* is not radical enough—is less radical, and of course less sceptical, than Shakespeare's interrogative perspectivism.

Here, we may notice the important and paradoxical sense in which *Macbeth* is 'Christian'. In *Mimesis* Erich Auerbach remarks of Augustine that 'The urgently impulsive element in his character makes it impossible for him to accommodate himself to the comparatively cool and rational procedure of the classical, and specifically of the Roman, style, which looks at and organises things from above' (72). The 'Christian', decidedly unclassical and unSenecan, character of *Macbeth* appears in its terrors, rather than in certitudes or assurances, and corresponds with that sense of the psyche as something stratified, vertiginous, which Auerbach analyses in Augustine and which is so conspicuous in Gerard Manley Hopkins' 'No worst, there is none':

> O, the mind, mind has mountains; cliffs of fall
> Frightful, sheer, no-man-fathomed. Hold them cheap
> May who ne'er hung there. Nor does long our small
> Durance deal with that steep or deep. Here! creep,
> Wretch, under a comfort serves in a whirlwind: all
> Life death does end and each day dies with sleep.

The consequent paradox is that the Christian-providentialist accounts of *Macbeth* make it seem less Christian and more classical, more Senecan: Macbeth is not infrequently likened to Tarquin in *The Rape of Lucrece*, even though the play is so much more radically inward in its conception of the self and in its poetic-dramatic articulation of Macbeth's own vertiginous inner dynamics.

So, the great soliloquy in 1.7 shows how Macbeth's mind is its own precipice. Whereas Racine's Phèdre can report on her disintegrative inner tumult—seeing it 'from above', in Auerbach's sense, with what is in its own way a no less terrifying lucidity—the convulsive, eruptive processes of Macbeth's tortured imagination are apprehended from within, in a supreme example of 'negative capability'. As the speech starts, the play on 'done'—

> If it were done, when 'tis done, then 'twer well,
> It were done quickly . . .

shows that his mind is still just where it was when his last aside provided access to its inner workings:

> yet let that bee,
> Which the Eye feares, when it is done to see.
>   (1.4.52–3)

And that same earlier speech, registering Macbeth's consternation at Malcolm's investiture, shows where the soliloquy's images of a 'jumpe' and a vault are issuing from:

> The Prince of Cumberland: that is a step,
> On which I must fall downe, or else o're-leape . . .

Indeed, the idea of issue and the processes of issuing prove to be crucial in the later soliloquy. The extended, subtle analysis in Molly Mahood's *Shakespeare's Wordplay* shows how words like *trammel*, *surcease* and *successe* tremble with those very potentialities of meaning which Macbeth is most anxious to suppress, as he strives to fit his thought to a trajectory appropriate to the stage-Machiavel or Senecan moral gangster. *Consequences* cannot be trammelled like young colts. *Surcease* could mean death, 'decease', something done and over, done with; but in Elizabethan law it was also the term for the merely temporary halting of a legal process. Even *success* has an equivocal force, when we remember that at this time the usage was not restricted to happy outcomes, so that one might still refer to a calamitous success.

The Folio reading 'Schoole', in

> Heere,
> But heere, upon this Banke and Schoole of time,
> Wee'ld jumpe the life to come . . .

may provide an especially baffling and extraordinary example of Shakespeare's, rather than Macbeth's, associative imagination. 'Schoole' could mean school, of course, but 'shoal' was often spelt this way. The idea of a shoal—a shallow, or sandbank—complements 'Banke' and yields the substance of Theobald's emendation and gloss: 'This *Shallow*, this *narrow Ford*, of humane Life, opposed to the *great abyss* of Eternity.' Doubtless the emendation was inspired, and expedient: although they could be spelt the same way the words for a school and a shoal were not homophones (as Mahood points out), so that no actor could keep both senses present in speaking the lines. And yet the associations of school are also alive in the speech: in 'we but teach Bloody Instructions' (whether or not we also remember that a 'Banke' could be a schoolbench), and in the reference to judgement, which also invokes the traditional idea of this world as a school or preparation for the life to come. The New Arden editor allows that the school/shoal crux may include an 'unconscious pun', without reflecting that there is something alarming (though possibly instructive) about a dramatic pun which can only register on the printed page; he then goes on to tell us that 'jumpe' is being used to mean 'risk', without asking why Shakespeare used the one word rather than the other. True, it is allowed that 'jumpe' 'might perhaps mean "skip over" or "evade" ', but this suggests that the matter is of little consequence—whereas what is pressing upon Macbeth's consciousness is the fear of the ultimate judgement, of what Banquo calls the 'deepest consequence' (1.3.126). If we are not careful, we lose sight of the whole crucial concentration of meaning when, even as Macbeth struggles to discount his fears, they throw up an image of a man jumping into eternity, damned and lost for all time.

Not only do such associations stand in a significant relation to each other—for example, as the suppressed sense of *surcease* joins with the unwanted but possible meaning of *success*. The supposedly 'secondary' sense, which Macbeth wants to suppress in the first part of the speech, resurface, with terrifying intensity, at the end of the speech. Normally, when we have occasion to remember that a word has more than one sense, the context will suggest which is primary, although a deliberately obscuring 'pun' may complicate matters (say, if we think of the French lady in Queneau's *Zazie dans le métro* who shows a fondness for German oaths after being occupied during the War). Here, the suppressed senses *become* primary, flooding Macbeth's mind when its battens will not hold. The 'jumpe' becomes the catastrophic vault. The horse-consequences, which were threatening to resist trammeling at the start, reappear as the horses of an annihilating Apocalypse—before that final, grotesquely tragi-comic image of the inadequately *spurred* rider who would *vault* into the saddle but *ore-leapes*, and *falles on th' other*. And the sceptical reader who resists any suggestion that *successe*, in the sense of issue, suggests that Macbeth's anxieties also involve Fleance and *his* children, might well ask where, the later image of a naked newborn babe is surfacing *from*. The verbal and associative complexities of the speech are labyrinthine, and astonish us by seeming beyond the reach of any consciously purposive creative intelligence: Shakespeare has so far sunk himself into the mindfalls of Macbeth's anguished imagination. But at the same time the speech's inner dynamics of repression and resurgence are as clear and coherent as those of any speech of Phèdre's. The difference is that we are so intimately involved in the inner workings and processes of Macbeth's thought and feeling; and that difference corresponds with Auerbach's distinction between classical and Christian modes of feeling. The question, why does Tarquin yield? could be answered proverbially, if not politely: 'A standing prick knows no conscience.' Yet any attempt to understand what pricks the sides of Macbeth's intent, or why he both yields and watches himself yield with that mesmerised but courageously attentive horror, involves confronting that radically internalised Christian sense of the self as precipice, of the mind's mountains and sheer cliffs of fall.

In other words, as the play catches us up in the unfolding processes of its exploratory modes of thinking, it challenges us to confront that gap or gulf between what is apprehended inwardly, as need or aspiration, and the comprehensive uncertainties of the terrifying *Macbeth*-world. This is why it is so important to see that Macbeth is destroyed not by 'Nature' but by *his* own nature and his attempts to deny its imperious inner promptings. To be sure, those promptings correspond with one conception of the nature of Nature; but the play's energies also summon—and unleash—the opposed conception. One sign of this play's unbounded imaginative freedom may be found in its extraordinarily eruptive puns. The daggers with which the gracious Duncan is butchered are 'unmannerly breech'd'. Macduff's son is an *Egge* in one line, *yong Fry* in the next. Old Siward, shattered by the loss of a beloved son, speaks of having as many sons as he has heirs/hairs. Macbeth, as he wishes that 'famine' would eat up the invading army, can still manage a dreadful kitchen pun on forcing/stuffing. It is as though, at those very moments of horror and pain from which a more timidly conventional mind would recoil, this play erupts into puns and an imaginative exuberance which altogether refuses to be confined by pious notions of decorum or decorous pieties—although criticism did recoil from this quality of imaginative exuberance, until Nietzsche's remarkable paragraphs on this play in the aptly titled *Daybreak*.

But here it will be clear, I hope, and without my resorting to the summary exercise of an 'Afterword', that I am returning again to the propositions outlined in the first paragraphs of this book's Preface. What Ted Hughes calls a 'quarrel about the nature of Nature' registers so intensely because the play's imaginative openness refuses to recognise boundaries and relishes the very terrors it unleashes. If we give some privileged, supra-dramatic significance to the properly Tudor pieties on kingship Macduff utters in Act Two, we shall not follow the lesser tragedy of Macduff, or see what force Shakespeare's development of the contrasts between the Macbeths and the Macduffs gives to that Blakean maxim, 'As a man is, so he sees'. The 'tragedy' is located in that radically sceptical perspectivism, and the play's thinking about man and Nature is irreducibly experiential, a process we live through. Here, once again, we see how different this unfolding, often jarringly contradictory process of 'poetic-dramatic thinking' is from the linear process of logical-discursive thought: in this sense *Macbeth* is no less a Shakespearean 'play of ideas' than *Troylus and Cressida* or *Measure for Measure*. Moreover, one advantage of reading *Troylus* with *Hamlet*, or *Measure* with *Othello*—that is, of reading the plays in sequence, without regard for generic compartmentalisation—is that we may be all the more impressed by the continuities within the *oeuvre* and by the way in which Shakespeare's more constant creative preoccupations recur and develop—not as 'themes' but rather as a nexus of related concerns which each play broaches differently and subjects to a more or less different process of 'dramatic thinking'.

Bibliography

Adamson, Jane, *'Othello' as Tragedy*, Cambridge, 1980.

Alexander, Nigel, *Poison, Play and Duel*, London, 1971.

Altizer, Alma B., *Self and Symbolism in the Poetry of Michelangelo, John Donne, and Agrippa d'Aubigné*, The Hague, 1973.

Amis, Kingsley, *What became of Jane Austen? and other questions*, London, 1970.

Aristotle, *The Poetics*, trans. Gerald Else, Michigan, 1967.

—— *The Nicomachean Ethics*, trans. David Ross, Oxford, 1925.

Auerbach, Erich, *Mimesis: the representation of reality in Western Literature*, trans. Willard Trask, Princeton, N.J., 1953.

—— *Literary Language and its public in Latin Antiquity and in the Middle Ages*, trans. Ralph Manheim, London, 1965.

Bacon, Francis, *Selected Writings*, ed. Hugh G. Dick, Modern Library edition, New York, 1955.

Bailey, Helen, *Hamlet in France: From Voltaire to Laforque*, Geneva, 1964.

Barish, Jonas, *Ben Jonson and the Language of Prose Comedy*, Oxford, 1960.

Barton, Anne, *Shakespeare and the Idea of the Play*, London, 1962.

Boccaccio, *The Decameron*, trans. G. H. McWilliam, London, 1972.

Booth, Stephen, *'King Lear', 'Macbeth', Indefinition and Tragedy*, New Haven, 1983.

Bradley, A. C., *Shakespearean Tragedy*, London, 1904.

Bradshaw, Graham, 'Donne's Challenge to the Prosodists', *Essays in Criticism*, vol.32 (1982), 338–60.

—— 'Hamlet in the Prison of Arden', *London Review of Books*, vol.4 (1982), no. 16, 12–14.

—— 'Verdi and Boito as Translators', 'Epilogue' to *Verdi's Falstaff*, by James Hepokoski, Cambridge, 1983, 152–71.

—— 'Leavis, Othello, and Self-Knowledge', *Dutch Quarterly Review*, vol. 9 (1981), 218–31.

Bright, Timothy, *A Treatise of Melancholy*, London, 1586.

Brooks, Harold (ed.), *A Midsummer Night's Dream* (New Arden edition), London, 1979.

Brown, John Russell, *Shakespeare and his Comedies*, London, 1962.

Bullough, Geoffrey, *Narrative and Dramatic Sources of Shakespeare*, 8 vols, London, 1957–75.

Calderwood, James, *Shakespearean Metadrama*, Minneapolis, 1971.

—— '*Macbeth:* Counter-*Hamlet*', *Shakespeare Studies*, vol. xvii (1985), 103–21.

Campbell, Lily, *Shakespeare's Tragic Heroes: Slaves of Passion*, Cambridge, 1930.

Campbell, O. J., *Comicall Satyre and Shakespeare's 'Troilus and Cressida'*, San Marino, California, 1938.

Cavell, Stanley, *Must We Mean What We Say?*, New York, 1969.

Chambers, R. W., *Man's Unconquerable Mind*, London, 1939.

Clemen, Wolfgang, *The Development of Shakespeare's Imagery*, London, 1951.

Coleridge, S. T., *Coleridge's Shakespearean Criticism*, ed. T. M. Raysor, 2 vols, London, 1930.

Danby, John F., *Shakespeare's Doctrine of Nature*, London, 1959.

Devlin, Patrick, *The Enforcement of Morals*, Oxford, 1965.

Dodds, E. R., *The Greeks and the Irrational*, Berkeley, California, 1951.

Dollimore, Jonathan, *Radical Tragedy*, Brighton, Sussex, 1984.

Donne, John, *Satyres, Epigrams and Verse Letters*, ed. W. Milgate, Oxford, 1967.

—— *The Elegies and the Songs and Sonnets*, ed. Helen Gardner, Oxford, 1965.

—— *Biathanatos*, London, 1646.

Dowden, Edward, *Shakespeare: A Critical Study of his Mind and Art*, London, 1875.

Dryden, John, *Essays of John Dryden*, ed. W. P. Ker, 2 vols, New York, 1961.

Duthie, G. I., *The 'Bad' Quarto of Hamlet*, Cambridge, 1941.

Eliot, T. S., 'Shakespeare and the Stoicism of Seneca' and 'Hamlet', *Selected Essays*, London, 1951.

Ellis-Fermor, Una, *Shakespeare's Drama*, London, 1980. Includes the essay on *Troilus and Cressida* (1945).

Elton, William, *'King Lear' and the Gods*, California, 1966.

Elyot, Thomas, *The Boke named the Governor*, London, 1531.

Empson, William, 'Hamlet when new', *Sewanee Review*, vol. 61 (1953), 15–42, 185–205.

Erasmus, *The Colloquies of Erasmus*, trans. Craig R. Thompson, Chicago, 1965.

Fender, Stephen, *Shakespeare: A Midsummer Night's Dream*, London, 1968.

Fenton, J. C., *The Gospel of St Matthew: Commentaries*, Penguin, London, 1964.

Fergusson, Francis, *The Idea of a Theater*, Princeton, N.J., 1949.

Fowler, Alastair, *Conceitful Thought: the interpretation of English Renaissance poems*, Edinburgh, 1975.

French, A. L., *Shakespeare and the Critics*, Cambridge, 1972.

Gascoigne, George, *Poems*, ed. John W. Cunliffe, Cambridge, 1907.

Geertz, Clifford, *The Interpretation of Cultures*, New York, 1973.

—— *Islam Observed*, Chicago, 1971.

Gless, Darryl, *Measure for Measure, the Law, and the Convent*, Princeton, N.J., 1979.

Goddard, Harold, *The Meaning of Shakespeare*, 2 vols, Chicago, 1951.

Goethe, *Wilhelm Meister's Apprenticeship*, trans. Carlyle, New York, 1917.

Goldberg, S. L., *An Essay on King Lear*, Cambridge, 1974.

—— 'Making Moral Sense of People', *Critical Review* 25 (1983), 25–49.

Gottschalk, Paul, *The Meanings of Hamlet*, New Mexico, 1972.

Greenblatt, Stephen, 'Murdering Peasants', *Representations* 1 (1967), 1–22.

—— *Renaissance Self-Fashioning: From More to Shakespeare*, Chicago, 1980.

Greg, W. W., 'Hamlet's Hallucination', *Modern Language Review*, vol. 12 (1917), 393–421.

Guilpin, Everard, *Skialetheia*, ed. D. Allen Carroll, North Carolina, 1974.

Gurr, Andrew, *Hamlet and the Distracted Globe*, Edinburgh, 1978.

Hall, Joseph, *Collected Poems*, ed. A. Davenport, Liverpool, 1949.

Harding, D. W., *Words into Rhythm: English speech rhythm in verse and prose*, Cambridge, 1976.

Hawkins, Harriett, *The Devil's Party: Critical Counter-interpretations of Shakespearean Drama*, Oxford, 1985.

Homer, *The Iliad*, trans. Robert Fitzgerald, New York, 1974.

Hooker, Richard, *Of the Laws of Ecclesiastical Polity*, 4 vols, London, 1907.

Hopkins, G. M., *Poems*, ed. W. H. Gardner and N. H. Mackenzie, 4th edn, London, 1967.

Hume, David, *Dialogues Concerning Natural Religion*, London, 1779.

Hughes, Ted, *A Choice of Shakespeare's Verse*, London, 1971.

Hunter, G. K., 'The Heroism of Hamlet', *Hamlet*, Stratford-upon-Avon Studies 5, ed. John Russell Brown and Bernard Harris, London, 1963, 90–109.

Jacobson, Howard and Sanders, Wilbur, *Shakespeare's Magnanimity*, London, 1978.

Janouch, Gustav, *Conversations with Kafka*, trans. Goronwy Reese, London, 1971.

Jenkins, Harold (ed.), *Hamlet* (New Arden edition), London, 1982.

Jespersen, Otto, 'Notes on Metre' (1900), reprinted in *The Structure of Verse: Modern Essays on Prosody*, ed. Harvey Gross, Greenwich, Connecticut, 1966, 111–30.

Johnson, S., *Dr Johnson on Shakespeare*, ed. W. K. Wimsatt, Penguin Shakespeare Library, London, 1969.

Jones, Emrys, *Scenic Form in Shakespeare*, Oxford, 1971.

Jones, Ernest, *Hamlet and Oedipus*, New York, 1959.

Jonson, Ben, *Ben Jonson*, ed. C. H. Herford, Percy and Evelyn Simpson, 11 vols, Oxford, 1925–52.

Kermode, Frank, 'Opinion, Truth and Value' (on *Troilus and Cressida*), *Essays in Criticism*, vol. 5 (1955), 181–7.

Knight, G. Wilson, *The Wheel of Fire*, London, 1930.

—— *Christ and Nietzsche*, London, 1948.

Knights, L. C., *An Approach to Hamlet*, London, 1960.

—— *Explorations*, London, 1946.

—— *'Hamlet' and Other Shakespearean Essays*, Cambridge, 1979.

Konner, Melvin, *The Tangled Wing: Biological constraints on the human spirit*, London, 1982.

Kott, Jan, *Shakespeare: our contemporary*, trans. Boleslaw Taborski, London, 1965.

Kozintsev, Grigori, *Shakespeare: Time and Conscience*, trans. Joyce Vining, New York, 1966.

Kyd, Thomas, *Works*, ed. F. S. Boas, Oxford, 1901.

Lascelles, Mary, *Shakespeare's 'Measure for Measure'*, London, 1953.

Lawrence, D. H., *Twilight in Italy*, Phoenix edn, London, 1956.

Leavis, F. R., 'Tragedy and the "Medium" ' and 'Diabolic Intellect', collected in *The Common Pursuit*, London, 1952.

Lever, J. W. (ed.), *Measure for Measure* (New Arden edition), London, 1965.

LeWinter, Oswald, *Shakespeare in Europe*, London, 1970.

Locke, John, *An Essay Concerning Human Understanding*, ed. A. C. Fraser, 2 vols, Oxford, 1894.

Long, Michael, *The Unnatural Scene*, London, 1976.

McAlindon, T. C., 'Language, Style and Meaning in *Troilus and Cressida*', *PMLA*, vol. 84 (1969), 29–43.

Machiavelli, Nicolo, *The Prince*, trans. George Bull, London, 1961.

—— *La Mandragola*, trans. Anne and Henry Paolucci, London, 1957.

Mackenzie, Henry, 'On the character of Hamlet' (1780), collected in *Shakespeare: The Critical Heritage: 1744–1801*, ed. Brian Vickers, London, 1981, 272–80.

Mackie, J. L., *Ethics: Inventing Right and Wrong*, London, 1977.

Mahood, Molly, *Shakespeare's Wordplay*, London, 1957.

Mander, R. and J. Mitchenson, *Hamlet through the Ages*, London, 1952.

Marston, John, *The Malcontent*, ed. G. K. Hunter, Manchester, 1975.

—— *The Fawn*, ed. David Blostein, Manchester, 1978.

Mason, H. A., 'An Introduction to Literary Criticism by way of Sidney's Apologie for Poetrie', *Cambridge Quarterly*, xii (1984), 77–173.

Melville, Herman, *Billy Budd, Sailor, & other stories*, ed. Harold Beaver, Penguin, London, 1968.

Middleton, Thomas, *Works*, ed. A. H. Bullen, 8 vols, London, 1885–86.

Montaigne, *Montaigne's Essays*, trans. John Florio, 3 vols, Everyman's Library, London, 1965.

Moody, A. D., *Shakespeare: The Merchant of Venice*, London, 1964.

Munday, Anthony, *Zelauto*, London, 1580.

Nietzsche, *The Birth of Tragedy* and *The Genealogy of Morals*, trans. Francis Golffing, New York, 1956.

—— *Daybreak: thoughts on the prejudices of morality*, trans. R. J. Hollingdale, Cambridge, 1982.

—— *The Anti-Christ*, in *The Portable Nietzsche*, trans. Walter Kaufman, New York, 1980.

—— *Human, All-too-human*, trans. M. Faber and S. Lehmann, Nebraska, 1984.

Nosworthy, J. B., *Shakespeare's Occasional Plays*, London, 1965.

Nowottny, Winifred, ' "Opinion" and "Value" ' in *Troilus and Cressida*, *Essays in Criticism*, vol. 4 (1954), 282–96.

Nuttall, A. D., '*Measure for Measure*: Quid pro Quo?', *Shake-*

speare Studies 4, ed. J. L. Barroll, Cincinnati, Ohio, 1968, 231–51.

Oates, Joyce Carol (writing as J. Oates Smith), 'Essence and Existence in Shakespeare's *Troilus and Cressida*', *Philological Quarterly*, vol. 46 (1967), 167–85.

Palmer, John, *Political and Comic Characters In Shakespeare*, London, 1964. Collects *Political Characters of Shakespeare* (1945) and *Comic Characters of Shakespeare* (1946).

Panofsky, Erwin, *Studies in Iconology*, New York, 1972.

Pasternak, Boris, *Safe Conduct*, trans. Alec Brown, London, 1959.

Pater, Walter, *Appreciations*, London, 1889.

Prosser, Eleanor, *Hamlet and Revenge*, Stanford, Cal., 1967.

Quiller-Couch, A. (ed.), *The Merchant of Venice* (Cambridge edition), Cambridge, 1962.

Rabkin, Norman, *Shakespeare and the Common Understanding*, London and New York, 1967.

—— *Shakespeare and the Problem of Meaning*, Chicago, 1981.

Righter, Anne: See Barton, Anne.

Robertson, J. M., *The Problem of 'Hamlet'*, London, 1919.

Robson, W. W., *Did the King see the Dumb-show?*, Edinburgh, 1975.

Rossiter, A. P., *Angel with Horns*, London, 1961.

Rowe, Eleanor, *Hamlet: A Window on Russia*, New York, 1976.

Sanders, Wilbur, *The Dramatist and the Received Idea*, Cambridge, 1968.

—— 'The "Strong Pessimism" of *Macbeth*', *Macbeth: A Casebook*, ed. John Wain, London, 1968, 255–75. First printed in the *Critical Review*, no. 9 (1966).

—— *Shakespeare's Magnanimity*. See entry for Howard Jacobson.

Schanzer, Ernest, *The Problem Plays of Shakespeare*, London, 1963.

Schlegel, A. W., 'Etwas über William Shakespeare, bei Gelegenheit Wilhelm Meisters' (1797), *Sprache und Poetik*, ed. Edgar Lohner, Stuttgart, 1962, 88–123.

—— *A Course of Lectures on Dramatic Art and Literature* (1808), trans. John Black, London, 1846.

Schoenberg, Arnold, *Style and Idea*, trans. Leonard Stein, London, 1975.

Schopenhauer, Arthur, *The World as Will and Idea*, trans. R. B. Haldane, and J. Kemp, New York, 1961.

Schücking, Levin, *Character Problems in Shakespeare's Plays*, London, 1922.

Sidney, Sir Philip, 'An Apologie for Poetrie', *Elizabethan Critical*

Essays, ed. G. Gregory Smith, 2 vols, Oxford, 1904, vol. 1, 150–207.

Silvayn, Alexander, *The Orator*, London, 1596.

Smith, Joyce Oates: see Oates, Joyce Carol.

Spencer, Theodore, *Shakespeare and the Nature of Man*, New York, 1942.

Spenser, Edmund, *Works*, 11 vols, Baltimore, MD, 1932–57.

Spurgeon, Caroline, *Shakespeare's Imagery and what it tells us*, Cambridge, 1935.

Stein, Arnold, *'Troilus and Cressida:* the disjunctive imagination', *ELH*, vol. 36 (1969), 145–67.

Stoll, E. E., *Hamlet: An historical and comparative study*, Research Publications of the University of Minnesota, vol. 8, no. 5, September 1919.

Strindberg, *Pre-Inferno Plays*, trans. Walter Johnson, Washington, 1970.

Tillyard, E. M. W., *The Elizabethan World Picture*, London, 1943.

—— *Shakespeare's Problem Plays*, Toronto, 1949.

Tolstoy, L., *War and Peace*, trans. Louise and Aylmer Maude, London, 1942.

Turgenev, 'Hamlet and Don Quixote': see entry for LeWinter.

Valéry, Paul, 'Poetry and Abstract Thought', *Paul Valéry: An Anthology*, ed. J. R. Lawler, London, 1977, 136–65.

Vives, Juan Luis, *Opera, in duos distincta tomos*, Basel, 1955.

Waldock, A. J. A., *Hamlet: A study in critical method*, Cambridge, 1931.

Weitz, Morris, *Hamlet and the Philosophy of Literary Criticism*, London, 1965.

West, Rebecca, *The Court and the Castle*, London, 1958.

Wheeler, Richard, *Shakespeare's Development and the Problem Comedies: Turn and counter-turn*, Berkeley, California, 1981.

Whetstone, George, *Promos and Cassandra*, London, 1578.

Wilde, Oscar, *Essays and Lectures*, 6th edn, London, 1928.

Wilson, Thomas, *Arte of rhetorique*, ed. Thomas Derrick, New York, 1982.

Wilson, John Dover, *Hamlet* (New Cambridge edition), Cambridge, 1934.

—— *The Manuscript of Shakespeare's 'Hamlet' and the Problems of its Transmission*, 2 vols, Cambridge, 1934.

—— *What Happens in 'Hamlet'*, Cambridge, 1935.

Winch, Peter, *Ethics in Action*, London, 1972.

Wittgenstein, Ludwig, *Culture and Value*, ed. G. H. von Wright, Oxford, 1980.

Index

DAVID GLENN HUNT
MEMORIAL LIBRARY
GALVESTON COLLEGE